MW00884159

# North To South

## A man, a bear and a bicycle

James Brooman

Cover photo: Amazon at dawn ©, by James Brooman
Illustrations by David Brooman

Copyright © 2014 James Brooman
All Rights Reserved.

# Acknowledgements

Few worthwhile things can be achieved without help, so I would sincerely like to thank the following people for their support and assistance to make my journey possible, my journey better, and in the creation of this book.

My wonderful family - David, Claudia and Tanya Brooman for their unerring support in both good times and bad. I couldn't have done any of this without you. David Brooman for his illustrations and finding Tolly the Bear as a companion (and to Christie Bears for providing him). Thanks to Alex Evans, Marcus Fernandes and Mark Asiedu for their home team support. Will Robins for helping start it all and Jon Cooper for his support on my return.

Gerrit Schadler, Jodie Stover, Alvaro Zamora, Marian Wolf and Sam the Dog for their riding companionship. Rowan, Brett, Thomas Wolf, Cat and Craig for making paradise perfect, and Alaskan Robin, Dennis Bieber and Erik Gunnar Counselman for their exemplary kindness. Nathalie Faucher and Elke Hauk for their warmth, humor and humanity, and Evan Haussmann, Alina Liberte, Ryan Hanrahan, Ruth Beck, Leonie and Stewart the Aussie for their friendship and general awesomeness.

Heartfelt thanks to the anonymous. The police officer who saved my life in California. The Alaskan truck driver who fed me. The Venezuelan pilot for his acrobatics and the many people who took a tired English cyclist into their home and offered him their hospitality.

Special thanks to Alexis Tosti, Rebecca Kanter, Mary Harries, Andrea Diamond, Meixi Chen and Tanya Brooman for their feedback and editing wisdom.

And *you*. Thank *you* for buying this book. I hope you enjoy it!

ONE

# The End

The end. It is a strange place to begin our time together, perhaps, but as I sat there at the edge of the world and looked out towards Antarctica with tears rolling down my cheeks, I thought as I do now of the journey I had finally completed. It had been a journey half way around the world, a journey through adventure and danger of which I could never have dreamed. To quote Tolkien, "It's a dangerous place out there, Frodo. If you don't keep your head, there's no telling where you might be swept off to." And swept off I had been for two long, hard and wonderful years. Perhaps that was the intention all along; my only miscalculations were both the difficulty and the duration. It had been 20,675 miles since the frozen shores of the Arctic Ocean, during which time I had been starved, chronically dehydrated, robbed, frozen, been rescued twice from forest fires, accidentally set myself on fire and almost drowned. I had also become lost in several deserts, been stung, bitten, psychologically traumatized and taken hostage by an Amazonian tribe to name some of the more interesting challenges. To add injury to insult, I had ridden my bicycle for a thousand miles with a dislocated back, suffered heat stroke quite a few times, torn the surface off both eyes and sliced my elbow down to the white bone beneath. Sitting on the thick wooden fence at the end of the world, though, ingloriously sipping tepid champagne through my ragged beard, I knew those memories to be pristine jewels of experience that I would treasure forever, for it is these terrifying, painful, desperate and dangerous moments which alone have the power to change the mind forever. Plus they also make the best stories!

There were an equal number of magnificent experiences as well as the terrible ones, of course, as life has a way of balancing good and bad if you let it. You need only open your eyes to opportunity. I stumbled unawares across many true wonders of the world, feeling those brief and rare moments when all one can do is smile like a village idiot and laugh out loud, as you are enveloped in bubble of pure euphoric happiness. For me, such experiences linger forever and are the moments which make all of life's problems 'worth it'.

Then there were the people whom I met along the way; extraordinary people, special and rare individuals, people who are unique in their abilities, kindness, character and deeds. Alvaro, my Spanish hero and fellow cyclist, Robin, the Alaskan mom with a heart of gold, the Californian police officer who saved my life; they inspired me to be better than I thought I could ever be. Not everyone I met was unique for positive attributes, however, and some encounters were notable for entirely different reasons. The money changer in Venezuela, the Costa Rican thief and the conspiracy theorist in Montana enabled me experience the full spectrum of humanity on my journey, from the very best to the very worst. Indeed, to meet both the angels and the demons who walk this Earth was yet another reason I resolved to undertake this challenge in the first place.

Sitting on that fence I thought also of endings and beginnings. Was this the end of my adventures or just a frightening beginning of the next stage in my life? Looking back, I believe it was both and neither. I had no plan to follow, no signposted path to glory laid out ahead, but for all my worrying I realized that beginning and ending are just words used to divide life into manageable chunks. A wise old biker, a genuine Hell's Angel with a white beard and black Harley Davidson whom I met at a convenience store in Utah, once said to me that life is not about the destination, it's about the journey. A cliché, perhaps, but he was right, plus he said it at lot better than I just did. All of life's pain and joy, wonder and love, fear and hope happens between those two little words, often on some dull Tuesday when you least expect it. This is a book about all those Tuesdays which became special, a book about chance encounters with the power to change my life, a book about the experiences, both wonderful and dreadful, which have made me 'me'. It is also a book that begins, as great adventures are apt to do, with a bar, a beer, and the spark of an idea.

# Christmas Revelation

New Year's Eve, London, 2002. I arrived unexpectedly early at a bar in the district of Farringdon, a consequence of my poor planning and, surprisingly, an on-time London Underground subway system. I vaguely knew the bar, but tonight I was the guest of a friend at a party whose organizers I didn't know, so as the Elves and Santas merrily bounced around putting up ever more tinsel and colorful fairly lights I pulled myself onto a bar stool and ordered a beer as my liquid companion. Although surrounded by the happy chatter I was in a reflective mood and merely watched the scene as an invisible spectator, a Dickensian orphan peering in through the snow edged window pane at the merriment unfolding beyond. I thought about the year that drew rapidly to a close.

"What have I achieved this year?" I wondered. "What great and marvelous new things had I experienced?" I thought about it for the first time in a long time, confronting questions which I had not wanted to ask. That year I had spent a stupendous amount of time at my desk, an unfortunate side-effect of being an investment banking analyst. True, I had helped to move the ownership of a large number of oil wells from some German people to some French people while simultaneously moving a billion Euros in the opposite direction. Pitifully few of them had been diverted by my employer to my personal account, especially given the sacrifices I had made for the job, and I reflected that if I was doing it for the money I'd picked the wrong career. I was making less per hour than my secretary, and if bankers were in the infamous 1% I certainly hadn't been invited to the club. The other junior bankers working beside me, the 'lucky few' who had survived several rounds of layoffs were in an equally dejected place. After creating an ungodly number of PowerPoint slides and equally painful financial models, my job felt like an auditor of paperclips. I guess it has to be done, but when everything has been recorded, reconciled and stacked neatly into little boxes, what value did it really add? It made me think about what I had achieved in those 365 days, and shielded from society's norms and expectations by an introspective Christmas-themed bubble I knew I knew the answer. It was an answer to be spoken only in dark, secret whispers lest it be overheard and condemned by the omnipotent and tyrannical conformism of the mainstream. I had achieved nothing.

This revelation resulted in an immediate and prejudiced revulsion at my career choice and current lifestyle. In that brief moment, driven by the rashness of youth, perhaps, I decided to resign with a singular new goal; to avoid the same answer in exactly one year's time. Of course, the next question was what the hell was I going to do instead, although I suspected that my next path was not going to involve a desk, PowerPoint or Excel. As a veil lifted from my eyes to reveal this bright new day I began to ponder the infinite myriad of choices now before me and glimpsed fleeting shadows of the outrageous and monumental possibilities they revealed.

"Well hello sir!" pieced a voice through the bar chatter, popping my bubble and bringing me back to the present. I turned and saw my friend Will approaching me along the bar. It was great to see him. We ordered some drinks, and as we chatted my revelation faded into the dark shadows of my mind. Faded but not forgotten. I didn't know it at the time, but I'd taken the first step of a journey, a journey not just of the proverbial one thousand miles, but of twenty.

# THREE

# If only Gandalf were here

How do you choose a quest? It's not an easy thing to do as I quickly discovered. A quest must be demanding yet not impossible, inspiring yet not esoteric, grueling yet not done merely for suffering's sake. Over several months I asked friends and family for their thoughts, and their ideas ranged between the impossible and nonsensical, the benign to the just plain dull. Yet an undercurrent pervaded these ideas as though pinned to substrate of my vision.

"If you are going to do something *crazy* like *that*, James," people would say, "then you should at least do something *you* really want to do. Follow your passion."

Ah, that word "passion". For me it's a catch-all term used in job interviews and newspapers as a placeholder for some ultimate motivator. Some people are indeed blessed to have that 'one thing', that one passion, be it to sail around the world, climb Mt Everest or collect every stamp ever issued. I envy them because I never had such a thing, no one thing that fit neatly into a box or a consuming pinnacle of focus. As I relaxed on the couch one night during that time, slugging at a cold bottle of beer as my feet softly poisoned the air in revenge for their day's imprisonment, I thought about how this could be true. How could I be a man without a passion after I'd made such sacrifices to achieve success at university and work? It was a paradox to me, until on that couch I discovered that that the problem was not with me, but with the question.

Passion is not the fundamental source of our motivations but merely a conduit; it's merely a projection used to correct a disconnect we can sometimes feel between the world that is and the world we think should be. I thought I must be in some way 'special', but that I hadn't yet proved to myself how I was so. Maybe many of us feel that way when we are children; find me a boy who hasn't once imagined that he has super powers. It is something very different from arrogance, a sense that in a world of such opportunity we surely must each be destined for something unique. For me, 'normal' tasted a lot like defeat. I looked at myself in my job, slipping inexorably into an abyss filled with the affluent and boring while never having proved to myself or the world what I am capable of, and some powerful purpose surged inside. I needed this quest to help give me some inner peace, and to do that it needed to be hard. Really hard. It needed to be epic.

An epic quest. My mind once again faltered, until inspiration appeared when I stopped looking for it, in a place I didn't expect. That March I read a book given to me by my parents, 'Into thin air' by Jon Krakauer, a book I'm sure many of you have also read. It is one gift they perhaps now regret. The story chronicles the ill-fated attempt of Krakauer, a freelance reporter writing for Outdoor Magazine, to climb Mt Everest as part of a guided climb in 1986. In a tragic case of wrong time, wrong place, wrong pretty much everything, he was caught in a now infamous storm which took the lives of 12 climbers, including several of his climbing party. Having spent time in the Himalaya during my university travels I found it utterly gripping.

One story in the book caught my attention in particular, the tale of a young climber from Sweden, Göran Kropp. For Göran, climbing the highest mountain on Earth was not enough; he needed to do it the hard way. Everything the hard way, in fact. Gathering all his equipment in Sweden, all 150lbs of it, he loaded it onto a bicycle and set off alone to the Base Camp of Mt Everest, some 8,000 miles distant in Nepal. Summiting and descending the mountain using a difficult and technical route, for good measure he rode the bicycle another 8,000 miles back to Sweden. The brief account of his cycling adventure was inspiring, shocking and utterly riveting.

The proverbial light bulb above my head burst into dazzling light; one of those rare moments of clarity when a solution just presents itself as pure and obvious simplicity. Ride a bicycle! I had earlier ruled out backpacking as too easy, especially as I'd done a fair bit of travelling already, but riding a bicycle across some far flung place would allow me to discover the reality of each country hidden behind its touristy façade. It was also a great challenge given that I wasn't an avid cyclist, or even a cyclist at all for that matter. My existing bicycle was some rusting old thing from the 1980s that my dad bought for me at a second hand sale, and I used to do 25 mile rides through the countryside on it once every few months when the weather was nice and I was feeling ambitious.

"No matter," I thought, considering my lack of experience and training as mere inconvenient details. I hopped off my bed in the little room where I grew up in in my parent's house and walked into an adjacent bedroom, where a large map of the world has hung from the wall for almost as long as I can remember.

With one finger on London and one on Nepal I did a quick check against the little scale diagram in the corner of the map. 4,000 miles, plus or minus, so maybe double that in all to account for winding roads and detours.

"8,000 miles, just like the book said," I mused. A hell of a long way, but at 1,000 miles a month it might be doable. I had zero idea whether 1,000 miles a month was even reasonable, but my mind was now set and the wheels were in motion, so to speak. Ride across Western Europe and the Balkans, traverse Turkey, negotiate my way through Iran and Pakistan, trundle across northern India and then finally up into Nepal. It was the perfect plan, and only war or famine could stop me now!

War dutifully arrived. Watching CNN's coverage of the American and British tanks thundering across the Pakistani border into Afghanistan a month later I seriously doubted the correspondent's jubilant declaration of victory. With a suspicion that my British passport would not be particularly welcome in Iran or Pakistan at that moment I returned to the wall map to formulate Plan B. The alternatives were initially uninspiring. I could likely still do the London-Nepal trip but with an additional 3,000 mile detour through the inhospitable deserts of Kazakhstan. Call me Mr. Picky, but that didn't appeal. I stared at the fading pastel colors of the map with index fingers outstretched, one finger of London, one on Nepal, and moved them in synchronized motions across the map trying to keep them the same distance apart to preserve the journey's length. Perth to Sydney? A whole lot of nothingness in the middle and too short a trip. London to Cape Town? Africa scared me. It would no doubt have been amazing, but for a first time biker that felt like a step too far into the unknown. Moscow to Vladivostok? Between these two emotive cities are vast tracts of nothing, not even roads, and I suspected it would have been a difficult journey in which to keep my sanity intact. I moved my fingers left across the map until they hovered over the Americas. The middle of North America to the middle of South America?

"Has potential," I thought, and moved my fingers a little further apart. How about the North of the North to the South of the South – and ride through Brazil, just for the audacity? The possibilities jumped off the wall at me, and I smiled.

I had found my quest.

# FOUR

# Preparation Prevents Poor Performance

How does one go about preparing for a two year solo bicycle journey? I had absolutely no idea. The furthest I'd ever cycled was 40 miles, and that single occasion was an accident when I got lost. I'd never even thought about doing a bike touring trip, let alone actually done one, and I didn't know anyone else who had either. In the end I just amalgamated various lists and accounts of other riders from the internet and formulated an idea of what I needed. First on the list was a bicycle. While it needed to have several key attributes, the most important was that it must be nearly indestructible. After much research I chose a front suspension mountain bike made by a US company called Jamis. Built from components selected for their toughness, this thing was generally considered to be bullet proof. The steel frame meant it could be fixed (if needed) by any metalworking shop in the middle of nowhere, while the front suspension would help absorb the bumps on the dirt roads. It also had a 'hardtail' back like a normal bike, which meant I could attach my luggage to it. Overall it was an excellent machine, apart from the saddle. They might have well have chosen to attach an anvil. Mentioning my saddle's utter lack of pliability to another cyclist I met on the trip, I was advised that it would eventually 'mold to me'. If anyone ever tells you that, ignore them. After a year we had indeed become molded together, except that I was the one who had changed shape rather than the saddle. It was a thing of evil and I still despise it.

With the bike chosen it was time to turn my attention to the equipment. Given my journey was expected to take me through some pretty remote places, the list of things I needed to bring was enormous. The camping gear alone took up a huge amount of space and weight. I brought a tent, sleeping mat, sleeping bag, camping stove, fuel bottle, cooking pots, cup, bowl - which for me was also the cooking pot - and a spork, a cross between a spoon and a fork. I saved weight wherever I could; for example, my pillow for two years was a pile of folded clothes.

Next were the spare bicycle parts and the tools to change them, including a spare foldable tire, several inner tubes in case of punctures and a pump. Some of the various other tools I needed were irritatingly specialized, including one especially heavy wrench whose only job was to enable the removal of one single bolt on the bike. In the end I did actually need to use it, so at least all the effort to carry it around was not wasted!

When it came to clothes I also economized, despite knowing that I'd be wearing the same stinky clothes for several days straight if things went wrong. I brought two pairs of cycling shorts and several pairs of board shorts with me, which I rotated with the two pieces of underwear I also carried. Completing the lower body I also took one pair of cargo pants and some fleece pants for warmth (and to keep the mosquitos off). For my upper body I owned one fleece, one cycling jersey, a couple of T-shirts and a rain jacket. I also carried three pairs of socks, a pair of flip flops and my running shoes. That was pretty much it. A single rain storm often condemned me to wear smelly wet clothes for the next week, but when grinding up steep mountains it was a trade-off I'd make every time.

Lastly there was the seemingly endless list of small but critical extras, little things that made the difference between abject misery and relative happiness. Sunscreen, mosquito repellant, a headlamp, contact lenses, a watch, penknife, mini towel, water bottle, soap, and water purification were critical, as was my bike lock and a cheap GPS device for those 'where the hell am I?' moments. I also carried a camera and a copy of the lonely planet guidebook which I periodically swapped out as I passed through each new region. In addition to all these bits there was one final item which deserves a special mention. As I prepared for my trip, word of my journey got around and one day my dad gave me a call.

"So I think I have found you a sponsor!" he told me. "Well, kind of. It turns out that the parents of one of the guys I work with own a teddy bear company called Christie Bears. They wondered if you would take one of their small teddy bears along with you and take some photos, maybe also write a blog. They will pay you some pocket money for it!" This sounded interesting.

"A teddy bear, eh? Well sure, I can do that. Just make sure it is *small*!" I replied, and my dad headed off to see what he could arrange. A few days later a box arrived.

I immediately noticed four things. First, they had indeed sent a small bear, maybe four or five inches high, and secondly, he was adorable. Third, they had made him a little passport so I could collect border stamps for him. They did a good job, even putting in a photo of the bear! Tolly was his name in the passport so Tolly he became. I discovered the fourth thing when I picked him up. He was *heavy*! In order to make him sit nicely on a table they had decided to fill his paws and body with lead shot. The damn thing weighed almost a pound. I mean, it wasn't like I was going to cycle half way around the world over a bunch of mountain ranges or anything, was it. Unfortunately, it was too late to change things so into my bag he went.

Fully loaded with untried and untested gear, an overweight toy bear and a bicycle in a box it was time to get on a flight and begin my journey. My starting point was a place I had always wanted to visit but never thought I would reach; one of the world's most evocative and remote locations.

I was going to Alaska.

# Land of the Wild

A land of unfathomable remoteness, of soaring mountains and deep fjords, of ice and bears, hardy wildlife and hardier people. A land of gold, oil and the midnight sun, a land whose very name is a synonym for the final frontier. Looking out of the window of Alaskan Airlines flight AL 50 I could see the Arctic tundra stretching away to the crystal blue horizon, a billion brown islands of meager grass marooned in a vast network of stagnant, mosquito-infested pools. Not a single building, road or any other sign of civilization was apparent, just an untouched and untamed desolation that was the very definition of the wild. The final frontier felt suddenly very frontier-like indeed.

Although deeply impressive and surprisingly moving, this utter lack of anything at all became somewhat troubling once the plane had begun its decent. I strained against the window for signs of civilization below and yet I still couldn't see anything to break the endless tundra. I'm not one for worrying, but at this point I had the distinct feeling I should have actually planned this part of the trip. It was only as we touched down on the short runway that I finally saw a couple of low buildings momentarily flash past the small oval windows on the opposite side of the plane. There was nothing on my side beyond the airport fence, so I figured those few buildings must the town. Welcome to Deadhorse, Alaska, the bleakest settlement on Earth.

Situated near the coast at the edge of a region called the North Slope, Deadhorse clings to life in the most inhospitable climate imaginable. Bitterly cold throughout the year, it is also so dry that the town is technically located in a desert. Its sole reason for existence is as a base for servicing the oil rigs and installations which are scattered over the adjacent ten thousand square miles.

As driving to the general store in a minus 50F winter blizzard is tricky at best, these rigs are mostly self-sufficient and so Deadhorse is small and sparsely populated, just a hodgepodge of large rusting work sheds on one side of the runway. There is also a small hotel, a tiny general store and a miniscule post office. That's it.

After saying all that, however, I must note that the town does have two worthy distinctions. The first is temperature, or rather the lack of it. The lowest wind chill-adjusted temperature recorded at Deadhorse was a nipple-shattering minus 102° Fahrenheit, or minus 75C. Cars have heaters built into the engine block to stop the oil from freezing solid, it's that cold. One guy I met said that in the olden days he had to make an actual bonfire under his truck to melt the oil before he could start it. Even in mid-June the temperature hovered around freezing point, but with the ever-present sun hovering above the horizon for 24 hours a day an eerie heat haze still shimmered across the tundra. It feels like the very edge of the world.

I had come to this forsaken place for the town's second distinction. Deadhorse is the most northerly town in the whole of the Americas to be permanently connected to the rest of the continent by road. This was my starting point, mile zero, page one. The Dalton Highway weaves 495 gravel-paved miles from Deadhorse to Fairbanks in central Alaska, and as well as being one of the remotest roads in North America it also happens to be one of the world's most dangerous. It was going to be a wild ride. Armed only with my bicycle, some money and what I hoped was the right equipment, I disembarked the plane with a handful of hope, a bag of naivety and a brimming glass of optimism. I immediately then realized I had no idea where I was going to stay.

"Hey there. Hey, are you doing alright? You look kinda lost," came a voice from behind me in the tiny arrivals hall where I was collecting my stuff. I spun round to see a middle-aged man with curly hair and a kind face looking at me.

"Um, yeah, sort of," I replied, which in British English means no. I was happy to have been asked, as I had no idea where I was going or what I was doing and the small crowd of arriving passengers had already dwindled to a few stragglers.

"So I heard there was a camping ground or something here," I asked hopefully.

"Uh, no, actually I don't think there is," he replied, "not that that I've heard of anyhow. Not a lot of anything around here! Looks like you need a hand; why don't you come with me, maybe we can sort something out." He looked past my shoulder at my pile of equipment. "Looks like you need two hands if nothing else."

It turned out that Rob was an angel sent from the heavens above. He drove me in his pickup truck the short distance from the airport to a large repair shed in the town.

"You can set yourself up inside here if you'd like; least it's got a roof," he said as he showed me through the heavy metal door into the large concrete-floored workshop. I couldn't have been happier if it had been a suite at the Four Seasons. It was a place to stay and somewhere get my bearings (and my mind right) before the long task ahead. As we talked in the entrance to the shed a couple of guys who worked there wandered over. They were tough men, with rough hands, thick mottled stubble and that tense distant look of those with hard lives. We chatted, and despite their gruff appearances they couldn't have been more welcoming. It was that kind of hospitality which comes from living in a place where not helping your neighbor means leaving him to die. Hard on the outside, soft in the middle and a core of iron.

One of these guys, Marty, turned out to be my second guardian angel of the day. A grizzled man of around 50 with wild graying hair, white stubble and a grip of steel, he was the very epitome of the Alaskan man.

"So I was wondering if there is a gas station around here?" I asked him, waving my camping stove fuel bottle in the air between us. "I need to get this bottle filled up before I head out. It burns pretty much anything, I think."

"Hmm. So we don't really have a proper gas station up here, apart from one that's way out towards the rigs," he replied a little quizzically, "but hey, leave it with me I will see what I can do," and took the red bottle with a mischievous grin, laying it on a nearby work bench to pick up later.

"Burns anything, right," he confirmed.

"I guess," I replied. "I've actually only used it once, but that's what the instructions said!" Meticulous planning once again, especially as I was about to set out across an endless wasteland with only rice to eat and thus dependent on an ability to boil water. Marty went off to do some errands and a few hours later I heard him knock on the shed door near where I was reading.

"Hey, I got it filled, man," he said, waving the bottle in is hand.

"Oh that's awesome!" I replied with a big grin. "Marty, you are a lifesaver, really." I took it from him and found a spot for it in one of my luggage bags.

"So what's in it, by the way?" I asked out of curiosity.

"Jet-A. I couldn't find anything else so I grabbed some from the hanger crew over the way," he replied with a cheeky grin. I laughed. He'd only gone and filled it up with jet fuel.

Later that afternoon I wandered the short distance from the repair shop to the only hotel in town. Although I knew it to be there, at $140 a night it was far too pricy for a guy trying to stretch his meager savings for the next two years. The hotel looked like an Antarctic research station from a movie. The single story building was raised on stilts a few feet off the permafrost while its thick wooden boarded exterior and metal door gave it a genuine 'pioneer chic' image. This place was the real deal. Unfortunately I had recently watched 'The Thing', a terrifying sci-fi horror movie set in an Antarctic research station, so my warm cuddly feelings towards it were slightly dulled, but no matter. Walking inside I was greeted by the friendly and helpful folks who ran it and any negative thoughts vanished. They were great. As we chatted I asked them about riding my bicycle to the coast, as I was planning to start my trip at the ocean shore. Sadly it turned out that riding to the ocean wasn't an option due to the security around the oil rigs; however, the hotel did run an official tour that went there and they were happy to let me bring my bicycle if I wanted. I signed right up.

# Colder than a Polar Bear's Privates

After a surprisingly restful night sleeping in the workshop I found myself outside the hotel in the clear and cold early morning, standing next to an old yellow US school bus with 15 or so intrepid tourists. The bus door opened and I stepped up to find myself face to face with a beautiful young woman, her blonde hair flowing down the side of her puffy jacket. There is a god after all, I thought, and after a quick double-take and a stumbling introduction in my finest English accent I asked her about getting my bicycle on board.

"No problem at all!" replied Angela, and asked the driver to open the back door. I lifted the bike into the back of the bus and took a seat at the rear as the rest of the passengers boarded, and we soon set off across the tundra along a well maintained dirt road, collectively marveling at the oil complexes and giant fireballs erupting from flaring towers into the pristine Arctic air. Despite a grimace from the pollution, the spectacle was undeniably stunning and the very definition of fire and ice. My inner pyromaniac found it cooler than Steve McQueen in a freezer.

Everything was going nicely on the bus ride, especially once I had introduced Tolly to the fawning crowd. I sat him next to me as we bumped along the road and made sure he was ready for his big photo shoot once we had arrived at the ocean itself, for which he was fortunately still appropriately clean and fluffy. We sat there listening to the tour commentary and distracted by the scenery, until Angela mentioned she had brought some towels.

Towels?

"So let me know if you want to join the Polar Bear Club," she continued. Looking at the towels she was piling on the front seat of the bus I put two and two together, but I still had to ask.

"Sure! It's when you swim in the Arctic Ocean," she replied, as though that was a normal answer to a normal question. "Now, there is also the Naked Polar Bear Club as well, and we do get the occasional person who does that."

This presented me with a problem. In typical fashion I had inexplicably picked that one day - that one day – to save on laundry and not wear any underwear, thus putting me in the Naked Polar Bear Club category by default. Hmmm, decisions, decisions. On the plus side, a once-in-a-lifetime opportunity. On the downside, I would be swimming naked in icy-cold water in front of Angela and an entire bus of people, so there was a high chance that I wasn't going to impress anyone. In the end there was only one realistic choice, the sensible choice, the prudent man's choice.

I chose the other option, and so a short time later shuffled out onto the ice stark naked in front of 15 bemused tourists and one hot 19 year old Arizonan girl. Not my most impressive moment in almost every way imaginable, but at the same time it felt incredibly liberating. With a deep breath of frigid air, a slow count to three and a leg raised in front of me, I stepped off the ice and into the void.

"Yaahh!"

Damn it was cold! Luckily it wasn't yet that deep, so I stood in thigh-deep water as the initial shock wore off, strangely aware of the soft silt under my feet. I turned to the crowd and raised my arms in celebration of this personal victory, an excellent move except for the minor detail that the water was only thigh deep and so was not quite high enough to protect any remaining modesty I might have still had. Ooops. There is nothing like murky ice water to obscure everything on your behalf, whether you want it obscured or not, so if ever there was a reason to suddenly submerge myself in the Arctic Ocean that was it.

Falling backwards into the water I joined the Polar Bear Club in style. I wouldn't trade the experience for anything, but the journey back was still awkward. Foiled again!

# The Beginning

11.14am Alaskan Time, June 26, 2003. I clipped a foot into the pedal cleat and stared out to the horizon, the tundra shimmering in the bright sunshine. Everything was quiet, the air still and cold. Before me was mile zero in the whole world. I looked at the gravel road disappear into the distance and wondered what lay ahead. Pain or pleasure? Adventure or boredom? Death or glory? Perhaps a little of each, with the hopeful exception of death.

Was I scared? Not really. I know that sounds strange, but it was far more a sense of anticipation rather than fear. The task was clear. I knew what to do and how to do it, so I faced the inevitable hurdles with confidence. All I had to do was ride, and that was simple enough. For me, it is a much greater fear to not to know the path, or not know if I can follow it once it is found; indeed, I found the uncertainty at the end of my journey far more fearful than the journey itself. In those beginning moments, though, the challenges ahead were at the front of my thoughts, a sense of burden and yet of expectation. It was time.

I took a couple of photos with myself and Tolly the Bear to mark the occasion, and then, with a push and a wobble, my 80lbs of equipment, bicycle, bear, food and water rolled tentatively onto the loose gravel road. The quest I had dreamed of was beginning for real now and everything on the line; the stakes high enough that death or glory were both possible outcomes. I was attempting something bigger than I was and adventure awaited. Nothing could stop me now!

I made it 20 miles before my first crash, and after picking myself up I promptly crashed again at mile 31. I guess something could stop me after all. With my knees bleeding and blood leaking from a sizable gash in the crease of my palm, a place so awkward it was still bleeding a month later, this was not an auspicious start. With no other option than to continue I wrapped my hand in toilet tissue as best I could and remounted the bike. Fortunately, they were the only crashes of the day as my riding became steadier and more confident as I adjusted to the sluggish reactions of such a heavy bicycle. By early evening I had covered 85 grueling miles to the edge of the North Slope where the flat tundra began to rise into the foothills of the Brooks mountain range ahead. Exhausted, I pulled off the road onto a wide grassy area and set up my tent as I watched tempestuous black clouds blanket the dark sky while thick veils of rain swept across the landscape, the light and color drained from the world like a pestilence across the land. Twilight was approaching and a light drizzle began to fall. I was now utterly alone and my prior optimism and euphoria were crushed in that dim solitude. I was beyond help, and for the first time I was scared. Sitting in the rain I cooked a woefully meager meal; one small bowl of rice and one small bowl of rehydrated chili con carne were my allotted rations for tonight's dinner, an inadequacy matched only by the similarly meager lunch and breakfast rations which I had planned for the next seven days. I had found misery.

I marveled at how spectacularly I had underestimated how hard this journey would be, how difficult the cycling, the quantity of food required, or how much training I should have done. Or that I thought it would be OK to hardly train at all. My preparation had consisted of riding to work and back, a seven mile round trip, for three days a week for the three weeks before my departure. Ironically, I stopped doing it because I felt that riding across London was too dangerous and too unpleasant. My total training mileage was less than that single first day, and boy was I paying the price. I knew I had bitten off too much, but I also knew I had no real alternative than to continue.

In those first eight days and 495 miles my fears became realities. I was burning more than 8,000 calories a day and eating only around 2,000, the equivalent of running two marathons each day for eight days without eating anything at all. Stopping at a tiny gas station on day three, the first and only first sign of humanity during the first six days, I ate 11 snickers bars in one go. It was mechanical, just unwrapping, chewing and swallowing them one after the other. Even with this calorie boost, by the time I reached civilization I had lost more than 15lb, nearly 10% of my body weight.

If this was not bad enough, the mosquitoes made it worse. Much worse. I had been told they were bad in Alaska, but they brought a new level of wretchedness, proof that God must have a twisted sense of humor. Billions upon billions of these sadistic little guys lie as dormant larvae through the winter, with antifreeze in their blood to keep them alive, before emerging at the start of summer in vast and voracious swarms. The migrating caribou, a smaller version of a moose, lose up to a liter of blood to mosquito bites *every day*, and sweet-smelling people like me don't stand a chance. To help fend them off I was wearing 100% pure DEET mosquito repellent, a chemical so strong that it dissolved the paint off my watch, plus thick head-to-toe fleece, gloves and a bee-keeper head net, and yet despite this I was still being bitten over a 100 times a day, every day. In fairness, I probably wasn't helping myself in this regard. I remember waking up one night urgently needing the call of nature, so rather than get fully dressed I decided to dash outside wearing only my boxer shorts.

"I'll only be out there for 60 seconds," I thought to myself, "If I keep moving, how bad could it be?" The answer is "Bad". I knew my plan might be an error when I touched the tent to open the flap and a loud buzzing noise erupted all around me as the swarm of bugs clinging to the outer surface were dislodged into the air. The entire tent was covered in a layer of them. I made my dash for it, and after diving back into the tent I spent the next 15 minutes killing all the mosquitoes which had followed me inside. I thought it had gone OK until the next morning when I counted my bites, which was easy enough to do as keeping track of them had become a new form of entertainment during my exile. It had not gone OK. 150 bites in under a minute is not what I call fun.

I arrived in Fairbanks an emotional and physical wreck. It was a new and shocking experience for me. I was physically drained, as weak as a bedridden hospital patient trying to move for the first time in months. For several days even the simplest of tasks was a trial. To climb the stairs in the hostel I had to take each step separately as I hauled myself upstairs using the bannister, my legs lifeless and weak. There was no fuel in the tank; the cumulative micro-tears in my muscle fibers from so much hard cycling had turned the insides of my legs to mush. For the first four days all I did was sleep for 14 hours a day, eat as much as I could and watch TV. Anything beyond this was a mental stress, compounded by god-only-knows what serious chemical imbalance I had created from my inadequate nutrition and severe calorie restrictions. I had left myself barely able to mentally cope with the situation and was at rock bottom, my motivation torched to cinders. I was once again scared, scared that for the next two years I would suffer as I had for the prior two weeks, scared that I also couldn't quit and keep my self-worth intact. I was trapped, and began falling into depression. Only a distraught phone call with my parents kept me from packing up and flying home. Both were sympathetic but both were also wiser than me. They knew the regret I would face if I gave up now, and my dad reminded me of a story he'd once told me, many years before.

"Do you remember when I ran the London Marathon?" he asked me. Yes, I replied. "Well, after 20 miles I was feeling awful, and I didn't think I had it in me to finish. But then, just when I was about to give up, I saw a big advertising billboard up ahead. Do you remember what it said? It said 'If you think it hurts now, think about how painful it will be if you quit.' It kept me going to the marathon finish, that did."

He was right, of course. I would have struggled to overcome the knowledge that I had quit, even if others didn't mind or care. My parents pulled me back for the edge, and the fire and drive I began with was slowly rekindled. I never really explained to my parents how pivotal that phone call was, but it saved me, and for that and about a million other things I will always be in their debt. I realized what it meant to have people willing to stand with you at the end of things, in those times when you just can't do it by yourself. I often say that 50% of people could do 90% of my trip, but it is that last 10% which is a big dividing line. Only with their help did I make it through.

Despite such suffering, I now look back on my time riding the Dalton Highway with fond memories of a wonderful experience. I saw two of continental America's remaining 40,000 musk ox, a rare type of bison, and stood on top of the Trans-Alaska pipeline just for a laugh. I experienced crossing the tree line, north of which no tree can grow, and saw glittering mirages on the icy tundra. I also met some very interesting individuals along the way, my favorite of which was an ice-road trucker. He was an older guy, probably late 50s, whose white-streaked scraggly hair, big calloused hands and weather-worn face spoke of a tough life in the wilderness. In true Alaskan style, though, his outward appearance belied his warm and hospitable nature. He stopped his truck for a chat and we stood by the cab of the huge orange juggernaut as I devoured a small tin of Del Monte fruit chunks he had kindly offered. I asked what it was like to be a trucker in Alaska.

"It's real dangerous for starters, man," he replied with a cool seriousness in his voice, "real dangerous. You gotta respect the road and the environment out here, man, 'cos if you don't it will turn round and bite you in the ass. You're a pioneer out here, you know," he continued, "and you have rely on yourself a lot of the time."

He explained that in Alaska, safety isn't just a topic on which inspectors write ignored notices about on an office wall. It's real and deadly serious. The rules here are for your own protection, and if you don't respect them your life expectancy is probably going to get shorter. A lot shorter. Even the toughest and strongest know it, and respect it.

He then asked about my trip, and as I told him about my plan to ride down to Argentina his face lit up.

"That's a great trip, man!" he exclaimed excitedly. "You know, back in '72 I rode a scooter around the world. That was a hell of an adventure!"

What! This guy was a legend amongst men. He did that trip before guide books or a backpacker trail, just him and his search for adventure. There, on the side of the road, hearing this story made me smile and it gave me hope. I told him so.

"Just keep on going, man, keep on truckin'!" he continued. "Yeah, you're gonna have a blast, man. There is some crazy stuff out there! You can do it, I know you can do it!"

My trucker friend gave me a prescription-size dose of much needed confidence, confidence that my trip wasn't just a fantasy, confidence that it could be done, and done by me, no less. For that - and the can of fruit - I wish him all the luck in the world. If you are ever in northern Alaska and meet a guy with big orange truck, please give him my eternal thanks.

# EIGHT

# Home of the Elves

Fairbanks was a nice enough place to spend time recovering from that first stretch, and each day my weight and strength recovered as my willpower and drive were slowly rekindled. Fatalistic pessimism morphed back into the 'I can do anything' state I had been in only days before, and eventually I felt ready to return to the road once more. I left Fairbanks on a pleasant summer's day, the warmth of the Alaskan interior contrasting with the frozen conditions beyond the mountains to the north, and I cruised along in shorts and T-shirt while enjoying the invigorating fresh smell of pine trees rising from the forest. I was heading for Canada, but with 350 miles to the border I suspected that my Alaskan adventures were not over. About the only thing I did not expect was to meet Santa Claus.

Alaska is a curious place. It is wild and unusual, and in some places just plain odd. That afternoon, as I rode east I arrived in a small town which exemplified this impression. I was puzzled to see that despite the July warmth virtually everything in the town had a Christmas theme. Lamp posts were painted like red-and-white candy canes and most of the trees in town were Christmas trees, complete with permanent fairy lights. In the winter snow it must look amazing, but surrounded by green summer grass it looked hilariously out of place. A short way into the town I finally passed a large sign which solved this mystery.

"Welcome!" it beckoned with grandiose satisfaction, "to the North Pole!" I had stumbled into North Pole, Alaska.

Every year, small children across America write wish lists to Santa, even if they have been bad.

"And where does Santa live?" ask their parents, once more playing this annual game.

"He lives in the North Pole, and that's in Alaska!" cry out misguided five year olds from California to Maine, and so that is what gets scribbled on envelopes in five year olds handwriting. 'Santa Claus, North Pole, Alaska'. With stamp affixed, eager young eyes watch their parents post the letters, and into the mail system they go. As I stood outside the town's enormous post office I could see where they ended up.

Seeing the post office gave me an idea for a cunning plan. I went into the small store inside the building and bought a postcard, which I then mailed to my parents in England.

"Your son had been a very good boy," it said, "Please get him a really nice present for Christmas, just in case I can't make it. Regards, Santa Claus."

My cunning deception didn't work, but at least my parents are now some of the only people in the world with a reply from Santa Claus, complete with the "North Pole" postmark to prove it. Definitely worth a try.

I was sad to have to leave this childhood theme park. I have always been quite fond of these childish things, perhaps because it allows me to be free and creative, an image of my life before the rules and pressures took over. Daft as it was, I know I would act like a 10 year old again if I returned there in winter. Maybe one day I will. In a small act of silliness before leaving, I sat Tolly the Bear on the post office sign and took a photo, thus making him a genuine polar bear for the day. I mean, only polar bears can visit the North Pole, right?

It was back to the highway once more, where after a night camping at the roadside I arrived in Tok, a small town strung out along the main highway. I pulled out my crappy map to look for a campsite, and as I did so a large SUV pulled up next to me. A friendly middle-aged woman with red-brown hair rolled down the window.

"Hello!" she asked chirpily. "Are you OK?" Being British and thus unused to the random friendliness of strangers (and even less so to the random friendliness of a women in an SUV) I was momentarily frozen, eventually stammering out some feeble response.

"Um, hi. Yeah, I think I'm doing OK. I think. Actually I'm just trying to figure out where there is campsite round here," I replied, holding up the map in an actually-I-have-no-idea-what-I'm-doing manner.

"So are you staying in town, then?" she asked. Clearly my response must have been woeful as a look of caring concern spread across her face. "You know, if you want a shower and a sandwich you are more than welcome to come back to our house."

Maybe it was my years of traveling experience gained the hard way, but it took me a few seconds to contemplate this offer. Was there a downside? She seemed nice and I couldn't imagine anything could go too wrong. Sometime it does, of course, but if you don't commit to such opportunities then none of the good things can happen either. That's a risk I'm usually willing to take, so I graciously accepted.

The nice woman turned out to be a truly wonderful woman. Her name was Robin and her family took me in for the night. Her husband Mark was a forest firefighter, a rugged Tom Selleck lookalike kind of guy, with a trim moustache and a wide smile. He was a down-to-earth fellow with a big heart and a very trusting disposition, which I discovered first hand when he came home in the late afternoon to find me sitting in his living room, drinking milk out of his fridge and watching his TV with his three young kids. Robin forgot to mention to him that there might be a strange British man in his house when he returned, but whereas most guys would have freaked out Mark took it all in his stride. A weary cyclist couldn't have asked for more hospitality and understanding. What a great family! It was also my birthday, so when Robin found out she actually went out and got me a cake! They even helped me get their phone number to my twin sister so we could talk on out birthday, even more impressive as she was in New Zealand at the time. I went to bed happier than I had been for a very long time, and I remain forever in their debt.

# There be Gold in Them Thar Hills

Canada. It's big. Really, really big. Big in a way that if you think you grasp how big it is, you probably don't. It *never* ends. You can't get a feel of the scale of it by looking at a map or even by flying over it. On a bicycle, big is demoralizing, and riding across Canada can be soul destroying. It is so vast and so sparsely populated that in some parts it can take two whole days merely to cycle between adjacent towns. The Yukon Territory alone is the size of the UK but only has 33,000 inhabitants, two thirds of which live in a single town. Ironically, after having ridden across part of it, for me the real puzzle was not why so few people live there but why so many. Despite its undeniable beauty it is remote, cold and dark in winter, difficult to live in and even harder to make a living in. Indeed, a recently as the late 19th century only a sparse handful of immigrants lived in the whole of the Yukon. They were a hardy bunch, mostly hunters, fur trappers and the occasional gold prospector on a mission to seek his fortune on the last great frontier. One such prospector was named 'Skookum' Jim, who in the late 1890s travelled far up the Yukon River in his search for gold and eventually reached the Yukon's confluence with the Klondike River. After navigating up the Klondike for several miles he turned from the main flow and panned for gold in a small tributary stream. It was in that creek, on August 16, 1896, that he finally hit pay dirt. The gold rush had begun.

A boom town called Dawson City sprang up near the discovery and quickly became the epicenter of the gold rush. As I cycled across Alaska and into Canada, this town was my next destination. After setting up my tent just across the river from the town I spent a few days in Dawson to recover. One of the best places to relax was in the original town saloon on Main St. Built early in the days of the town's beginnings it became the place to spend newly found wealth. Successful prospectors were known to throw gold nuggets into the bar spittoon purely for the entertainment of seeing less fortunate souls fishing them out. With such a history of human suffering, disaster and triumph combined with its location on the farthest frontier, Dawson is a fascinating place, still authentic with its dirt streets, subsiding old buildings, wooden board sidewalks and a saloon bar still with its original swing doors. It's a little exaggerated for the tourists, I suppose, but that sense of history is still there. It felt like the end of the road, as indeed it was for many of the people who arrived there to seek their fortune.

The hardship and dangers that faced those attempting the long journey to the Klondike in the winter of 1897 was eclipsed only by the staggering wealth that the gold rush created. Approximately 20 million ounces of gold have been recovered from the area since the original discovery, worth $30 billion at today's prices. It is said that the first few ships that docked in San Francisco and Seattle from the Yukon after the discovery carried a billion dollars of gold between them. Some of the richest mines unleashed a torrent. One story has it that a particular prospector became angry when his rocking box, a device used to separate the gold from the dirt, had broken after only two hours working on his new claim. He dismantled it impatiently and in the bottom of the machine found what had caused the malfunction. 800oz of gold, worth $1.5 million today, had clogged up the sifting mechanism. In two hours. Even now, the tributary stream of the original discovery, appropriately named Bonanza Creek, glitters from billions of microscopic flecks of gold glimmering in the river bed. It was so alluring that I was suddenly overcome with gold fever! I spent 10 vigorous minutes panning the creek with a Frisbee, sadly coming away empty handed. My reward was the experience of prospecting for gold at the very epicenter of a place that changed so many lives forever, the place that started it all. Although I was still sad to be about 115 years too late.

To reach Dawson from the ocean ships which brought them to Alaska, many of those first prospectors made the treacherous climb over the mountains along the infamous Chilkoot trail. I had wanted to hike this trail for many years, but first I needed to get to its start near the town of Skagway on the Alaskan coast. I left Dawson and headed south. Riding towards Whitehorse, the only sizeable town in the Yukon, I happened to meet a wonderful German couple riding in the same direction, and so for the next two weeks I was thrilled to be able to enjoy their company. Gerrit owned a bike shop in Germany, and his strength and talent for cycling was much needed as they had decided to bring another member of the family. Gerrit's bike was loaded with bags like mine, but behind the bike he also towed a trailer onto which was strapped a kennel, and in the kennel sat Sam, their miniature husky! What a cool dog he was, sometimes running like a white wolf through the forest alongside us as we roamed the sparsely travelled roads in this part of the world. For much of the time, though, and especially when there was traffic, he added a ton of weight to Gerrit's bike as he was towed around, but the joy of having him along was more than worth it. At least for me!

It was a blessed relief to finally have some genuine company on my ride. Long stretches since Deadhorse had been intensely lonely, and although I often enjoyed the peace and solitude I also missed the ability to share my experiences. I also found it hard to constantly maintain a positive emotional state, and sometimes became depressed or worked up into a pointless frenzy over nothing. With no other human input, the past conversations I repeated in my head became emotional spirals both up and down. Now, finally, with some good company I could find balance and enjoy some much missed laughter.

We stopped one evening outside a restaurant in the middle of nowhere that was famous for its cinnamon rolls, at least according to the billboards we had seen along the roadside for the previous 100 miles. Scarcely had we set up our tents at the back of the building when we heard violent barking nearby and from around the corner of the building ran two large Rottweilers, teeth bared and coming straight for us. We were done for. Suddenly, a white flash appeared from the side and I turned to see Sam the Dog run out in front of us to intercept them! All three dogs came to a halt between us and after a quick dog-sniff greeting they ran off together into the surrounding undergrowth. We were saved! I felt like I had been rescued by Lassie.

It was a wonderful few weeks until our routes diverged and we were forced to finally part company. It had truly been a great experience to cycle with them, easy and stress free days with fabulous and inspiring people. I said my sad goodbye, before taking a right at the junction and descending towards Alaska and the Chilcoot trail.

# The Right Man for the Job

Nestled in a steep valley amongst the milky blue-green fjords, Skagway looks and feels like an Alaskan cliché. Beyond the low wooden buildings of the town rises the White Pass, a foreboding notch in the coastal mountains between the ocean and the Klondike gold fields beyond. In 1897, a railway to the top of the pass was commissioned to help reach the gold, and thousands of men worked in temperatures down to minus 50°F (minus 46C) to build the tunnels, bridges and track along the nearly sheer cliffs. One part of the passage was even named Dead Horse Gulch for the thousands of horses which perished during the construction. It was a task so difficult and dangerous that it was almost not completed, and yet it was. Travelling along the railway by steam train, the wind carrying a hint of smoke through the old open air carriage as the train hugs the cliffs towards the glistening fjord and the town far below, is one of the world's great train rides. It is a spectacular testament to spirit over adversity, and to man's greed for gold.

On the road from Dawson I finally reached the border at the top of the White Pass and was treated to a glorious downhill to the town before spending the next four days relaxing at an 'authentic' hostel that was basically a family's house. I enjoyed a wonderful time there, only marred by one strange experience. I awoke on one particular day in a terrible mood. Nothing would cheer me from this strangely foul temperament, and by early afternoon I could stand it no longer. Leaving the homely living room of the hostel I put on my cycling gear and walked outside into the overcast drizzle. I mounted my bicycle, put on my headphones and selected the training montage from Rocky IV on my Walkman. I hit play as I reached the bottom of the pass and it blasted forth at maximum volume as I charged up the mountain in a rage. I climbed uninterrupted for 2,885ft to the top of the pass and the Canadian border, before turning around and zooming straight back down to town.

By the time I arrived in Skagway again I was feeling fabulous, and I really mean fabulous. It was like one of those rare days when you wake up feeling like a million dollars; it's your day, you can *feel* it, today you are a *winner*! I realized later that the morning's despair was no coincidence. It was a withdrawal symptom. The exercise of the prior weeks was something new to my body and had created an addiction known as a 'runner's high'. The brain releases natural chemicals in response to exercise which act like a happiness drug, and with enough exercise over enough time you can become addicted. It was weird to be affected on such a deep and fundamental level by something so simplistic, but it was the only explanation. It was a peculiar window on the soul indeed. As I acclimatized to my exertion levels over the following months and years the addiction disappeared, yet I will never forget the feeling of that strange afternoon.

On the fifth day in Skagway I packed a bag and headed to the Chilkoot trail, a three or four day hike over a mountain ridge to a lake beyond. It was a beautiful walk. The scenery changed with each day as I progressed higher and further into the interior until I was eventually faced with the final climb to the crest. It was here, on the barren scree and rocks, that I *felt* the gold rush for the first time. Much of the original machinery used for a makeshift cable car lies abandoned and rusting on the ground, and relics from the original prospectors still lie there untouched. I even saw some old leather boots in a crevice between the rocks. I found it moving to know that this history was real and that it happened right there, beneath my very feet.

Beyond the summit of the Chilcoot pass the trail descends to Bennett Lake, a lake with an outlet which becomes a tributary of the Yukon River. During the gold rush, prospectors where required to build their own boat for the trip into the interior, hence the need for the cable car to lift their supplies to the top of the ridge. Luckily for me I was heading instead back to Skagway and could let the steam train take the strain. Back in town I spent a couple more days relaxing before leaving again, this time for good.

There was never a set time I planned to stay in each place, but rather it was an organic process, a balance of the forces. The 'stickiness' of each place generally depended on the amount of rest I needed, how much there was to see and do, and the people I met, while the pressure of my journey forever pulled me back to the road. I had an 18 month window between the Alaskan summer and the South American summer, and thoughts of the immense distance still to cover were never far away. In each place, sometimes after a day, a week or a month, the time came when it felt right to leave. In Skagway, that time had now come.

I said my goodbyes to Alaska for the second and final time and climbed once more up the White Pass towards the wilderness of Canada. There is no road along the coast of north western Canada as the rugged landscape and jagged fjords make it difficult and uneconomical to build one, so the most westerly route to the south is the Stewart-Cassiar Highway, a 543 mile inland dirt road running from north nowhere to south nowhere. I turned onto it with low expectations of fun and high expectations of misery. The first night was spent at a small campsite on the banks of the surprisingly idyllic Bow Lake, a large clear lake surrounded by pine covered hills about 40 miles from the junction. I was almost alone at the lake and as normal I found camping in the far north a lonely prospect. Before sunset you can often sit outside and relax with a well-earned cup of coffee and a snack while admiring the frequently spectacular views. However, at sunset the mosquito hoards arrive and you cook quickly before the temperature falls with the coming darkness. Then it is time to retire to the tent where there is nothing to do but write a quick journal entry, read or re-read a few pages of the lonely planet guide book and check the map for the next day's ride. I was usually pretty exhausted by then and despite such enthralling entertainments I normally went to sleep quite early. Coping with this loneliness was one of the hardest parts of the journey, even if you have a little toy bear as a companion. It is amazing what you can get used to.

While that first evening on the Cassiar Highway was normal, the next morning was a different story. A stormy tempest had arrived during the night and the weather was now awful. Luckily the rain was sparse, but it was cold and a strong wind howled incessantly. As a cyclist you can acclimatize to most kinds of weather or at least suffer them with moderate ambivalence. Starting to snow? You dress up warmly and ride carefully. Been raining for days? Your life will suck but ultimately you won't dissolve, just most of your clothes and half your equipment. Burning in the desert sun? You drink more and sweat more. Windy? Now you are in trouble. Wind is a different animal. To a cyclist it is a black beast born of Nebuchadnezzar himself. It is evil, a nemesis, the bringer of suffering and Lord of Injustice. Every ounce of effort expended to ride into a headwind is lost forever. Unfortunately, due to my poor planning, the number of days when I cycled into a headwind far outnumbered the days with a tailwind due to my route against the trade winds. At times I felt like Sisyphus, the mythical Greek king condemned by the Gods to push a boulder up a mountain for all eternity. That day on the Cassiar was no exception.

Tall trees sheltered the road a little from the maelstrom but by early afternoon I was exhausted and desperate for a rest. Crossing a small bridge I rode through some wide gates into a large and deserted tree-covered glade along the opposite river bank. I had entered the Dease River Crossing RV Park and Campground. A small picnic table stood in a grove of large pine trees about 30 yards from a small house, and I quickly sat down to rest my legs and make a large stack of peanut butter sandwiches. I was half way through eating them when I heard the thwack of a screen door bang shut and looked up to see a large man walking casually over towards me. He wore a worn pair of denim dungarees and a checked cowboy shirt, as though he had dressed up to make the whole occasion especially authentic. I assumed he was the owner and was briefly concerned as to what his reaction to me might be, but I needn't have worried.

"Hi there!" he greeted me warmly, extending his big, weathered hand. "My name's Dennis. Welcome to my place. I guess you look like you could use a rest!"

Any worry or concerns quickly vanished. Dennis was as hospitable as you can get, and as honest, hardworking and generous as they come. He had been a dairy farmer for many years in his native Illinois in the US before selling up and moving north to settle in this remote part of Canada. I asked him why he made such a move, but before he could answer there was a deafening 'Crack!' followed by a splintering sound. I spun to my left just in time to see a large tree fall onto Dennis's house!

I momentarily froze in disbelief before jumping up from the table and uttering something I probably can't repeat in type. I turned to look at Dennis, expecting him to be freaking out as well, but instead I saw him calmly rise from the table.

"Ah, that doesn't look so great. Hang on there for a bit, won't you," he said, "I'll be back in a minute," and with that he set off across the grass before disappearing behind the house. For the next 15 minutes I witnessed a marvel of efficiency and one man's raw ability to get things done. In that short time he had fetched his slightly rusty little yellow fork lift truck from the nearby barn, tied a piece of rope to the tree and carefully winched it off the roof. Clambering out of the cab he picked up the chainsaw he had also retrieved, coaxed it into life without missing a step, and like a professional lumberjack methodically de-branched the trunk before sawing it into 3ft logs. Once done, Dennis got back into the fork lift and stacked the logs up next to his house for firewood before dragging the remaining branches to a large fire pit over in the corner of the yard. After a quick inspection of the damage to the house - luckily just some broken guttering - he returned his equipment and rejoined me on the bench. 15 minutes, I kid you not.

"Sorry 'bout that, guess these things happen," he said with the upbeat continuity of a man who is unaware of his latest miracle. "Now, where were we?"

I often wonder why the world doesn't collapse into chaos every five minutes, given the staggering number of things that can go wrong in a world subjected to mankind's unsurpassed capacity for stupidity (as anyone who has watched various videos on YouTube can confirm). Why don't planes crash every day or power stations occasionally explode? This is not as difficult as you might imagine. A great friend told me a story from when he was manning the skeleton crew of a night shift at a large power station in England. At 3.00am an emergency alarm rang out from the automated control room, threatening to shut down the power grid in the northeast of England. The cause? An overzealous janitor had looked with disdain at the dirty computer keyboards in the control room and decided to clean them by putting them *all* in the kitchen unit dishwasher. No joke. As the red warning lights multiplied my friend had to frantically search for a dry keyboard to plug into the control console, which he managed to do before the plant shut down. Faced with such incidents I had no answer to our survival puzzle until I saw Dennis in action. It was the missing link. It is the rare individuals like Dennis who keep things functioning and prevent these overzealous power station janitors from causing too much damage. May the Dennis's of the world live forever, for all our sakes.

# ELEVEN

# An Alien Encounter

I said a fond farewell to Dennis and to the sound of crunching gravel beneath my tires I pulled back onto the windswept road to resume the day's torture. Distracted by the suffering, it was only after two hours that I noticed something was wrong. One of those eerie, "Did I leave the oven on?" feelings where you know something is 'off', but not sure what. I stopped and did an inventory check. All my bags were still attached, all my valuables were present and correct, and I confirmed no wolves were stalking me either, just to be sure. Straddling my bike I ran my fingers through my hair in puzzlement, only then noticing that this was surprisingly easy to do given I hadn't yet taken off my cycling helmet. Damn. I'd left the bloody thing on the picnic table! I briefly considered abandoning it there but knew my mother would kill me if she found out, plus it had already saved me more than once. There was nothing to do but to go back and get it, so with a howl of frustration I wrenched the bike around and began the 15 mile journey back the way I had come.

At 5.30pm a surprised Dennis watched me arrive for the second time that day. I pointed to the cycle helmet still sitting on the picnic table, and after he stopped chuckling I asked if I could camp in the glen for the night.

"You are more than welcome to," he replied, "but I have a better idea," and with a grin he turned and led me past his house to a nearby two story wooden building. Inside on the ground floor there was a large woodworking shop covered with wood shavings while upstairs there were some very basic rooms with bare floor boards and an old bed in each.

"You're more than welcome to stay here free of charge if you'd like," continued Dennis, "Should keep you out of the wind at least. Why don't you get yourself sorted, and afterwards my wife and I would love for you to join us for dinner." I heartily accepted both offers.

His wife Lana was as cheery a character as Dennis. She made us the best grilled cheese sandwich of all time and we sat at the kitchen table in his rustic cabin and talked about this and that. I asked Dennis about running a place like this, so far from anywhere.

"Ah, you know," he replied, putting down his knife and fork, "it's pretty good. But it's not without some challenges. Like the tree today."

"Right!" I replied. "There must be all kinds of crazy things happening up here. Things like bears! Do you get many of them around here?"

"Oh yeah. Actually we get lots of them and you have to be careful. Once they figure out you've got food, well, then you have a bear problem. We had a grizzly break in here once," he continued, getting up from the table and walking over to the far window. "It took out the whole wall here to get in," and traced his hand from the floor to the ceiling, then about 10ft across the wall above the window and back to the floor. "Lucky we were out - the damn thing turned the place inside out. I had to shoot it in the end." He reached over to a sideboard near the wood burning stove and rummaged around in drawer for a couple of seconds before pulling out two photos. Retaking his seat he placed the first one in front of me. It was a picture of the dead bear with a rope around its legs hanging upside down from his yellow fork lift truck. To say this bear was enormous would be an understatement.

"No way," I exclaimed, disbelievingly pointing and moving the photo closer, "That thing is massive!" Dennis nodded.

"13 feet tall, that guy, weighed 'bout 700 pounds. Pain in the backside to move."

To put that in perspective, 13ft tall is an NBA basketball player standing on the shoulders of another NBA player. 700lbs weighs the same as a man sitting on a Harley Davidson. If it reared up you'd be staring at its belly button. I didn't fancy my chances in a one-on-one situation. Dennis then handed me the second photo.

"Here's a picture of its paw," he said. It looked fake but it wasn't. The bear's ankle was far thicker than my thigh and the paw itself was well over a foot across. On each claw was a fearsome six inch blade which looked to be designed for the specific purpose of disemboweling cyclists. Bears may look all cute and fluffy but after seeing those photos I was going to treat them with more respect from now on. They run faster than us and can climb trees. Or uproot them. The US National Park Service recommends staying at least 400 yards away from them and I could see why. Luckily, my first bear encounter in Canada was at about this distance. Unluckily, my second was at about three yards.

This encounter happened on the Cassiar Highway not far from Dennis's place. Cresting a small hill I saw a black bear sitting at the bottom of the little valley at the side of the road ahead, absent-mindedly eating little yellow flowers and enjoying the sunshine. My getaway speed up the other side of the hill was going to be about four miles an hour but I had no option than to ride right past it with my fingers crossed. As I pedaled slowly past I looked at the bear, which sat up and looked back at me. We were so close I could see its individual whiskers, the shine in its dark eyes and the small flowers still sticking out of its mouth. It was having a grand old time with those flowers and fortunately seemed to regard me with a nonchalant disinterest. The experience was invigorating but it also nearly cost me my underwear.

As I ate the grilled cheese in Dennis's kitchen the tail of the storm left us and the weather quickly became still, clear and cool. We continued our merry conversation until the silence outside was broken by the sound of tires rolling on the gravel path. It was Friday night and five of Dennis's friends had driven up to visit from the town of Dease Lake, about 30 miles to the south. We walked outside and a red plastic SOLO cup full of whiskey and coke was immediately thrust into my hand; one of the guys was already distributing them from the tailgate of his pickup truck. I was heartily welcomed as one of the group – this was Canada, after all!

Two of the group became particularly good friends. Amanda was a woman in her late 20s who worked as a school teacher. She was super fun and yet also represented the saner part of a group who worked hard and played harder in what was essentially still the last frontier. Cody was a young guy about my age, as tough and solid as they come, with a big heart, a bigger hand shake and a gregarious personality. He was dressed in a light brown knitted sweater peppered with holes earned the hard way from his career in the construction industry. He was a man's man and the typical alpha-male, but with none of the usually associated arrogance. I liked him immediately.

As the evening wore on and the Jack Daniels continued to flow, the guys lit a roaring fire and we sat for hours next to the hot crackling logs while we laughed, drank and swapped stories under the darkening twilight sky. We were still in the far north, and at that latitude in July the sun set for only a few hours each night. I was in one of those relaxed, happy states, and as the fire burned down I lay on my back just outside the circle, warming my toes and gazing up at the billion stars strung along the Milky Way. It was only as my eyes adjusted to the darkness that I could see that something was wrong with the sky. It was shimmering. Almost imperceptible at first, the darkness had a subtle green hue that oscillated through the sky like waves on the ocean.

"Hey Cody," I said, while still staring up at the sky, "I don't suppose you see the sky wobbling, do you?"

"I don't think so, eh," came his answer from somewhere around the fire. "Probably just the sky getting lighter, it comes up really early these days. Or maybe it's just the fire or something."

"Hmmm, yeah." I replied as I continued watching. "Yeah, it's probably me." Except that it wasn't.

"Hey, are you guys seeing this?" I asked again a short time later, and this time they were. The sky really was shimmering and the brightness increased until huge sheets of vivid electric green sparkles hung across the sky, wavering like curtains billowing in a phantom breeze. We all lay there memorized as we watched the Aurora Borealis, the Northern Lights, in all their glory.

It was truly remarkable. The most stunning aspect happens to be the one thing you can't appreciate from the photos. The Northern Lights are three dimensional. Cosmic rays come whizzing in from space along the Earth's magnetic field and react with the upper atmosphere to emit light. These rays create sheets that look like a waterfall of sparkles. We must have moved right underneath the main point where the rays entered the atmosphere as a small area above us slowly became brighter and brighter until an intense green spot burned above us. Green laser beams seemed to fire in every direction from its center and it looked exactly like an alien spaceship was beaming us on board (I imagine!). It was science fiction, but reality. I lay there in my lucid bubble with the biggest of smiles, totally stunned at what I was seeing. Even the locals were amazed; Amanda said it was one of the best she had seen for over 10 years. If this is what an alien abduction looks like, sign me up.

# Ice

The next morning I graciously accepted the group's invitation to go fishing. We loaded up a small aluminum boat at the bank of the river and were soon speeding through the narrow streams with Cody manning the outboard motor. Reaching a secret spot at a bend in the river, we tried spinning for pike by a submerged tree and soon enough had landed some decent sized fish. It was a genuine Canadian adventure, and the kind of experience which had inspired me to undertake my cycle journey in the first place. Feeling the wind in my hair as we rushed across the water I felt so lucky to be there, and smiled with a genuine happiness based in deepest gratitude.

By 1.00pm we were back at the Dease River Crossing RV Park, and while the others drove their trucks back to town I hopped back on the bicycle and rode to meet them there. Cody was gracious enough to give me a bed for the night at his parent's log cabin. He said his dream was to build his own cabin just like it and I would be surprised if he doesn't manage it.

Next morning it really was time to leave. I still had 170 miles of the Cassiar highway to go before turning back onto the main road, and a whopping 835 miles before my next planned rest in the small mountain town of Jasper. Along the way I passed the famous Mt Robson, which was completely obscured in rain and cloud as I rode by. I did see what it should look like from the postcards in the visitor center, though! So near and yet so far. Apart from that, the remaining miles were generally scenic but uneventful, with the exception of the RVs. Oh, the RVs.

By virtue of its natural beauty, its location as the start of the Icefields Parkway, and regrettably probably also due to the golf course, Jasper attracts tourists by the RV load. For those not familiar with 'Recreational Vehicles', they are mobile homes used mainly by vacationers and retirees who sell up and spend their later years migrating between the north and south along with the seasons. RVs are a blessing for their users and a curse for pretty much everyone else, primarily by making wilderness travel in the US far too comfortable. Their facilities in the most extreme cases include flat screen TVs, satellite channels, internet, full barbecue capabilities, refrigerator, air conditioning, shower, toilet facilities, full beds and sometimes even a dishwasher. The biggest problem with wilderness travel for these adventurers becomes running out of ice or difficulty in getting Netflix. My big problem with them is that people who shouldn't be allowed to drive a shopping cart are often behind the wheel. While I met some lovely RV'ers on my travels, I also had many near misses and been run off the road numerous times by incompetent and dangerous drivers. I've been told I have a less-than-charitable viewpoint when it comes to RVs, but after spending several months dealing with them as a road hazard and being kept awake in campsites by their generators I think I can be allowed a lack of charitable forgiveness just this once. Their very existence was an omnipresent fear.

I reached the main highway turn off for Jasper early one afternoon. The junction has a single traffic light, the first I had seen for 300 miles, and as I reached the light I was greeted by an unusual sight. A car and an RV rested in the middle of the road surrounded by pieces of headlight, bumper and fender. People stood at the side of the road talking on their phones, no doubt waiting for the nearest tow truck to arrive, probably also 300 miles away. After learning that no one had been hurt I looked at the carnage with just a hint of an ironic smile in the corner of my lips. One traffic light in 300 miles, eh.

I was excited to reach Jasper, at it marked the start of a very special stretch of road indeed. Extending 180 miles between the towns of Jasper and Banff, the Icefields Parkway follows two rivers past tall snow-capped mountains flanked with fluorescent green and baby blue lakes. Dense pine forests cover the hills and valleys as moose, beavers, eagles and elk occasionally materialize into view. After the first day of riding though this postcard scenery I stopped at the Beauty Creek hostel, a tiny wooden cabin situated off the road on the banks of the wide river below Stanley Falls, a stunning cascade through a mountain canyon. The hostel was fantastic. Run by a French couple, it was part frontier cabin, part gourmet pancake parlor. In the morning, surrounded by knick-knacks on the walls and the faint haze of wood smoke, they would make pancakes for the guests. And when I say pancakes, I mean *pancakes*. Maybe I was just hungry, but they rank up there with the very best pancakes anywhere. Unlimited numbers were made to order, and with your choice of chocolate, blueberries or seasonal fruit inside the secret batter recipe it was an endless plate of heaven. Sitting at the tiny kitchen bench looking out of the window at the mountains and river outside I had found breakfast paradise.

Beyond the hostel the road climbed up past the cascade to a plateau where I was greeted by one of the highlights of the Icefields Parkway, the Athabasca Glacier. From its beginnings in the distant Columbia ice field, a 1,200ft deep lake of ice nestled in the Rockies, it descends through a wide valley and finishes near the road. I rode my bicycle along the well-trodden dirt path up to the glacier before walking the short rocky climb to the ice itself. Standing on the blue ice as you stare into seemingly bottomless crevasses is a humbling sight, and hearing the creaks and moans of the ice moving imperceptibly yet continually beneath your feet gives an overwhelming sense that some things are infinitely older than we can appreciate. Glaciers are beautiful. And yet as I learned years before, they can also be deadly.

During my undergrad years I was lucky enough to be part of an expedition to Pakistan, our goal being to cross the longest stretch of ice outside the poles. It was an arduous 27 day trek up the Biafo glacier, across a vast ice field called Snow Lake and back to civilization down another glacier called the Hispar. It was here that I learned just how treacherous glaciers can be. After crossing the 17,200ft pass from Snow Lake we descended to the night's camping area on the moraine at the edge of the Hispar. Wary of crevasses, our group was roped together for the walk and we progressed carefully through several miles of heavily broken ice until we approached the edge. It looked flat and safe for the last few hundred yards so we unroped to speed things up. Big mistake. After barely 20 yards I found myself buried in snow up to my armpits and yet I could feel my legs swinging in thin air. I had partially fallen through a snow bridge and was suspended above the jaws of a huge crevasse. The team quickly threw me a rope and hauled me out, and after reaching solid ice we all walked along the edge to look at what had nearly claimed me. The smooth vertical walls of ice disappeared into the darkness far below, but I joked with the others about my near escape, a reaction I can only put down to adrenaline. It was only later that night when I felt a shiver of dread that I realized how fortunate I had been. The snow bridge should never have held my weight and if it hadn't I would likely have died either from the fall or from hypothermia during the rescue. It was a close call and not an experience I would care to repeat.

Back on the Athabasca Glacier and with that memory close at hand I decided to take it easy and returned to the bike. I had seen enough ice for one day.

# THIRTEEN

# The Man on the Grassy Knoll

From the Athabasca Glacier I passed through wonderful scenery and the touristy village of Lake Louise before reaching the town of Banff. Banff is as beautiful in summer as it is fun in winter, and well worth a visit in either season for its picturesque mountain surroundings, nearby skiing or the famous film festival held there each year. I spent a few days resting and partying - if that is simultaneously possible - and felt pretty damn fabulous about pretty much everything. I even won the hostel pool championship, an outcome which was beyond a miracle and something I will never come close to repeating. Those were good times with good people, a time in my life that I now remember with unequivocal fondness. I had no worries or stress, life being an easy combination of deep relaxation and hedonism with the right people to share both of those with. I was devastated to leave my new friends, but as always I had no real choice in the matter. Onward, to the United States!

The US border involved the usual hassle. Indeed, in a recent survey of the world's most intimidating border crossings the US was ranked as the worst, behind such places as Venezuela and Israel. Despite following the exact advice given to me by an Alaskan US immigration officer it still took two hours of questions and negotiations to get a 90 day visa, a necessity given the time it would take me to cycle across the US to reach Mexico. To their credit they did eventually acquiesce to the full 90 days, and then was in Montana! I had cycled clean across Canada!

I must admit that I was ready for a change. After 3,000 miles of rolling hills and spruce trees I had had enough. Despite the few dramatic sections, the scenery had, to be honest, become a bit boring. Maybe I get bored easily, but in any case some variety was needed. With that in mind, as well as a desire to see parts of the United States I might never otherwise visit, I shunned the conventional route down the west coast and continued directly south towards the deserts of the Southwest. In my path lay the states of Montana and Wyoming.

Once in Montana I took an off-road route towards the town of Whitefish along the Continental Divide trail, but after a few hundred miles I got frustrated with the total desolation and the difficulties of the route so rejoined the road close to Helena, the state capital. I passed through the city in the morning and back to the open road, and it was late in the afternoon when I started to look for a camping spot. The light had begun to wane and the wind picked up as dark clouds ahead foretold of an approaching storm. For mile upon mile the barbed wire fences came right up to the roadside without a break, and at the first spits of rain I reluctantly turned into an RV park to see if I could throw up my tent.

"Yeah, for a $15 donation you can," said the miserable old bastard who ran the place as he peered out of his half open trailer door dressed in a dirty white vest. I begrudgingly crossed his price-gouging palm with some crumpled old notes and then found a small shelter which covered a picnic table and patch of ground just big enough for a tent. I set up as the rain began to come down hard and in the apocalyptic gloom sat at the table to cook some food. I watched the lightning in the distance and tried to read a book by torchlight as I huddled in my clothes for warmth. It sucked, and I forlornly wished that something would distract me from this misery.

Be careful what you wish for. After some time I heard the sound of an engine and I looked up into the darkness to see a van roll slowly into the complex. It looked like something from a secret government agency, with black paint, black tinted windows, black wheel rims and no front license plate. It was completely unmarked without even a brand badge. The van came to a stop several yards away from me and in the gloom a man slowly climbed out. Dressed in tattered army fatigues and heavy black boots, his long greasy dark hair flowed from beneath an old baseball cap to obscure his face in further shadow. Framed by the darkness and illuminated by lightning this was a scene right out of a horror film, at the bit when they are trying to bury the body in a forest. As we all know, and as I was thinking right then, that scene rarely ends well. The man walked towards the shelter and took a seat directly across from me at my table. We sat there, alone and in silence. Eventually he spoke.

"Hello," he said.

"Uh, hi," I replied. And then more silence. We stared at each other until I felt I should muster some courage and ask him a question.

"Where are you from?"

"I'm from Alabama, man," he replied slowly in a thick southern accent, "But I ain't going back there. Oh no. You can't get up in the South, man, the gov'ment is keeping us down. That's why the South is always strugglin', man, always fightin' but not getting its dues, man. But hell, that won't make *no* difference no more as we're all doomed anyhow, you know, nuclear war is coming, I've seen the signs, man! Gotta be careful, you know, gotta keep safe."

Ah. All this without prompting. In the stormy darkness I had found myself a real life genuine conspiracy theorist. He proceeded to tell me that he wouldn't go back to the east coast because he had seen signs in the bible that nuclear war was coming and only the western states were safe.

"Those blue helmets like what the UN people wear, those are a *sign*, man! 'Those in blue shall precedeth the wrath of God,' man," he offered. Not a great conversation starter in my book, but given the circumstances it would do. I was a little apprehensive at what was happening but not particularly frightened. Sadly that was not to last.

"Back in the '70s I was in the Army, you know. After 'Nam they stationed me out in Korea, man, yeah that was a tough gig.

There was this whole secret war going on with North Korea, man, but the gov'ment ain't gonna tell you *that*! No way, man. We were doing missions into North Korea, you know, going over at night into all the villages. I've been there a ton of times, man."

The few Vietnam vets I've met are usually both good guys and a little quirky, and the far end of the Vietnam vet quirky scale is very quirky indeed. This guy was beyond the usual scale, a view which was reinforced when he pulled out a 12 inch hunting knife.

"We used to sneak in through tunnels, man, and kill those sons of bitches," he continued, while enthusiastically waving the knife around. This wasn't exactly what I had planned for the evening's entertainment. He then listed out a multitude of government conspiracies, from such classics as the JFK assassination ("The gov'ment did it, man, the *gov'ment*!") to the Iraq war ("The oil, man, the *oil*!"). He was unlike anyone else I'd ever met, and although it was scary it was also actually kind of interesting.

Then it got creepy.

"Hey, you wanna meet my daughter?" he asked out of the blue, probably 45 minutes after he'd sat down at the table.

"Um. Sure. Uh, what?" I replied, definitely not sure at all. What did he mean by 'his daughter?' It turned out he meant exactly that.

"Hey April!" he called out, "Come and say hi to the man." A few short moments later the van's side door slid quietly open and a girl took a single step out. In the shadows I saw a teenage girl with long black hair, dressed in a black jacket, jeans and high leather boots. With her features obscured by her black hair and the darkness she stared at both of us for before raising her hand towards me with a small, timid movement. She looked like the evil spirit girl in the horror film 'The Ring' who climbs out of the TV to get you.

"Hi," she said in a quiet voice.

"Hi," I replied, but before a conversation could even begin she retreated into the van and disappeared as the door slid quietly shut. I sat there kind of stunned, wondering what on earth was going on. It was surreal.

The Conspiracy Theorist continued to talk for a while longer about Korea until he suddenly rose from his seat.

"Hey, I'm going to call it a night, man," he informed me, and walked to the back of the van before returning with a small lantern. "In case you want to read a bit more or something. Hey, good talking to you, man, sleep well!" he said, and with that parting act of kindness he vanished back into in the vehicle. I never saw him again.

# FOURTEEN

# Bombs and Barbecues

Perhaps I'd judged the Conspiracy Theorist a little unfairly, just another example of jumping to conclusions based on a stereotype. It's easy to forget that ultimately most of us want the same things, like safety, opportunity and equality, even if we go about getting them in very different ways. If this book has a purpose beyond introducing a long list of inadvisable things to do, it is perhaps to help impart an appreciation that walking a mile in another man's shoes is something quite different from guessing his shoe size. In all my encounters over the years I have done my best not to judge others from the first impression, and one chance meeting in particular stands above the rest as a demonstration as to why you should rarely judge a book by its cover. To meet this fascinating person we must take a brief detour away from my bicycle and the hills of Montana to my backpacking days and the tribal areas of Pakistan.

The tribal lands of western Pakistan lie trapped between Afghanistan and Pakistan as a semi-autonomous region which is beyond the control of either. They are wild lands, governed by the vagaries of tribal law and controlled by a combination of war lords and elders. Fierce tribal loyalties and an exceptionally hardy population have made this place ungovernable for two thousand years. Alexander the Great, the British Empire, the Mughals of Babur, the Mongols of Tamerlane and the Soviet Union all tried and failed to conquer the area, and it was not a coincidence that Osama Bin Laden hid here right after the 2001 atrocities. I journeyed there to visit the infamous Khyber Pass, a route across the mountains which connects Pakistan with Afghanistan, and was fortunate enough to arrive at this volatile and dangerous place during an uncommon period of peace.

As every man worth his salt in the tribes needed three important things – a Pashtu flat cap, a long beard and, most relevant for us, an assault rifle, we were required to take an armed guard with us in our tour jeep from Pakistan. This made additional sense when we passed a large sign hanging from the imposing barbed wire fence at the tribal area border. Written in large red lettering on a white background in both Urdu and English, it proclaimed a dire warning.

"Warning!" it shouted. "You are now beyond the assistance of the Pakistani Army and Security Forces! Warning! Enter at your own risk!" They are not joking; cross that line and you really are on your own.

Immediately through the gates I noticed a near-continuous line of shops running along the road for several hundred yards, in contrast to the sparsely built Pakistani side of the border. These basic, single story buildings sold just two kinds of products - guns and ammunition. And when I say guns, I mean the kind of weaponry which would put a Texas gun store to shame. Want a Kalashnikov AK47 assault rifle? There are so many for sale that shopkeepers prop them up on racks outside their stores. Want a US Army M16 machine gun? No problem, would you like a real one or a working copy? Perhaps you are in the market for a rocket launcher? Most of the shops we passed had several in the window, along with a selection of rockets. Need a truck-mounted anti-tank gun? I saw one of those as well. Having grown up in England and thus virtually never having seen a gun before this was a bit of a culture shock, and frankly a bit scary. The world's biggest gun show with exactly zero controls on anything at all. Luckily, according to my armed guard at least, tribal rules dictate that a man should only use their weapon "appropriately", to quote his exact word. I never found out what circumstances were "appropriate", but he did assure me that that randomly shooting a tourist was generally considered "inappropriate". Lucky me.

The Khyber Pass was fascinating, and treading in the very footsteps of Alexander the Great himself was stirring. Highlights included watching local tribesmen stacking stolen VCR recorders and large sacks of pungent hashish against a wall at the roadside, and peeking inside the fortified compound of the local war lord who had left the gate open. Eventually we reached a hill overlooking the Afghanistan border where I took a photo holding the guard's machine gun with the crossing behind me as a memento. The trip went off without incident, and in the late afternoon we returned to Peshawar, the Pakistani frontier city from where I had begun the tour.

The air was dry and still hot in the purple twilight as I walked out of the hotel in search of food in the city's Old Quarter. The wide and dusty main road was lined almost exclusively with metal working shops, and the white glare of strip lights hanging in the open fronted shops competed with the searing blue arc welding flashes as men in filthy torn vests toiled in the heat. The world had stepped back in time in that place. After much wandering I smelled a rare pleasant odor amongst the faint but ever present background smell of hot sewerage and humanity. Someone was barbecuing chicken! Following my nose I stumbled upon a small restaurant amongst a row of poorly maintained brick buildings. Open to the street, its fluorescent lights brightly illuminated the interior white tiles on the walls and floor, while in front of the restaurant stood a grill made from two halves of an oil drum, each full of smoldering coals. A man stood over the fire with his back to the lights, illuminated only by a devilish glow from the coals. I walked past him into the small restaurant, noting an AK47 assault rifle hanging from his shoulder. I thought about mentioning the dangers of barbecuing with live ammo, but I decided to let it go and took a seat at a table covered with a red and white checked plastic tablecloth. I ordered from the boy who worked there and soon enough my chicken arrived, delivered by none other than the cook from outside.

In the light I got my first good look of him, and it was an imposing sight. He was tall, well over six feet, and wore a traditional knee length grey brown garment called a Salwar Kameez. His long face was accentuated by a deep black beard and his dark skin looked etched by a hard life. From beneath his traditional flat cap burned deep hazelnut eyes. Oh, those eyes! They sparkled and glowed with a fire which is hard to describe, as a thousand years of pain and history and glorious bloody revenge shone out from their depths. At their centers his pupils were black and dead, like a shark's eyes. Horror seemed to live there, a sense that they had seen things no man should see. I was transfixed. Slowly he lowered his AK47 and extended a huge calloused hand.

"Salaam Alaikum, and good evening to you, young sir!" he said slowly and clearly in surprisingly good English, every word beautifully measured. "I hope you are very well. My name is Jahangir Hussein. May I join you?" he asked.

"Walaikum Salaam," I replied, returning the traditional greeting with a broad smile and shaking his hand warmly. "I am very well, thank you. Of course, please join, it would be my pleasure," and rose from my seat as I gestured for him to sit. Despite his frightening appearance, Jahangir's manner was one of kindness itself and he quickly put me at ease. He was professional, if that description makes sense. I soon discovered that he was Afghan and had come to Pakistan in the early 1990s. I asked him why.

"I came to Pakistan many years ago after my family had been killed by Russian soldiers," he replied. "They attacked my village and many people were killed. My wife and four children also."

I sat still for a few seconds. I had not expected such an appalling answer.

"But that's terrible," I replied, "I am very sorry. I can't imagine what something so terrible can be like. I mean, what did you do then?" I asked. I was not expecting his next reply either.

"I joined the Mujahideen."

The Mujahideen! I was stunned. The world "Mujahideen" translates from Arabic as "strugglers", which itself has its origins as a religious struggle in the name of Islam. While there have been several groups through history that can be called Mujahideen, it most commonly refers to the Afghan guerilla fighters who resisted the Soviet invasion during the 1980s. Their resistance was so ruthless, so disruptive and so determined that eventually the Russians gave up after losing 15,000 men, declaring on exit that the country was ungovernable. I remember watching them on the BBC News when I was very young and never thought in a million years that I would actually meet one. And yet here sat Jahangir in front of me, watching me eat his grilled chicken.

"I know this might sound rude," I said, "and I wish no offence, but what was it like to be in the Mujahideen?" flashing a quick sideways glance at the AK47 leaning against the wall.

"No offence at all, young sir," He replied. "It was our duty to fight in any way we could. We had to resist. We wanted peace and safety for our families, the chance to live our lives as Allah intended," he continued, with a calm seriousness in his voice. "After we had achieved victory I decided there was nothing left for me in my homeland, and so came here to Pakistan."

We talked further about his experiences and it became evident to me that despite our differences we had the same basic needs, needs like safety, justice, and the opportunity to build a life for ourselves. The big difference was that Jahangir had to work hard and suffer greatly in order to find these things, things that I could easily take for granted. A focus on our superficial differences is a dangerous distraction and carrying an assault rifle and having a long beard doesn't change that one bit. It is all too easy to be obsessed by the obvious and understand only the 'what' of things, rather than the 'why'.

I spoke to Jahangir for several more minutes until he glanced outside at the grill and rose from the table.

"Young sir, it has been a pleasure speaking with you. I wish you many successes, Inshallah. Now I must return to my duties - there is a fire which needs attending!" And with a final sparkle of his eyes he shook my hand with a strong grip, slung the weapon back across his shoulder and disappeared back into the darkness to become a wraith once more.

FIFTEEN

# Cold Air and Hot Water

Back in the mountains of Montana I awoke in the RV park the next morning to find that the storm had passed. The van of the Conspiracy Theorist remained parked close by, black and silent, and remained that way as I ate a quick breakfast and packed. Soon I was back on the road and heading south towards Wyoming and the famous Yellowstone National Park. I decided to spend the night in the town of West Yellowstone at the park's northwestern edge, and the place I stayed at was both one of the main gift shops on Main St and a small hostel, making it very peculiar indeed. Coming down from my room into the shop in the morning felt like walking onto a John Wayne movie set. Antlers covered the wooden walls of the cramped space while old pieces of machinery, traditional carvings and Native American art sat in every nook on every shelf. It was actually quite charming and really gave me the sensation of being in the American West. After breakfast at the local diner to keep up with the American theme I was back on the bike and crossed the state border into Wyoming and the park.

Luckily it was October and while there was some traffic it certainly wasn't ridiculous. By Yellowstone's standards, ridiculous really means just that - in summer there are so many visitors they can create possibly the largest traffic jam in the world. One person stops to photograph a buffalo and boom! 50,000 vehicles behind them also stop. This is so common they are actually called Buffalo Jams. Authorities recently reintroduced grey wolves to the park to restore the original habitat and "keep the elk population under control", but after learning of the traffic problem I suspected that the real plan is similar but with the word "elk" replaced with "tourist".

The west of the park was a pretty affair, with trees interspersed amongst the high altitude grassy meadows. The park averages around 8,000ft above sea level so the air was cool and the riding pleasant. After an hour I came across a long line of stationary cars in the road and as I filtered past to the front I discovered why they had stopped. Buffalo Jam! A large herd was walking along the road towards us and I suddenly remembered the warnings to avoid them. It was buffalo rutting season and every year a few unheeding tourists get too close and are injured. Posters were all over the park to advise people to stay several hundred yards away at a minimum, so when the buffalo got to within 50ft I decided I was in trouble. The expansive plains on either side of the road offered no protection so I looked around in increasing desperation. Finally I saw a narrow gap between two cars at the front of the traffic jam and I went for it, wedging myself in just as the buffalo walked right by. It was a nerve-racking experience to be so close to these huge and primeval looking animals. That said, I couldn't resist leaning over and touching one of the little ones, giving it the fright of its life. James 1, Buffalo 0, but I'm not going to try that again.

After the herd had passed by I continued on to Yellowstone's most popular attraction, the majestic geyser called Old Faithful. Boiling water and steam erupt a hundred and fifty feet into the air once every 91 minutes, and it was well worth the trip to see it. The only drawback was how far away they make you stand, ostensibly to protect you from falling through the thin ground and into the boiling pools below. Having visited a geyser in Iceland where you can get right up to the bubbling pools of crystal blue water I admit to being a little disappointed to be kept so far back. However, I had also discovered in Iceland that if you stand *too* close then hot sulfurous water showers down onto you during the eruption. Perhaps being kept a safe distance away wasn't such a bad thing after all. I watched two eruptions and then hopped back on the bike. Unfortunately, I hadn't researched the park beforehand and completely missed the famous colored pools which lie close to the geyser, a fact which haunts me a little every time I see a picture of them. It's a long way to go back. In any case, I had to reach the campsite by the day's end, and I arrived as the sun was setting to discover a new and unexpected problem.

Planning what equipment to bring is always a problem through such varied terrain. Beginning in the icy conditions of Alaska and heading towards the tropics clearly called for a steady purge of cold weather clothes and equipment, except that things like high altitudes and deserts throw a large wrench into that otherwise reasonable plan. In the warmth of Montana I'd sent home my thick fleece and warm sleeping bag, thus finding myself with only thin shell cargo pants and a microfleece as temperatures fell well past freezing point on the high Yellowstone plateau. That night of camping was one of the worst of my life as I lay in my tent wearing everything I owned and still unable to sleep in the brutal cold. Seconds dragged on like minutes, minutes like hours. In the morning I crawled out at the first rays of light and sat next to my tent as I tried to heat up some food, my numb fingers barely able to work the stove. As I struggled with this new misery I heard the door of the RV next to me open.

"Hey, are you OK?" said the middle aged woman who emerged, "You look frozen. We thought you might like this," she continued, and handed me a steaming cup of hot chocolate. I would have married her if she had asked. It was glorious to feel the hot liquid run inside me and restore life to my frozen body. Just shows you, for every night there is a dawn. I sat there for a long time as the sun warmed the forest around me before eventually packing and saying an emotional goodbye to my saviors. I was soon at the exit to the park and heading down towards the comparative warmth of lower altitudes.

# SIXTEEN

# The Places In Between

After descending from the plateau I was greeted by the clear waters of Jenny Lake and the towering Teton mountain range which dominates the skyline in this part of Wyoming. To see these mountains rise many thousands of feet above the flat plain gave ever more credence to the Wild West image that this state holds to with a passionate grip. Underneath the Tetons lies the resort town of Jackson Hole, which does nothing to dispel this cliché. It is pleasant country, though remote, with endless miles of grassland stretching to the southern horizon. My only companions through this section were Pronghorn antelope, bouncy and elusive little guys that run in herds across the high altitude plains. They were my riding buddies in some strange way and I became really quite fond of them. As such, arriving at the only gas station for a hundred miles to find that half the floor area in its adjacent general store was dedicated to guns and bows with which to shoot these poor little things didn't improve my opinion on hunting. It did remind me, though, that I was still in America.

The next (and only) town of any size along this stretch was a mining settlement called Rock Springs. I immediately disliked it. If I ever visit a more dejected town I will be sad indeed. It is crap, an ugly, soulless, strip-mall infested vomit stain of a town. As an example, I tried to find somewhere which sold coffee and after almost two hours of looking I gave up. Some of the gas stations don't even bother to sell it, and if you are after anything more advanced than plain drip coffee in this town then you are pretty much out of luck. Here, the height of sophistication is Applebee's. Not that there is much wrong with Applebee's, it's just not a cultural pinnacle as far as I can tell. After the coffee failure I couldn't take it anymore so despite the late hour I rode out along the freeway and back into the desert rather than stay the night.

With no other road I was now forced to ride on the freeway. Surprisingly, it was a stress free experience with a nice wide shoulder that made it quite a lot less scary than most other roads. It is illegal to ride a bicycle on the freeway in the US unless it is the only available route, but I think this one counted. Even so, one very kind gentleman pulled over and asked if I needed a ride. Bless him. Americans might sometimes have the desire to kill anything which moves (including each other), but they can also be a wonderfully kind and welcoming bunch. After the disappointment of Rock Springs this guy certainly helped to improve my mood.

After 10 miles on the freeway I reached a junction and turned left to begin the climb up onto the plateau from the wide U-shaped valley below. The utter desolation of this road made the prior high altitude road seem like a buzzing thoroughfare. I had a feeling it was going to be one of those pitiful nights of camping, and sure enough the snow started blowing up the valley behind me as the sun drew low. Just wonderful. I put up my tent in a ditch at the roadside and lay inside, cold and alone as I listened to the snow brushing gently against the fabric walls. To make matters worse I was almost out of food and water after my restocking failure in Rock Springs, and a mars bar and my last precious sip of water were my evening meal before I fell into a hungry sleep.

A howl woke me with a start. Outside it was now silent and my heightened senses strained for noise. Had I really heard that? Sure enough I eventually heard a faint rustle. Something was moving outside, quiet but near. Then another rustle on the opposite side from the first and a howl from somewhere close. I froze, gripped by fear. I daren't move or call out as I sat there and listened to the creatures moving around my tent in the darkness. Wolves? Coyotes? Were coyotes dangerous? I had no idea. I wanted to assume the best rather than confirm the worst, until I could take it no longer and mustered my courage to call out. Silence. For the next 10 minutes I heard nothing and the adrenaline wore off as I slowly slipped back into sleep.

At the first rays of sun I was awake and crawled out of my tent. The night's snow had barely settled in the stubby brown grass and recorded no evidence of the intrusion. To this day I'll never know what those creatures were, although I still think the experience was preferable to staying in Rock Springs. I packed up quickly and with no food or water I started out towards Utah.

# SEVENTEEN

# Unexpected Wisdom

The next small part of civilization along the road was the tiny settlement of Dutch John, which lay beyond a deep valley and high mountain pass. The ride was beautiful but my lack of food, and more importantly of water, was a critical distraction. The temperature was rising fast and drinking almost no water for 24 hours while riding 80 miles over a mountain is not what I would consider a great situation. By midday I was really struggling and beyond thirsty, visiting a strange place where your brain decides that it needs to take matters into its own hands. It began to conserve water in involuntary and increasingly unpleasant ways, such as stopping me from sweating and dramatically limiting my athletic capacity to reduce my core temperature. These are both big problems when you still need to climb a desert mountain, so by the time I reached the summit I was in dire straits. It was clear that I was getting heat stroke, and without the cooling breeze on the downhill ride and the appearance of a gas station in Dutch John I'm not sure what would have happened.

Eventually I was rehydrated, and the rest of the day's ride was a glorious joy. It was just so nice to have a change of scenery and some real warmth for the first time in a long time. The ravines and lake of Flaming Gorge were an oasis compared to the high altitude deserts and I was simply happy to be in the sun. The change of scenery gave me optimism and for the first time in a while I felt like I was making progress. That afternoon I reached the town of Vernal and by late evening I found myself approaching the town of Price. Finding a spot on the top of a bluff overlooking the town, I set up a tent and watched the sunset.

I was riding shortly after dawn and had done 10 or so miles by the time I pulled up outside a 7-11 convenience store on the edge of town. It was time to stop for coffee and a breakfast snack. Sitting on the curb outside the store I looked out at the faux-landscaped roads and green verges that contrasted against the light browns of the surrounding desert, the very stereotype of suburbia in the western United States. I pondered this view and drank my coffee until I heard the faint single cylinder thumping of a motorbike in the distance. The volume gradually increased until I watched a Harley Davidson roar into the parking lot and stop a couple of spots from where I sat. A heavy set man wearing a black leather jacket, jeans and heavy black boots shut off the engine and dismounted the bike. His whitening hair was hidden by the bandanna he wore in place of a crash helmet and his sun-worn face sported a '70s style handlebar moustache. He walked into the store with the slow purposeful stride of a man walking to a gunfight. This guy was the real deal, the original rebel. You definitely didn't want to spill your beer on him in a bar.

A few minutes later he walked out of the store with his coffee and stopped beside me. Turning slowly, he looked down at me staring back at him.

"Hi there," he growled.

"Uh hi, how's it going?" I replied, hoping that this innocuous phrase wasn't somehow offensive in Utah Biker Speak.

"It's going not too bad, thank you for asking," he replied, a little less gruffly. "Where are you heading?"

"Down to Monument Valley," I replied warily, "I heard it's pretty spectacular down there." I figured a compliment on his local landscape might be a good start.

"Oh yeah? Well you got that right, it's a great ride this time of year. Been down there a few times myself over the years," he answered. "So where are you from with that accent? Australia?"

"Actually I'm from England," I replied, and as I did I saw a smile move across his face.

"England! Ah that's great. I spent some time over there back in the '70s."

And so we struck up a conversation about London, the weather in London and the 1970s until eventually we got to the question of why I was sitting on the curb in bicycle shorts. I explained what I was doing and why.

It turned out that my new biker friend was one of those rare and unusual men who have absorbed the experiences of a lifetime and turned that knowledge into wisdom, in much the same way as had my trucker friend on the Dalton Highway in Alaska. A modern day sage, if you like. I don't usually remember conversations word for word, but as we talked he said a phrase that burned itself in for the rest of my life.

"You know, the house and the car, and all the *stuff*," he said, as we discussed the merits of my journey, "It's all just icing on the cake. The things in life that really matter, the things which are *actually* important are your family, your friends and your experiences."

Now of course everyone has their own view about what is important in life, whether it is making money, becoming famous, painting pictures, following a football team or hitting a little white ball over some grass into a hole with a stick. Listening to his particular philosophy though, well, it resonated with me. I have spent quite a lot of my life focusing on the experience part of the equation, yet why I have done so is a good question. I never used to think that way. When I was in high school my dream was inexplicably 'to be a businessman' and earn $80,000 a year, an arbitrary number which at the time felt like a stupendously large sum of money. To achieve these goals I figured I had to be smarter than all the rest so that was where my focus and hard work went. It was only at university, where I was fortunate enough to meet some intrepid friends were my eyes really opened to the world. Since that time I have realized that having more and more things didn't make me any happier. They don't make me laugh any harder, or make me smile like an idiot. Only intense experiences can do that, and acquiring them has become a cornerstone of who I am. As I watched my biker friend roar off into the distance I felt a renewed excitement and a sense of purpose. New experiences were waiting, so I clipped into my pedals once more and rode out to meet them.

# EIGHTEEN

# Calorie Counting

Several hundred more miles of hard and lonely riding through barren desert lay ahead as I aimed for Moab, a town in the south of Utah nestled near the banks of the Colorado River. Nearly a week later I found myself at the tiny hamlet of Green River with just one more day to go. The map showed 55 miles to Moab, 30 miles east and then a 90 degree turn southwards for the remaining 25 miles to town. Luckily today I had a trick up my sleeve. The previous night I had fortuitously met an employee of the local tourist office who had told me about a shortcut through the desert.

"Just remember to take a left at the sign!" he said, "It's a couple of miles in from the highway. Once you are on that it will take you straight to Moab."

With no traffic and better scenery than the road I wondered what could possibly go wrong, and so began my brutal lesson about shortcuts as I confirmed the old adage that if a shortcut really was shorter than the main path it would *be* the main path. I turned off the highway as instructed and kept an eagle eye open for the sign. Three miles. Four miles. Six miles. I wondered whether I had misheard the distance he told me so without a better option I continued along the trail as it wound deeper and deeper into the wilderness. I was going south, after all, which was roughly the right way. Increasingly difficult terrain eventually left me at the bottom of a deep canyon, out of water and laboring in the 100F (38C) heat to drag my heavily laden bicycle through the soft sand on the canyon floor. At this point I was 20 miles from the road and after a fall on the way down I had a broken pedal and a bleeding leg into the bargain. Not awesome. Dragging my bicycle through the sand was a nearly impossible task and I was making less than 12 inches of progress for each herculean effort.

Even at that pace my GPS recorded that I dragged the bike for 1.2 miles before finally deciding that with no water and no map it was prudent to turn back. Angrily I wrenched the bike around and dragged it 1.2 miles back through the sand before riding out of the canyon and then the rest of the 20 miles to the road. It was agony, made worse when a few miles from the highway I finally saw the trail I was supposed to have taken! Next to the turning there was a small square hole in the ground; someone had removed the sign post.

By now I was a broken man. Beyond broken. I wasn't scared but I had some dim awareness of my precarious position. I had no water, no more food, I had stopped sweating and I barely had enough energy to stand, let alone ride. My pedal was broken and I still had 50 miles to go. With no other honorable choice I thus began the grind towards Moab, one pedal push at a time. The world became like a dream, as though I was looking at it through a frosted window. The only reality on my side of that window was pain. It was like the final mile of a marathon, where you can see the crowd but in that moment all you notice is the weight of your legs and the tightness in your lungs.

I spent two hours in that bubble until, down the arrow straight road, I could see in a distance a mirage through the shimmering heat. I saw a white building. Was I hallucinating? I honestly couldn't be sure. Riding now with a glimmer of hope, the mirage resolved itself to reveal a white building next to a bridge across the road. It was a gas station! I was saved! After what seemed like an eternity I finally reached it and staggered inside before sitting on the floor against the glass-fronted refrigerator with door open behind me as I bathed in the cool air and tried not to puke as I downed half a gallon of Gatorade. It was horrible feeling, but was overwhelmed by the knowledge that I might actually now be OK.

For the last 25 miles to Moab I was like a dead man riding. In my stupor I even left my wallet in the next gas station, an expensive mistake that really crowned the day. In the end though

I did reach Moab, upon which I checked into the hostel, made a quick dash to the nearest supermarket and then crashed into bed. It was 6.00pm.

14 ½ hours later I woke up feeling much, much better. I was starving, a man on a mission to eat, so I went downstairs to the common kitchen area to make some breakfast. Looking back, I hadn't eaten enough in the weeks prior to my ordeal and now my body was about to make sure it didn't run out of energy stores again. What follows is a description of what I ate that day. To clarify before I begin, mainly because I get this question a lot, what I ate just vanished inside me. No puking, no "issues", no nothing. Had I not written it down I wouldn't have believed it. Here is the list in full:

Breakfast - 9.00am: A whole large box of granola plus an omelet made with six eggs and the entire ½ lb block of cheddar cheese. I also drank a full pot of coffee. My hunger was briefly beaten back but it soon returned.

Mid-morning snack - 10.30am: Six toasted bagels with the entire 1lb tub of Philadelphia full fat cream cheese. I started and just kept going, frankly only stopping because I ran out of bagels.

Lunch - 12 midday: I walked the half mile or so into town and straight into Burger King, where they were doing a special deal on triple cheeseburgers. I ordered three triple cheeseburger supersized meals, including the fries and drink, but I guess the burgers were empty calories after all as I was still hungry. I couldn't face another Burger King meal so I walked directly across the street and into McDonalds, where I ordered two double cheeseburgers just to compare. No contest. Burger King reigned as the King.

Afternoon snack - 3.00pm: A quick haircut and I returned to the hostel. I watched TV and absentmindedly ate my way through an entire 36 cookie multipack of Oreos washed down with glasses upon glasses of milk. Between breakfast and my snack I drank a gallon.

Dinner - 6.00pm: It was time to slay the hunger beast once and for all. The first course was an entire box of pasta and a jar of sauce, followed by a second course of two 12 inch deep pan pepperoni pizzas. The beast was almost slain.

Evening snack - 8.00pm: In the killer blow I ate two large tubs of Ben & Jerry's Ice Cream straight out of the tub while watching 'Indiana Jones and the Last Crusade' in the hostel common room. Finally I felt full.

My energy intake for that day was 20,000 calories, eight days of the recommended food intake for an average man under US guidelines. That much energy can boil 68 gallons of water or power me to run seven marathons. The human body is an amazing thing. I do still wonder how mine still works, though. I've had a pretty good go at trying to break it.

After a few days of mooching around the hostel to recover I had gained enough strength and motivation to get out and explore the rest of Moab. Situated in dramatic red rock scenery, the canyon of the Colorado River contrasts with towering spires of red sandstone. The landscape is arrestingly powerful. My first port of call was high on the ridge above town at the start of the famous Slickrock mountain bike trail, 11 miles of preposterously steep and technical track undulating over prehistoric sand dunes which have solidified into hard Navajo sandstone. On the cliff edge a thousand feet above the Colorado River canyon you fly down 40 degree slopes and swoop around a tight bends, only to then grind to the top of the next dune and repeat the process. It was terrifying. I have never enjoyed mountain biking due to the guarantee of pain and this was no exception as I jammed on the front brake during the second steep downhill and vaulted unceremoniously over the handlebars. With my obligatory blood sacrifice to the mountain bike gods out of the way I felt a little braver, and the rest of this intense ride was actually fun. There was even a surprise bonus when a Navy jet fighter howled through the canyon beneath me, its deafening scream a primitive and fitting tribute to the raw landscape. It was a sublime joy to be there.

Abject misery to sublime joy in three days. That is travelling in a nutshell.

# NINETEEN

# The First Wonder of the United States

Situated south of Moab at the crossroads of four States lies Monument Valley, a wild land where huge sandstone monoliths rise above the cacti and red sand desert below, scenery that is the very epitome of the American Southwest. One arrow straight road in particular leads past an outcrop of those imposing and improbable rock pillars and is an iconic image of the United States. Since I was a young boy I had wanted to visit Monument valley after seeing a picture, and now finally this was my chance.

Travelling along this unique road I found the place where those images were taken and dismounted the bicycle to just stand there and marvel at the view as a storm rolled across the land, the sky black to the horizon. Great sheets of rain fell on the desert as if in slow motion while dramatic forks of lightning struck the famous sandstone towers ahead. Thunder echoed constantly like a drumroll. If normal photos of this place were out of this world then this was another galaxy. Soon those great sheets of rain reached me and the road disappeared in a fizz of raindrops bouncing back up from the pavement. It was an epic drenching but I didn't care; to see such a display of nature is this place I was more than happy to get wet. Indeed, after the previous night's tribulations I was just happy to be here at all.

I'd set up camp behind a small tourist store in the tiny town of Magic Hat, finding a small flat area on a wood chip verge next to a small fence. I fell asleep as the rising wind foretold of an approaching storm. It wasn't kidding. I woke up in the night to find myself trapped in what felt like a hurricane. The roof of my tent was bent down towards my face by the ferocity of the wind and I lay there spread-eagled as I tried to prevent it from being uprooted with me inside. It was genuinely frightening to be helpless in this stalemate. After a long time the wind eased just a little and as I finally felt I had its measure nature once again proved me wrong.

The sound of an explosion ripped through the tent as a brilliant flash of light shone through the fabric like bright daylight. Imagine standing right next to one of those 'flash-bang' military grenades when it goes off; that is the only comparison I can think of which could do it justice. I was disorientated and it took a moment for me to come to my senses. What had happened? I had no idea and so decided to take a risk and look outside. With difficulty I unzipped the tent against the wind and peered out. It was dark and deserted. In the singular glow of a distant light bulb I could only see a nearby fence and a tall metal pole protruding from the ground about 15ft away, a pole to which I had originally tied my tent earlier that day. At the last minute I decided to untie and move it to the less bumpy ground where I currently lay, a decision which now proved highly fortuitous. The pole had been hit by lightning! I wasn't scared, although I continued to listen with a heightened awareness to every clap of thunder as the storm passed into the distance and I was safe once more.

People have told me I have an unusual reaction to these kinds of one-off events. They just don't freak me out. Sure, I will do a reassessment of the risks based on what happened, but I am as often as not equally likely to do again whatever it was that almost got me the first time. I have been in several close calls with lightning over the years and each time I was left unperturbed. After a bolt hit the hostel roof terrace in Florence while I sat there, every other person dashed for cover apart from me. I figured that the chances of it hitting twice were nearly zero and the first one hadn't even hit us. So why worry? Perhaps it is that outlook which had enabled me to overcome the psychological difficulties of my journey so far. Either way, waking next morning I was as happy with my situation then as I had been the night before.

From the postcard photo spot in Monument Valley I pushed on through the rain and passed into Arizona as the weather cleared. The ride alternated between deep canyons cutting through the desert plateau and steep pine-tree covered mountains which rose like great dividers across the moonscape. It was only slightly spoiled by the crappy town of Kayenta, where my time was marked only by having to endure the least glamorous camping spot of my whole trip in a Laundromat car park. Given the number of roadside ditches I had slept in, that is saying something. The only thing which made it interesting was being woken up at 2.00am by a horse walking past my tent, a mysterious occurrence given where I was. Welcome to Arizona.

I rode through the unworldly scenery for several more days until I arrived late one afternoon at a large and beautifully landscaped car park woven amongst the pines. Propping my bicycle against a tree I walked along a short path to a small building just beyond the parking spaces, intent on determining where the hell I was. Passing around the building I discovered to my surprise that there was a large hole in the ground on the far side. It was 10 miles wide, 30 miles long and a mile deep. I had stumbled upon the Grand Canyon. I mean, I knew it was around there *somewhere* but thought it further away than it was. That was quite a surprise, let me tell you!

That first moment of disbelief when you set eyes on the Grand Canyon is for me the real wonder of the place. It is that feeling of looking at something that shouldn't exist. For me it was not so much the vast scale but rather the abrupt change from the gradual flat terrain which surrounds it. I had some sense of climbing onto a high plateau through the physical exertion of the ride, but even that didn't prepare me for arriving at the edge and watching the ground drop precipitously away for 5,000 vertical feet. For 10 minutes I just stood there amazed as my mind tried to process what it was seeing.

Once it had been processed, though, I felt my perception of the Grand Canyon change, somehow demoted from a "wonder of the world" to "very good". It was though maintaining this unfathomable sense of scale was too difficult to rationally appreciate and my brain gave up. Or maybe it was the opposite and my brain decided that it wasn't quite big *enough*. I have stared vertically down over 10,000ft to the floor of Colca canyon in Peru as condors circled past, and in the Himalaya I've seen a mountain face rise unbroken for 15,000ft above the surrounding valley. The Grand Canyon for me just couldn't hold its place in such company, so while it remains in the "super cool" camp I can't put it in my Global Top 10. First wonder of the United States, though? Very possibly.

The camping area was several miles further along the canyon rim and I planned the next day before settling in for a quiet night. It was supposed to be a rest day so I decided to hike the trail down into the Canyon and back out, a round trip of 23 miles. Oops. Early the next morning I filled a single bottle of water and began the descent into the Canyon along the South Kaibab trail, a spectacular zig-zagging path down a steep face towards the canyon floor. It took several hours and by the time I reached the river the air had gone from pleasantly warm at the rim to stifling hot. I'd been told it gets hotter as you go lower but I never really believed it. Boy, is it true. I stopped briefly for some relief at the small cafe in Phantom Ranch and admired where I was. Red and yellow sandstone cliffs blended with the golden desert grass and the warm brown of the river, pastel colors broken only by the sharp blue sky at the canyon rim above. There was an aura of peace in this refuge far from the tourist world far above. I lingered for a while but all too soon it was time to start the climb back to civilization. A long, long climb. As the sun shone low in the sky I finally clambered back onto the rim, exhausted and thirsty. I must have slept deeply as I have no recollection of that evening, but no matter. It was a wonderful day!

Before leaving the next morning I had a quick job to do - take a picture of Tolly the Bear at the Grand Canyon. After placing carefully him on the edge I was lining up the picture when through the lens I saw him start to fall backwards. It seems as though it happened in slow motion, yet before I could react he was gone! I mean, what is the point of putting half a pound of lead shot in him for stability if he is going to fall over at exactly the wrong moment! Expecting to see nothing I skipped to the edge and looked down. There, on a small ledge a few feet below me, was Tolly. He had survived the impossible, just like Indiana Jones! Luckily I was able to climb down and retrieve him, not a smart move but a necessary one. Once back we tried the photo shoot again and this time with success. No harm, no foul.

# TWENTY

# Hotter than the Sun

From the Grand Canyon I was heading downhill for a change, this time to a university town in northern Arizona called Flagstaff. I liked it. It even had a little civilization and some night life, something which I had been missing for a long, long time. For the first time in what felt like an age I was also totally clean, showered and shaved, wearing a brand new T-shirt and newly washed jeans. I felt like a million dollars. It sounds strange to be so imbued with something so basic, but after going endlessly from campsite to roadside and back again, just to feel fully clean was a joyous novelty. At the hostel I met a nice group of people, four pretty girls as it happened, and later that evening we took a walk through town. At the first bar I was barred from entering because the bouncer didn't believe my passport was mine, so we kept wandering and in the end found a much better place to drink. I sat at a table sipping a gin & tonic and felt a calming wave of contentment wash over me. No stress, no worries, just contentment. This was a good night turning into a great one. I'm sure from the girl's perspective my manic smiling looked like that of a serial killer, but at that moment I didn't care. Two gorgeous girls then got up on the bar and started dancing to complete the picture. It was like I was in some music video, those ones where the rapper sits in a booth surrounded by beautiful women and knows he is the main event. Good times were rolling.

It was then that I noticed one of the girls on the bar had unzipped her shiny silver pants to show her expensive little G string underwear to the appreciative crowd. Nothing odd about that, per se, but what was odd was that this zip was on the back of her pants rather than the front. That means she must have gone out *intending* to climb onto a bar and show her underwear to everyone, otherwise why wear them? Who does that! Sadly I never got to find out as we left soon afterwards and my night hit a bump as I walked straight into a cop while carrying a bottle of beer that I had smuggled out of the bar. In Arizona that is a bad move.

"Step this way sir," he demanded sternly. "Do you know there is a $125 fine for drinking in public, sir?"

Time to use the English card, and for once I played it to perfection.

"Oh I am *terribly* sorry, officer," I began in my finest accent, "I had no idea it was illegal here, you see I am from *England*. It is legal there and I didn't think about it." Of course I had no idea if it was legal in England or not, but that was beside the point.

"England! I went there a few years ago," replied a second police officer who had now pulled up in the car. Hook, line and sinker.

"Oh really!" I replied in feigned shock and impressed wonder. "That's just *wonderful*! Where did you visit? How was the weather? Did you see the Queen?" Blah blah blah.

In the end he merely made me pour out the beer and that was it. A good night after all!

The next morning, somewhat worse for wear, I left Flagstaff on the final stretch towards the mythical State of California. Unfortunately, between us lay a large and rather nasty desert called the Mojave, which as anyone who has done the Los Angeles to Las Vegas drive can tell you, might be hotter than the sun. To confirm this notion, halfway between them in the small town of Baker stands the world's tallest thermometer. It lights up by an additional one foot for every degree Fahrenheit and extends a colossal 134ft into the air. Why 134ft? 134F, or 57C, is the highest temperature ever recorded on Earth, in a small town not far from Baker named Furnace Creek. This was in the same desert through which I was now attempting to ride a bicycle on a sunny day at the end of summer. What could possibly go wrong?

On the Arizona / California border where the Mojave begins I loaded up my bike with nine quarts of water, guessing this would be enough for the 93 mile crossing. It was early in the morning but already hot as I rode out of town. The air had that unmistakable sweet smell of the desert when it is still heating up. Today was going to be a scorcher.

The first 20 miles along the nearly deserted road were tough and I was sweating profusely as a red pickup truck roared past me before gently slowing to a stop ahead. A stout man of about 50 years old with graying stubble and a friendly face climbed out of the cab and waited for me to reach him.

"Morning!" he said cheerfully as he extended me a big hand as I stopped next to him. "How are you getting on? Need any help?"

"Hi," I replied breathlessly as I unclipped from the pedals and offered my clammy hand to shake his. "Yeah I'm doing OK. Pretty damn hot out, though, eh?"

"Yyyyyep!" replied the man with a chuckle. "That's why I'm here! I patrol the road on days like this to make sure folks don't get into trouble when they break down and such." He pointed to his truck, on the side of which was written PATROL in large white lettering. Wiping the sweat from my eyes I could see why he was needed.

"This heat'll kill you if you give it the chance," he continued. "Tell you what. I'd hate to see you get in trouble. Take this," and he reached over the tailgate of his truck to lift out a one gallon plastic jug of water. "Now, about 20 miles up the road you'll see a little tree on the right of the road. There's only one tree for miles around so you can't miss it. I'll stick another one of these jugs under it on my way past, just in case."

Despite my usual "It'll be alright on the night" philosophy, in that heat and hot sun his idea seemed like a sensible one and I was happy to take him up on it. In the end that was a critical decision. By the time I arrived at the small tree it was well over 100°F in the shade, which was cool compared to the temperatures I suffered as I climbed over the hills in the direct sun. I had already finished my original nine quarts and had begun to drink his first one gallon installment. I still faced 40 miles of total isolation to the next water source, and it was going to be touch and go whether I could make it. Finally, as the sun dipped behind the horizon and the temperatures began to retreat I pulled into the parking lot of the Joshua Tree National Park headquarters, my destination for the night and the first evidence of civilization I had seen since Parker. I had made it but was now dangerously dehydrated. I desperately searched for water and saw a garden hose lying on the manicured verge. I drank straight out of it, potable or not, sucking down half a gallon in one go. What a relief!

In total that day I drank over five gallons, or 40 pints, of water in just 16 hours without taking any electrolytes or supplements. That is over one quarter of my body weight. I don't really know how it was possible. The risk of heat stroke or hyponatremia, which is a chemical imbalance due to a lack of salt, must have been astoundingly high. I guess it is just another example of the unbelievable tolerance and resilience of the human body.

I do also sometimes wonder what I would have done without the help of the patrol guy. I am certain I could not have finished the ride to Joshua Tree and would have become another heat stroke victim lying out in the desert, waiting for a rescue. Maybe by the same guy, who knows! Either way, it does prove that even if you think you are doing something on your own, you never really are. Both angels and demons are following you.

# TWENTY ONE

# Fire? What Fire?

After a quick hike in the morning to check out the Joshua Tree National Park, I rode out of the park and into rural southern California. San Diego was the goal now. As I rode through dry, pine covered scenery under bright blue and sunny skies I wasn't expecting any drama, and so was surprised when a car pulled up next to me and a middle-aged woman rolled down the window.

"Hi there!" she began, in the usual chirpy Californian style. "Hey, are there any forest fires ahead?" she then asked, which wasn't a question I was expecting. I looked up into the clear sky and replied that there weren't. Not looking very reassured the woman then rolled the window back up and sped off down the road.

Still pondering this odd encounter I arrived at the picturesque and quaint town of Julian, the self-proclaimed apple capital of California. In Utah I had heard about this place, or more accurately, I had heard about the Julian Pie Company, which apparently made some of the best apple pie in the world. It was a claim I was keen to put to the test and I quickly found the cafe attached to the small factory. Taking a seat I ordered a huge slice of fresh pie and a dollop of their home made cinnamon ice cream. With apprehension and expectation I raised a spoonful of pie to my mouth and took the first bite. The rumors were true. It was unbelievable, and really might actually be the best apple pie in the world. People have fought wars over less. I eventually left the store proclaiming that I would send my sister there immediately, all the way from England. With a full tummy I remounted the bike and headed towards my planned resting place for that night, a state park campground about 30 miles to the south, where I arrived just before 5.00pm.

'Sorry, but we're shut because of the fires," said the woman in the entrance booth and pointed at the barrier across the path ahead. Pointing at the clear sky I tried to remonstrate but to no avail. "You'll have to ride down to the desert in the valley, it's only about 20 miles," was her reply when I asked what my options were. I thanked her, turned tail and rode out of the park towards safety.

After three miles I had had enough. I was exhausted, bored and wanted to stop. I rounded a sweeping bend into a narrow valley to see a small car park at a trail head leading up into a forest at the edge of the grassland. Beyond was a small clearing around a telephone pole that was the perfect spot to put up a tent, hidden from view by the surrounding tall grass and a good distance from the road. The setting was beautiful, with a steep rise of pine trees ascending for several hundred yards to the top of a ridge on one side and a similar ridge ascending on the opposite side of the road. I assembled my tent, made some food and called it a night.

Several hours later I was woken by a voice in the silent darkness outside.

"Hey there," said a man authoritatively as I watched the spot of his flashlight shining on the tent fabric above me. "Is anyone in there? This is the police."

Damn! I couldn't believe I'd been discovered. He had found me despite not looking, spotting my green tent hidden amongst green grass in the dark at least 20 yards from the road in a place no-one was supposed to be. Once he'd seen it he also then turned his truck around and came back to investigate. What were the chances? Maybe one in a hundred? Less?

"Um, hi," I replied, "Yeah, I'm really sorry about camping here like this officer but the campground was shut when I got there and I was just so tired that I had to pull over."

"Well, I guess no harm, no foul," he replied, which came as a pleasant surprise. "At least I know you are here in case we have to evacuate because of the forest fires." That was less pleasant, but in my sleepy state it didn't really register. I heard his patrol truck speed off and I fell back asleep, disgruntled that I had been disturbed from my dreams for no good reason.

The voice jolted me awake once again. It seemed like I had dosed for only few minutes, but my watch now said 3.30am.

"You have to get up right now," the voice commanded. "The fire is coming this way so get packed. I'll be back in 20 minutes."

"Urrr, yeah, sure, I'll be ready. Thanks," I replied, and he acknowledged my answer before speeding off once more to leave me enveloped in silence.

"Bastard," I said to myself, "there's no fire! Bet he did that just to piss me off," and I snuggled deeper into my sleeping bag. I was convinced he had woken me up just to teach me a lesson for illegal camping so I went back to sleep. 15 minutes later I woke up once more with the officer's command playing on my mind, and reluctantly decided that I should at least get out of the tent to avoid being yelled at when he returned. Then he could have his fun and I could finally go back to bed. Extracting an arm out of my sleeping bag into the frigid desert air I unzipped the tent flap and flung it open.

Oh boy. While the sky directly above me glittered with stars in the deep black, a vast and impenetrable wall rose from the opposite ridge and flickered with a hellish glow of oranges, reds and yellows. It looked tolkeinesque, like a portal to hell itself had been opened. Demons danced in the trees as they burned everything in their path while illuminating the wall of smoke and ash. The entire ridge above me was on fire.

Breaking the world record for the fastest tent packing in history I finished just as the cop sped around the corner and screeched to a halt.

"We gotta go. Quick, let's throw your bike in the back of the truck," he said, and helped me lift my gear into the back of the pickup. I hopped into the cab and with a screech of tires we hurtled towards the lowland desert. Despite being hundreds of yards away from the flames I could feel their heat through the truck window as we drove past the burning hillside. It was a surreal, unreal experience. I listened to the police radio as it chattered with frantic talk of evacuation and rescue. At one point there was a dispatch to our patrol car.

"Be advised," said the voice, "The fire is expected to cross Highway 87, estimated time 06.30am."

Highway 87 was where I had been camping and my alarm was set for 7.00am. Sleeping in a highly flammable nylon tent in a dry grassy meadow located in a narrow valley surrounded by pine trees is not a good place to be in a forest fire. Nowhere to run. The only reason I was alive was that against the odds I had been found. Lady Luck hadn't just smiled on me, she had unzipped the back of her silver pants and danced for me on the bar.

At daybreak we reached the desert and the main freeway into San Diego. The road had been closed and the area surrounding the junction was like a war zone refugee camp. Perhaps a thousand people were parked on every available piece of ground and many of the cars were jammed full of possessions. You could see a few clothes, perhaps an antique lamp or some photographs through the windows. The cop dropped me off unceremoniously at the edge of the congregation and headed back up the road, so I made myself a little space and talked to people as we waited for the freeway to reopen. For those forced to abandon their houses the things in their car were all they had left. The devastation and the raw emotion of people in that place was something I will never forget. Amongst such trauma, though, I also saw their fortitude and stoic resolution. Their support for one another was unconditional. I reflected that while my faith in humanity had sometimes been drained by difficult encounters, those people showed me once again how people can come together in times of need and help their fellow man. It gave me back my faith.

In the brightening daylight we could see that the road to the coast was blocked by a similar vertical wall of smoke to the one I had seen from my tent. It was so vast it looked like a barrier placed there by the gods. After several hours the authorities decided to reopen the freeway, although I wasn't allowed to cycle and was forced to hitch hike instead. Eventually a college student in a Ford pickup truck stopped and offered me a ride, so after loading my gear in the back we pulled onto the freeway. I remember vividly the moment we entered that wall of smoke. A thick haze quickly dimmed the sun to a dull red, while white ash fell like snow. Great lines of fire burned on distant hillsides and once again I could feel the heat radiating through the windows.

After 30 miles or so he dropped me off at a 7-11 convenience store in the town of El Cajon, on the outskirts of San Diego. It was still only 7.30am so I went in to get coffee and a muffin. 15 minutes later I walked out of the store and had to brush off the thick layer of ash which had accumulated on the saddle. It was apocalyptic.

The remaining 30 miles to the ocean was dense with smoke, and only the bright red of the traffic lights blazed through the haze as yellow and green light was filtered out. The sun was clearly visible as a deep red sphere. You could comfortably look at it with the naked eye, and when I did so I saw a small black spot on the lower left of its surface. Throughout the morning I watched that spot slowly rotate around the sun. I must have been looking at either a sun spot or a planet traversing the sun, and seeing either of those with the naked eye is not something you do every day. Surreal indeed.

At the ocean the weather was brighter and the smoke thinner. A couple of blocks from the beach I checked into a hostel, finding myself officially recorded as an 'evacuee', which I guess I actually was. On the plus side that got me my room for free! A very charitable man also came by at lunchtime and brought something like 50 McDonald's hamburgers for the evacuees and everyone else, so I also got some free food into the bargain. I spent the afternoon resting in the common room as I watched news of the fire on CNN. It was terrible to see the destruction that had been wrought in the places I had just visited. One clip showed footage of the firefighters battling the blaze just outside the town of Julian and I could see the pie shop in the background, barely 12 hours after I'd been eating there. Strangely, those visuals gave the day's events an additional reality. Guess it isn't true unless you see it on TV.

That fire was the worst in the modern history of California. Named the Cedar Fire, over 438 square miles were burned, 2,820 buildings destroyed and 15 people killed. Surreal and terribly sad.

# TWENTY TWO

# Intrepid New Friends

In the few days I spent in San Diego I met three other intrepid bicyclists who were also planning to ride down the Baja peninsula, just as I was. Small world. First was a Spanish guy named Alvaro whom I liked immediately. Alvaro is a man cast from the mold of a Spartan warrior with the body of a titan and a will of iron, and whose physical achievements over the years are as numerous as they are fantastical. He has run one of the most brutal foot races on the planet, the fabled Marathon Des Sables where competitors run 150 miles across the Sahara desert in eight days. Each runner must carry all of their own food, clothing and emergency equipment for the entire distance, a task so arduous that of the 600 extremely tough men and women who begin barely 200 finish. Alvaro came 25th and beat Spain's top marathon runner in the process. He has also ridden a motorbike in the Paris-Dakar rally, another fabled race which begins in Paris and ends in Senegal. It is by all accounts equally brutal, with a physical hammering so violent that competitors sometimes pee blood after several of the stages. Inspirational stuff, in my book at least. Even on this trip Alvaro was attempting twice my ride by cycling around the whole world; that's 35,000 miles on a bicycle.

Also in the hostel was one of my friends from before my trip, Jodie. She was great. I'd met her travelling in Thailand and I had stayed with her in Anchorage before I started my trip all those months ago. She was born and raised in Alaska and had one of those adventurous free spirits. From her ride's beginning in the US she eventually made it all the way to the south of Argentina, an incredibly impressive feat as she rode solo through most of South America. My journey gave her a little spark of inspiration to head out of the door, and the rest she did herself.

Finally there was Marian. Meeting Marian cycling across North America was like finding a goblin serving you in Starbucks, i.e. not very likely. He was an older guy, fit and also young at heart, who was on a journey to fulfill a childhood ambition. Like me he had little experience of bicycle touring before beginning on this trip somewhere in the US, but the similarity ended when it came to our philosophies on how to do it. My minimalist, bare necessities philosophy meant that although I sometimes got in trouble because of a lack of gear, at least it was easy to carry. Marian took the opposite approach and brought everything including the kitchen sink. This guy was travelling in style.

With great company and nice weather I found San Diego to be one of the most pleasant cities in America. After the smoke and ash had subsided it was a wonderful place to relax. Although the city is less manageable or varied than San Francisco and less frenetic and action-packed than New York, the glory of its warm sunshine, beaches and quirky laid back atmosphere give it a very special niche. It represents some of the best of California and of course I was sad to leave, but now joined by my new and old friends it was time to head onwards to Mexico!

# TWENTY THREE

# Baja and Bullet Holes

Mexico is a fascinating country of opposites. It is a place where the best meets the worst with everything else imaginable sandwiched in the middle. The wild hedonism of Cancun glitters against the backdrop of ancient of Mayan ruins and a largely conservative society. Murderous drug cartels operate against a backdrop of tranquil and stunning beaches. Traditional tribes are surrounded by tourist resorts. Mexico was both exactly and nothing like I expected.

As the first developing country I was to cycle through on this journey, and indeed ever, I approached the border with some apprehension. I was happy to have company for the crossing and the reassurance that additional numbers can bring. We had chosen to enter Mexico about 40 miles inland from San Diego at the town of Tecate, which despite some few warnings was, by most accounts, still infinitely better than Tijuana, a legendary bastion of ill repute, muggings and general chaos on the coast. We passed through the border control with virtually no fuss and that was it – I had ridden clean across the United States and now I was in Mexico!

The place didn't feel terribly different. A fraction poorer and slightly more ramshackle in appearance, perhaps, but that was it. A different currency was returned when you bought something but otherwise it felt pretty much the same as the part of town lying a few hundred yards away across the border.

After a night in Tecate we turned briefly towards the coast and then south. Once beyond the border things changed rapidly, as the civilization of the modern world slowly burned away in the wild desert heat and the real Mexico emerged. This was the peninsular of Baja California, an overlooked sliver of land stretching a thousand miles from the US border to its southern tip. For much of its length a single road is the only evidence that mankind has attempted to tame this harsh landscape. Baja seems forgotten by time, a wild place straight out of an old western movie. Cacti, saguaros and Joshua trees vie for toeholds in a parched desert framed by distant blue mountains, while at the coast the crystal waves crash onto yellow sand beaches hidden in isolated coves. I found it arrestingly beautiful.

During our second afternoon we arrived in Ensenada, the last coastal town before we headed into the interior for a while. With a long and difficult stretch of dirt road ahead we reviewed our gear, and in particular we reviewed Marian's gear. He had been riding very slowly in those first two days since San Diego so Alvaro offered to see if he could help Marian cut down some weight. We sat on the beds in the hotel room as Alvaro removed items from Marian's bags and introduced us to the 'Kitchen Sink' packing philosophy. Some of the objects were mind boggling.

The first item out of the bag was a small axe.

"In case I need to cut down firewood," offered Marian as his reason for carrying it. In the forests of Canada this *might* have been a reasonable item to bring, but as we were now riding through a treeless desert it seemed a little superfluous. Onto the 'don't need' pile it went. Alvaro reached into the bag once more and this time pulled out a Maglite torch. Not one of the small ones but the biggest one they make. It takes four DDD batteries and weighed 5 lbs.

"But it is really bright!" was Marian's protest as Alvaro moved it to the 'don't need' pile and reached in again. Out came a large and luxurious beach towel weighing at least a pound.

"I guess that is almost OK," said Alvaro as he placed it on the bed before reaching into the bag again, "but oh, what's this?" he exclaimed as he pulled out another identical beach towel.

"In case one is damp," came Marian's answer. Not a good enough reason for Alvaro and both were set aside. I had to agree. I hadn't owned a towel for five months.

With one bag checked Alvaro moved onto the next. The first item out of this bag was a frying pan. Not one of those light weight cooking pans designed for hiking but a proper full sized frying pan. Alvaro didn't even wait for a response before putting on the throw away pile. The removal, discussion, protests, laughing and discarding of items continued for an hour. To make it even funnier, Marian kept trying to sneak items back into the 'keep' pile without us noticing. I think he managed to get one of the towels back in but that was about it. In all, Alvaro cut out over 20lbs of equipment, a monumental saving when you have to carry it over a mountain. And you know what? It worked. On the next ride we could hardly keep up with Marian and even he had to admit that Alvaro had been right. Tough love at its best.

The journey through Baja California took a month. It was wonderful desert scenery and rural hospitality all the way, a journey purely concerned with riding and camping in a calm solitude and serene remoteness far from the troubles of the world. We would stop in small villages along the way and eat at tiny cafes or stalls set out along the roadside. At one place we were staying in an unfinished building next to a small cafe, and in the morning the owner was ecstatic about showing us that his Huevos Rancheros breakfast dish was famous. He even showed us the magazine to prove it, and sure enough there was the article all about it. Of course, by that point there was only one thing we could order whether we wanted to or not, and I must admit it was pretty damn good! The only real moment of worry during these thousand miles was when we cycled through a swarm of bees, as both Alvaro and Marian were allergic to bee stings. They weren't too happy when it happened, but luckily we passed through unscathed.

It was nice to be riding with company once again. Although I had become quite used to the solitude of riding alone it was never easy. I am still a social creature at heart, as most of us are. The ability to share the sunset with others, to take my mind of a difficulty with a conversation, to enjoy stories and learn about someone else were things I had been missing for a long time. They are normal things which most of us have as a fundamental tenant of living, yet a lack of social company is something I learned to tolerate. It was a wonderful change to embrace these simple actions and I was lucky to have such a good group to travel with.

After a month we emerged back into civilization at the city of La Paz. It was a shock to the system as we rushed through town and boarded the first ferry out of the port to the Mexican mainland. The ferry ride was long, some 15 hours or so, but not unpleasant. Standing on the deck of the ship looking at the clear blue waters all around I was astounded to see a huge pod of dolphins, perhaps a hundred strong, playing in the wake of the ship. It looked like a lot of fun. They stayed with the ship until night fell, whereupon we found some space inside on the main deck and slept until the ferry docked early next morning in Mazatlan. At this junction our planned directions diverged. Jodie and I wanted to ride into the interior whereas Alvaro and Marian preferred the coastal route. I had enjoyed their company very much in those few weeks and I hoped I would meet them again.

"The world is much smaller than you think," Alvaro reminded me, "I am sure we shall meet again soon." Maybe he was right, but I still left Mazatlan with a sad heart mixed with anticipation. Or perhaps it was trepidation, for this stretch of road had a sinister reputation and an ominous name. "El Espinazo del Diablo," The Spine of the Devil. Rising from the ocean to over 10,000ft in just 40 miles, the road weaves through the knife-edged mountain spires of the Sierra Madre range as it climbs through the state of Sinaloa, an area notorious for drugs and gang violence. I had been cautioned about this road by pretty much every local I'd met but I didn't give the warnings much credence until Jodie and I stopped to rest outside an isolated roadside cafe in the hills. I bought a snack and was sitting on the curb outside in the sunshine when I noticed a car parked outside the cafe a few feet away. It was beaten up and wholly unremarkable except for a large number of small holes in the driver side door. I thought it odd and edged closer for a better look until I realized what they were. They were bullet holes. Drugs and violence, Mexico has it all, and in the uniquely Mexican way of doing things, they then drive the evidence to the store to get groceries.

The road and the climb were as dramatic as the name suggested. It was also quite slow going and impossible to camp due to the sheer cliffs. As the sun set on the second night we knocked on a random house door in a tiny village straddling the cliffs between two mountain spires and were given shelter by a family. They even gave us one of their son's beds for the night, despite my protestations. In the morning we said a heartfelt goodbye and continued on before stopping a short time later at a roadside shack selling coffee and pastries. Perched at the saddle point of the peaks this cafe had vast drops on either side into the valleys 5,000ft below. Sitting on a low brick wall with my legs dangling over the void I decided that this was about as unique a place I could think of to have my morning coffee.

The road continued to rise and the environment changed from lush coastal vegetation to fragrant pine forest. After what seemed like endless climbing we eventually crested at almost 10,000ft and topped out on the central plateau. Respite at last! For the next two days the terrain became rolling hills through a forested landscape until we arrived at the historic city of Durango. It was pleasant enough but not so pleasant as to justify much time, so after one night we turned south across the plateau to the small town of Hidalgo.

Hidalgo is small but important. It was here, on the steps of the town church on September 16, 1810, that Miguel Hidalgo y Costilla, a priest turned revolutionary leader, gave a rousing call now known as the Grito de Dolores and began Mexico's path to independence from Spain. Standing on those very steps I couldn't resist the temptation to declare that Mexico was now part of the British Empire. It didn't work. Right place, bad idea, 200 years too late. Can't win them all I guess.

In Hidalgo it was also time for Jodie and I to go our separate ways. It had been a genuine pleasure to ride with her for those six weeks but I was now feeling an increasingly powerful desire to strike out on my own once more. I'd learned that one of the difficulties with long distance adventure cycling was proximity. It is a 24 hours a day relationship. Even if one of you rides slowly and the other rides hard it is difficult to build more than a few miles of separation. Often the whole day is spent within view of one other. You eat together, ride together and camp together, all day, every day. The smallest annoyance can become a dagger of frustration; the most minor disagreements a festering war. Jodie is a fabulous person but I wasn't prepared for such non-stop company and it was now time for us to part ways with a smile, so we said our fond goodbyes and she turned west towards the coast as I continued south to Guanajuato.

# TWENTY FOUR

# The X Factor

The history of Guanajuato and indeed of Mexico is as unlikely as it is fascinating. Before the colonization of Latin America by the Spanish and Portuguese in the 16th century, Mexico had the 10th largest population in the world, and yet despite this great size the territory was ultimately subjugated by what was in comparison a mere handful of Spaniards. Hardened mercenaries, these conquerors were driven by a desire for power and the glory of Spain, of course, but above all by their desire for riches and the glittering allure of silver and gold. This search for riches has left a permanent and deep legacy, not least through language, culture and demographics, but also in more physical ways. With substantial deposits of silver found in the surrounding mountains and in one ravine in particular, the founding of Guanajuato is one of those legacies. The street plan of the old city appears to be little changed in centuries, with improbably narrow alleyways, stairs and dead ends weaving around Mexican baroque architecture in a tangled and delightful mess. More than once I took a wrong turn and found myself standing on the roof of somebody's house. It is a city totally unsuited to the modern world and thus a fascinating place to visit.

I stayed at a guesthouse in the center of the city which had a roof terrace and a view of the cathedral. It was a pleasant backdrop against which to sit in the sun and drink beer. I'm not saying that I took full advantage of this, but suffice to say that even with beer at $0.50 a pint, my beer tab was more than the cost of my accommodation. Helping me in my quest to drink the hostel dry was an eclectic and random group of fellow travelers, including a quirky Japanese guy with some break dancing skills.

He was particularly good at spinning on his head and actually traveled with a skateboard helmet which he would bring with him to bars in case he needed to bust out some moves. Also in the group were two young Americans who had made some cash in the tech bubble in the 1990s and decided that the good life was in Mexico. They had spent quite a lot of time developing their ability to party, a fact which contributed to my somewhat tipsy state for the duration of my stay.

After a long afternoon session on the roof we found ourselves that night in one of Guanajuato's larger nightclubs. We were feeling good and ready to get the groove on. The club had a modest décor but a large open dance floor, with a narrow stage stretching across the far side. For the record, stages and I have a complicated relationship. I must admit that I can be quite exhibitionist at times and will do anything for a good view, all of which draws me to dancing on a stage like a moth to a flame. Just like the moth and the flame, though, I also often end up in a fiery death spiral of embarrassment. After getting our drinks and supporting our Japanese friend's attempt to spin on his head - which he did superbly, I must say - I of course ended up on the stage. Looking through the laser illuminated crowd I was in my own dreamy bubble as I danced like a man being tasered. I was happy and free without a care in the world, and when I thought it couldn't get any better, it didn't. It got weird.

As I danced, I momentarily caught sight of a guy in the crowd who was taking his shirt off. I was sweating hard from all my "awesome" dance moves and it suddenly gave me the idea to cool off somewhat by aerating my T-Shirt. And hey, why not do some funky stripper-type dance moves at the same time - I was on a stage after all! As I was front-and-center this meant I was effectively flashing my torso to the whole club, although in my defense this was mostly unintentional. Mostly.

"Look at this guy," came a voice in Spanish, somehow cutting through the pounding music. At first I could kind of hear the voice but couldn't figure out either where it was coming from or what it was saying. Then two things happened in quick succession and I sobered up rapidly. Firstly, I realized the voice could cut through the music because it was the DJ, and secondly, when I looked away from the lights and down to the crowd I realized that he was talking about me. 400 people were staring in my direction.

"Hey girls, who wants to see him take his shirt off?!" asked the DJ, and a high-pitched shout went up from the crowd. "I'm gonna stop the music until you do it, amigo," he continued and then he actually did, I kid you not. 400 pairs of eyes waited for me in the silence to take off my shirt, the girls presumably for the modest abs I had accumulated in the prior seven months and the guys to get the music back on. It was, without a doubt, one of the strangest moments in my life. The feeling from the crowd was intense and for the briefest of moments I was a rock star. I could feel the weight and pressure of so many eyes pushing into me, a sensation similar to the pressure you feel to avert your eyes in an awkward conversation, but multiplied a thousand times. In that instant I felt the allure, the power and the fear of fame. It was utterly thrilling and utterly terrifying.

There was nothing to do but make the most of it, of course, so I reached down from the stage and grasped the hands of two attractive young women in the "audience" below, lifting them beside me on the stage in one swoop. Keeping their hands in mine I gripped the base of my T-shirt on each side and after a 3-2-1 countdown they pulled it off. A wave of disappointment washed across the crowd and the music sprang back to life as quickly as it had stopped. The moment was over as quickly as it had begun, but it remains a moment I will never forget.

# TWENTY FIVE

# Wake-up Call, Mexican Style

The next day I left the shattered remnants of my dignity in Guanajuato and began a traverse across the broad central plateau of central Mexico, a tiring seven day stretch. On the eighth day I reached the edge of the plateau and swept nearly 8,000 vertical feet down to the Gulf coast. At dusk I found a camping spot in a small clearing behind an abandoned warehouse located at the end of a short driveway leading to the main road. Despite being hidden from view by the thick surrounding jungle it still gave me a strangely uneasy feeling. It was almost like a sixth sense that things weren't quite right, and I wrote about the sensation in my journal before falling into a restless sleep.

"Hola?"

I opened my eyes to see a faint glow inside my tent as shards of light from the rising sun gently illuminated the surrounding foliage. It was early, around 6.00am. A little adrenaline surged from having an unexpected visitor.

"Que passar aqui? Que hace?" demanded the voice. "What's going on here? What are you doing?"

"Uh, hola," I replied, "Momento, momento," and squeezed out of my sleeping bag. Crawling over to unzip the tent flap I really hoped this would turn out for the best. It didn't.

I pushed back the fabric to find myself staring straight into the barrel of a shotgun that was being pointed at my face. This was definitely not a good sign. I was in a remote part of Mexico, alone and hidden from view. With nothing else to do I eased slowly out of the tent with my hands in full view with the hope that this gunman considered it bad sport to shoot an unarmed man on all fours. I slowly stood up and greeted him properly.

He was short, maybe 5'4", and dressed in a black jacket, beige pants and a baseball cap. We stood close as he talked in rapid, animated Spanish while waving the gun around. I didn't understand much of what he was saying as I was mostly focused on the gun, but after a few minutes I had pieced together that he had seen my tent from up on the hill and had come to investigate. Only then did I look at him more closely. On his baseball cap was written 'Policia Federal' in large white lettering. He was a cop. That made me feel better, although not much better given where I was. We continued talking for a few more minutes as I tried a few stuttered replies in broken Spanish to explain why I was there, until without warning he lowered the gun and reached out his hand to shake mine vigorously before turning away with a smile and scampering off down the path.

With this abrupt departure I just stood there and watched him leave until my wits came back and I decided that what I really needed to do was get the hell out of there before he came back. I packed my stuff like a man possessed and rode off cursing myself for not listening to my instincts the previous night. Another lucky escape and another lesson learned.

# TWENTY SIX

# Chafing the Dream

The seasons had continued their inexorable march forward as I travelled south to avoid them, and in Mexico I now passed beyond the reach of winter. It was late December and the Gulf coast was warm and pleasant. Continuing along the coastal road I passed the very spot where the Spaniards had first landed in the New World. Upon their arrival in 1519 they founded the small village of Villa Rica de la Vera Cruz, where a quaint little church still stands overlooking the tiny town square in its center. Its architecture is very basic and quite nondescript, a cube-looking building with thick walls and a bright whitewashed exterior. What makes it special, however, is not its architecture but its history, as this is believed to be the first ever church built on the Latin American mainland. Knowing the conquest of a continent which followed I found it a reflective experience to sit on the steps of the place where it all began.

From Villa Rica I continued along the coast to the city of Veracruz. I had ridden for 13 ½ straight days and almost a thousand miles without a rest at this point and my body was feeling the effects, not least of which was due to the saddle. I'd heard about saddle sores before my trip but until I experienced them I barely imagined how stunningly unpleasant they can be. The sores are formed when the constant pressure of the saddle against the pelvis damages the blood flow to the skin and the muscle trapped between bone and saddle. Skin abrasions are common and often an abscess forms within the muscle itself. Both become terribly painful to the touch, which is a problem when you still have to sit on it. Wearing padded cycle shorts helps, but during such a long stretch my shorts became so revolting that I was forced to cycle for the last few days wearing unpadded board shorts instead. Excruciating. Choosing between riding standing up for hours on end and the pain of sitting was not a win-win result, let me tell you, and I have rarely been happier to arrive at my destination and get off the bike. As bad as they were, however, I knew that it could be so much worse after a monumental journey I had suffered through in rural South East Asia several years before. The bus I took on that one particular stretch was a converted pick-up truck with a makeshift tarp over the back into which a crush of passengers was hemmed until movement was impossible. We bounced and banged through the mountains of Laos, jarred on every rut by the overloaded and broken suspension as each pothole sent my hard wooden seat dropping sharply downwards, only to rebound ferociously and impact onto to my now descending bottom. It was like being beaten with a heavy wooden board for nine hours straight. By the end I was oozing blood from where the label of my underwear had rubbed between my skin and the back of the seat; a mere inconvenience compared to how the muscle beneath my pelvis was feeling. It had been internally pulverized to mush, leaving me with two cavities inside. I was unable to sit down for the next month and the scars remain to this day.

Back in Veracruz, to take my mind off the saddle sores the next morning I explored the harbor. I heard there was a famous coffee shop with a special twist here, so I went to find it. Called the Gran Cafe De La Parroquia, it has been serving coffee for an incredible 204 years. Walking past the vast container ships I eventually found it at the start of one of the docking piers and went in. Surprisingly for such a modest looking place it was packed. I took a seat and figured out the rules. A waiter, immaculately dressed in a white jacket and black bow tie, would emerge from within the thick crowd to pass by your table carrying two large silver kettles with long spouts. One kettle held coffee and the other held milk. To request a coffee you merely tapped a spoon on your glass; a quick 'dink-dink' and the waiter would fill or refill your cup with a combination from both pots.

It was fantastic, like drinking coffee at the Ritz in London only far more exciting and much less expensive. The coffee was excellent and almost as good as the opportunity to people watch. An eclectic mix of tourists, retired gentlemen, sailors and local businessmen all sat together, hemmed in as one. For some reason I felt very much at ease as I drank an inadvisable amount of coffee and let the pains of the prior few weeks ebb into the back of my mind. It was an invigorating place to relax.

With saddle sores healing it was time for me to cross the Isthmus of Tabasco, the narrowest part of Mexico which separates the Pacific Ocean from the Caribbean Sea. Here the mountain range takes a break, so the 63 mile journey from one shore to the other was physically easy, at least on a relative basis. Only one thing made it special, which was that today was Christmas day. That evening I camped on a low cliff above a quarry and enjoyed the surprisingly good view of the mountains which rose in the distant north. Christmas dinner consisted of some avocados and rice washed down with a couple of warm beers and a Romeo and Juliet cigar for desert, which I had picked up after randomly passing the factory a few days before. Although I don't really like cigars, for a couple of dollars I couldn't pass up the opportunity. Watching the silhouettes of fruit bats masked against a purple sunset I felt in command of my destiny. Life was good. The only emotion which detracted from this contented beauty was loneliness. I was unable to contact my family that day, and although I knew it was technically just a day like any other I still felt isolated and a long way from a loving cuddle. In a sharp and unexpected wave of emotion I briefly cried, soon wiping away the tears as I realized how silly I must look to the bats. I missed my family a lot, in good times as well as in bad. It made me realize that there is a difference between knowing you are loved and feeling that love first hand. I knew that my family was thinking of me while I thought of them, though, and that gave me comfort. It may not have been a perfect Christmas but it was undeniably one to remember.

The next morning I left the coastal plains and ascended once more into the hills. The town of San Cristobal de las Casas, nestled in the mountains above the Yucatan peninsula, was the next destination. The culture of San Cristobal is heavily influenced by the tribes from the surrounding area, making for both a vibrant atmosphere and some deep tensions. In January 1994 the tension between the local tribes and central government boiled over into armed conflict as a group of separatists named the Zapatistas took control of the city. Under the command of the still-unidentified Sub-Comandante Marcos, the occupation held out for 11 days until a ceasefire was brokered and the Mexican military regained control of the area. Despite this defeat the Zapatistas had succeeded in bringing the persecution and segregation of the local indigenous population to the attention of Mexicans across the country. Not everyone was sympathetic, though, and feelings towards the Zapatistas were still strongly polarized ten years later when I arrived. Part of the country and most of San Cristobal considers them heroes; the other part considers them terrorists. The group's completely black, balaclava-wearing, gun-toting uniform didn't do much to refute that last comparison. Local adoration of the Zapatistas was clear to see though as I walked through the winding maze of narrow walkways of the town's central market, a strange place that seemed half for the locals and half for the tourists. I passed stalls selling everything from delicious tacos and kitchen utensils to touristy knick-knacks. There seemed no logic to their arrangement, and wandering along one alleyway I looked over and saw one particular stall which stood out. Manned by two old women wearing colorful local dresses, it sold just one type of product. In an age of Al Qaida and Osama Bin Laden this stall only sold Zapatista dolls. In 2004 these terrorist dolls, dressed in their long black coats and carrying small wooden machine guns, might have been the world's most unusual souvenir. I couldn't pass up the opportunity to get a couple and so a six inch tall terrorist doll now sits in my parent's living room display cabinet.

# TWENTY SEVEN

# It's just a Flesh Wound

It was once more New Year's Eve and I was relaxing in the hostel courtyard, a place with a large terracotta tile floor surrounded by thick stone walls and heavy wooden doors leading to the bedrooms. A random mix of guests had started drinking early while laying out sunbathing in the courtyard, myself included. In the warm sun I thought of the year which had passed. It had been 365 days since I made the promise to myself about doing something with my year, and I reflected on what I had achieved. While I could make a list of the individual new things I had done, I realized that I had only really achieved two things. Personal growth and a new understanding of risk. I had learned so much about so many things, heard the stories of so many people, seen and experienced so many unique places and events. I had also gained an appreciation of what is possible if you persevere and never give up, while also learning to judge those circumstances when you are onto a loser, no matter what. I had grown as a person, and that is all I could ever ask for in this life. In my book at least, if you aren't growing you are waiting to die. Promise fulfilled.

I lay relaxing in the courtyard. Beyond the usual coming and going of people, nothing much was happening until a Canadian fellow named Nick disappeared into his room and returned with an oddity. Two 20 inch thin metal chains hung from his fingers, each with a rubber ball on the end and a leather finger loop to hold each chain with. I asked him what they were.

"They're Poi," he explained, "It's this traditional Maori thing from New Zealand, but it's got pretty popular all over the place." With that non-descriptive explanation he moved into a sunny part of the courtyard and with hands gripping the loops he began spinning them around his body. The complex patterns and rhythmic movements were mesmerizing.

"Hey, could you teach me how to do that?" I pleaded with him, "It looks awesome!" He kindly agreed and spent the next few minutes teaching me the basics. It was pretty good fun but surprisingly difficult, so I spent the rest of the afternoon accidentally smacking myself in the face with them until I got the hang of it.

Night fell and the temperature dropped sharply. People grabbed thicker clothes from their rooms and returned to the now illuminated courtyard to continue partying. Nick returned with more clothes, some different poi and a bottle of gasoline, into which he dunked the poi heads before setting them on fire. Watching the arcs of flame trail around his body was even more mesmerizing than the afternoon's show and I knew I had to try it! After some more pleading he reluctantly agreed and we went to a corner where Nick showed me how to douse them in the fuel. I did a bit messily due to my tipsy state but eventually we got things sorted out and they were soon attached to my fingers, ready to ignite. Nick held the lighter underneath and 'whoosh!' up went the flames. My adrenaline surged. I started to spin them around my body and that at moment nothing else in the universe existed, only the fire flying past my head. Flames controlled by my whimsical bidding, what could be more primordial than that? I was doing everything Nick had taught me and it was going well. And then I set my pants on fire.

With the adrenaline pumping and my mind focused I was completely oblivious to what was happening as the flames flickered up from the material and reached my back. Nick finally had to rush in and slap them out. The flames burnt a two inch hole through my pants, right over one side of my bottom, but luckily I was otherwise unscathed. The lesson of the day became 'Don't wipe gasoline on your clothes before brushing fire over them.' No real harm was done, except that those pants were my only pair and because it was wash day I didn't have any underwear on underneath them either. Fortunately though, these pants were a beige color that exactly matched my skin so the hole was actually quite difficult to see against the pale shades beneath. I guess I could have borrowed another pair but I everyone was leaving and I didn't have time. Leaving things as they were I headed out to the bars with the others. Not one person we met seemed to notice, although I vaguely remember telling a few people what I had done. It's not every day you have a story about setting yourself on fire. Either way I celebrated the arrival of the New Year as though nothing had happened. As you can tell, I'm a classy guy.

# TWENTY EIGHT

# Mushroom Men and Mayans

By now I had been immersed in Mexican culture for 10 weeks and I was ready for a change. The promise of Belize, a former British colony on the Caribbean coast, was exactly what I needed but to reach the laid back Rastafarian vibe I still had to navigate a route through the rest of Chiapas and the Yucatan Peninsula. The first key destination along this final Mexican stretch was Palenque, one of the three great cities of the Mayan civilization before its demise. This would be my first encounter with the Mayan civilization and I was excited to see it.

The ruins of Palenque stand as a lookout from the final steep mountain foothills of Chiapas before the unending flat land of the Yucatan. Now a national park, there is only a single entry road with a great gate at its boundary, some distance from the ruins themselves. Preferring to stay nearby rather than in the non-descript town several miles away I had luckily heard of a hostel located right at the entrance, yet when I arrived at the place I saw nothing except for a small path past an electric substation that led into the thick jungle beyond. I was about to give up and head back to town when along the path came a couple. They were without doubt the backpacking types, so I figured I might have the right spot after all. Wheeling my bicycle up the path, after perhaps a hundred yards I discovered to my surprise possibly the strangest backpacker hostel in the world.

The hostel was so enveloped in nature that even the entrance was difficult to find, as I had just discovered. The cabins, camping areas and hammock spaces were all woven into and through the jungle itself, and the only real evidence of civilization was the compound's large open air restaurant. It looked like a five star resort compound where millions have been spent to make it look authentic and tropical, except that this place was naturally like that. My stay there was like being on a rainforest trek, except with more people, better banana milkshakes and a lot more beer.

The highlight of my stay was the old Mexican guy who lived there along with his guitar. He carried it around with him all day, and was often joined by groups of the more hippy types in some secluded corner of the jungle where he would play music deep into the small hours of the morning. On my second or third night there I randomly stumbled on this group and the old man as I walked back from the restaurant bar, and joined them for no reason other than that the bar was shut and I didn't yet want to go to back to my hammock. It was like joining a club which was half a Cuban jazz appreciation society and half a jungle hippy commune, only better. Much better. I was totally blown away by his talent. Sitting on the dirt floor in the open air, illuminated by a single lantern and surrounded by buzzing jungle, I experienced pure magic. When he played "Chan Chan" by Buena Vista Social Club I had one of those can't-help-but-smile moments as my eyes teared up with happiness. I thought I would burst; a strange tense sensation in my chest as every nerve tingled with joy. I felt like a million dollars. No, a billion dollars. When people ask why I care so little for five star hotels I remember that moment in the jungle. It was better than any show in any resort in the world.

There was one final surprise that still awaited me. Allow me to introduce you to the Mushroom Man, a strange figure I'd heard about from a random traveler with whom I had crossed paths many miles before.

"So, when you stay at this place - and you've *got* to stay at this place," said the traveler, "there's this guy called the Mushroom Man. It's crazy, man. You walk through the park entrance and then along the road for a bit until you hear him call, and then this guy comes out of the bushes if you call back."

A small group of us departed for the ruins early in the morning and soon passed through the park gates. I swear they are a replica of the gates in the Jurassic Park movie, a surreal sight which is strangely in keeping with the surroundings. From the gates we walked about half a mile along the jungle-bordered road until sure enough we heard a rustle in the undergrowth ahead. We stopped and listened to the silence. Finally, faintly, we heard a voice.

"Mushrooms?" came a nervous whisper. Then a pause.

"Mushrooms?" he called again, a little more urgently.

We called out to him and explained we were tourists. There was another short silence before a portly middle-aged man in a dirty white T-shirt clambered out of the dense forest about 10 yards away. He stopped and one of the Spanish speaking guys in our group walked up to negotiate. After a brief discussion the man disappeared back into the forest and our friend returned with a bulging old brown paper bag full of slimy looking brown mushrooms. The Mushroom Man indeed!

While I generally draw the line at eating unidentified psychedelic mushrooms provided by a strange man emerging from a strange forest in a strange country, several of the group were not so shy. In the hostel bar later that evening one of them described the experience.

"I have to say, man, it was freaky!" he enthused. "I was just sitting there, you know, on the top of the Mayan temple looking down on the people walked around, and suddenly all of them were dressed as Mayans! Full on! They were all wearing the headdress, the clothes, everything! And then I looked at me and I was dressed as a Mayan! It was like I had been transported back 1,000 years or something! I sat there for hours, man, and just watched all the Mayans walking around and doing Mayan things," he continued. "Freaky!"

I have to agree.

Mushrooms or no mushrooms, Palenque was well worth the visit and I begrudgingly left the jungle hostel a couple of days later. Wheeling down from the low hill and onto the Yucatan itself I was now faced with 60 miles of completely straight road raised above the flat and featureless marshland that lay on either side. With dusk coming after a monotonous ride and still nowhere to pull off I finally arrived at a tiny village on one side of the road. It was the first I had seen for many tens of miles and this was my only option for the night. The first building in town was a small non-descript concrete box which was happened to be the village school. I put my tent up on one side and started to make a quick dinner. Someone had seen me arrive, of course, so the entire village came to investigate. It was a little unnerving and yet an invigoratingly pleasant experience. The villagers were all very nice and the little kids were curious about everything. We struggled in sign language for a while as I showed the kids various bit of my equipment until it was time for me to sleep. I enjoy those kinds of encounters despite never feeling quite comfortable. You never know what will happen, both good and bad. In many ways it was a fitting last day for me in Mexico, a reflection of the prior 10 weeks. Sometimes a bit unnerving and yet often invigoratingly pleasant. And always fascinating.

# TWENTY NINE

# Would you Belize it

I reached the Belizean border before noon the next day. Passing through the frontier was like warping through space and time. Everything changed. English and a distinctive Caribbean accent instantly replaced Spanish as the language of conversation, while the conservative style of dress seen across Mexico was suddenly replaced by fake Tommy Hilfiger hats and Bob Marley T-Shirts. Evidence of African heritage immediately became apparent.

My goal was to reach the islands off the coast of Belize. Called cayes (pronounced "keys") they form the world's second largest reef after the Great Barrier Reef in Australia. Unfortunately, to get a boat to the cayes I had to suffer the necessary evil of Belize City. Entering the city felt like arriving on the film set of Pirates of the Caribbean. Of the places I've visited on my travels, Belize City rates near the top on my Scale of Dodginess. Everyone seems to be continuously trying to hustle everyone else. It is probably OK if you are a local, as each man's hustling cancels out the next, but beware of playing the role of tourist in this place. Preferred activities seem to include trying to steal your stuff, selling you drugs or working an elaborate con, all of which I experienced in my two days there. I remember attempting to walk to a museum at the far end of a small peninsular where the cruise ships docked, perhaps 600 yards from the small tourist area by the river where I bought my ticket to the islands. I started down a deserted wide street in the approximate direction of the museum when a heavily armed policeman stepped out in front of me. He was wearing a bullet proof vest and helmet, and carried a machine gun.

"Sir!" he commanded as he stared me in the eyes. "You can't go down that street. You will get robbed."

"Really?" I asked, somewhat surprised as I looked along the sun-drenched street and then at my watch. It was 2.00pm on a Sunday.

"Yes," he replied matter-of-factly and then briskly escorted me step by step the 20 yards back to the "safe" area where I had started. If anyone else can find me a city where 20 yards makes the difference I would love to know where it is. Rio de Janeiro doesn't come close and even the slums of Lima and Mumbai didn't seem that bad. My advice for travelling in Belize City is to leave the Rolex at home. And everything else.

All that general sketchiness evaporates the moment you board the triple-engined speedboat and depart for the islands. 900 horsepower of pure terror rocketed me through the maze of inner atolls, and for two hours we sliced through the azure water of the Caribbean Sea to Caye Caulker. With only golf carts on its few sand streets this small island exudes a genuine Caribbean charm. With a couple of laid-back bars, a smattering of seafood shacks right on the beach, reggae music playing everywhere and friendly people, I quickly discovered that Caye Caulker was my kind of place.

The caye has an interesting recent history. Originally a single island, in 1961 the waves and storm surge from Hurricane Hattie created a channel which literally split the island in two. Since then both ocean currents and human help has kept the channel open and it is now simply referred to as "The Split." A beach bar there called the Lazy Lizard has become *the* spot to watch the sunset, so in good weather most of the island's tourists turn up at around 4.00pm for the party. One afternoon I was there as usual, except that this time I had brought Tolly the Bear for his photo. As Tolly sat guarding my camera on the weather worn wooden bar a couple of Rastafarians sat down next to us. These guys were the real deal. One had dreadlocks, the other wearing clothes in green, red and yellow. One was a large fellow and the other smaller. Both looked intimidating. I looked down at Tolly and I hoped I wouldn't need to fish him out of the sea in the near future, and as I did so the eyes of one of the guys followed mine.

"Ay man, what is that!" he cried out, and shook his buddy's arm to get his attention before reaching a great hand across the bar and grabbing hold of Tolly.

"It's Tolly, my bear," I explained, "I'm taking pictures of him in the places we are visiting."

"Yeah?! Ha he looks like one *wicked* bear," replied the first Rasta, and starting playing with him. Watching this huge Rastafarian walking him along the bar by moving his little legs up and down was hilarious. So much for throwing him in the sea, I couldn't have been more wrong about these guys. They were great. In the end I took some photos of Tolly which included one of them giving him a kiss. Ahh, cute.

Beyond the bars and restaurants, Caye Caulker has some other great attractions, including an opportunity to 'feed' the local sharks. A small boat takes you about a mile offshore to a small break in the outer coral reef which lies at the transition between the shallow island plateau and the deep waters beyond. Fishermen use this break to cross the reef without running aground, and once back in the lagoon's calmer waters they prepare their catch before docking. Discarded bits of fish are thrown overboard to the waiting sharks, which are thus trained to meet arriving boats, and it wasn't long after we arrived before

I was looking into the water at a group of nurse sharks. That was the easy part. The harder part was that our skipper was keen for us to swim with them.

"Jump now!" he shouted, but apparently I hesitated – can't imagine why - so he pushed me in. I landed right on top of one of the sharks. I wasn't too scared because nurse sharks don't have real teeth, or so I thought. It turns out they do, albeit a thousand small ones which are highly specialized for eating crustaceans and mollusks. Fortunately the shark didn't bite, but that will be the last time I jump onto one. Once not-bitten, twice shy as they say.

My favorite restaurant on the island was right on the beach, with the tables and chairs literally on the sand, and one evening I found myself there with about other 10 random people I had met at the Lazy Lizard that afternoon. A spritely young girl took our orders and I remarked to her that it was very impressive she managed to do it without using a notepad.

"I have done this for seven years," she replied, "It's easy!"

"Really?" I responded, "I'm still impressed though, this order is getting pretty complicated," which it really was. "I have to be honest, I will believe it when I see it!"

She defended her abilities a little more and then took the rest of the order before scampering off to the kitchen. We quickly received our drinks and a little later the food arrived. Not a single order was correct, not one! Luckily though, the grilled whole fish that turned up in front of me was utterly fabulous and almost certainly better than what I had actually ordered. This pretty much was the case with everyone's food so we let it go and got on with the businesses of enjoying our meal as we listened to the sound of gentle tropical waves lapping on our beach. Tough life.

Much merriment was had in those days. I arrived tired from the riding, but now, newly invigorated by the tropical atmosphere I once again felt like I was actually getting somewhere on my journey. This place sure looked different from Alaska. All too soon, though, it was time to board a boat back to the mainland.

# THIRTY

# Ruins in the Mist

I was excited about the next country along my route. It is a place where the sparkling morning light shines through deep blue skies, where the clean air is rarified and cool. It is a place where ornate colonial buildings flank cobbled and deserted streets, where barren black pyramids rise high above the icy lakes and small isolated villages to dominate the skyline, their volcanic smoke and ash floating silently in the air. It is a place where dense rainforests hide the ancient secrets of a lost civilization and where great stone temples grow through the trees to emerge as islands in a sea of pristine green. It is a place where dangerous and genuine friendships are sometimes hard to separate, but also a place where human troubles seem smoothed by a landscape and culture which measures time not in years but in eons. This place is Guatemala. It is raw Latin America, a true traveler's destination. It is a place where the days are rarely dull, for either good reasons or bad.

Entering from Belize into the far northeast of the country I rode a battered old road towards the Mayan ruins of Tikal. The undulating landscape in the lowlands was mostly farmed until I passed into the large national park that surrounds Tikal and found myself immersed in dense rainforest. As with Palenque, the gates were reminiscent of Jurassic Park and offered a fitting threshold, for beyond them I became enveloped by the screeches and clicks of invisible things. The place feels primeval and alive.

Reaching the center of the park many miles from the gate I was fortunate to be able to stay in a small dormitory only a few yards from the entrance to the ruins themselves. The facilities consisted of a line of mattresses on the floor in a low building framed with slatted wooden walls. Only thin mosquito netting across the entire interior shielded the occupants from a billion insects, and as night fell I lay there and listened to the cacophony of buzzing and zinging from every direction. I had walked through a secret door and into a different world. Coming from a civilization constructed out of concrete, air conditioning and Starbucks it was a deeply calming experience.

The gates to the ruins themselves are opened at 6.00am and I was damn well going to be the first one in. I was greedy and wanted to have it all to myself, even if just briefly. I also wanted to make it in time to greet the rising sun; something which I had been told was a nice experience. At 5.58am I stood alone at the entrance in the misty pre-dawn gloom, the forest calm and quiet. I had 30 minutes before sunrise at the top of Temple IV and I was impatient for the ruins to open. I didn't have to wait long. At 6.00am precisely a security guard walked out his little guard hut and opened the main gate. I was still alone. Without a map and unable to see further than 10 or 20 yards in the dark mist I jogged along the soft, leaf strewn paths. Long-tailed raccoons along the verge scampered away from me in surprise as I quickly became lost. Ancient stone pyramids, covered in a thousand years of jungle, emerged at the side of the path like illusions. It was an unusual feeling, a real sense of discovery, and looking at those pyramids untouched for a thousand years it really did feel as though I was the first explorer to find them. On those endless paths I became Indiana Jones as I escaped from forgotten temples. Magical.

I may have been Indiana Jones, but I was still lost! After a long time and increasingly fast jogging the path finally became wider and more defined until I arrived at a large manicured grass area flanked by two towering Mayan pyramids. I had reached the center of Tikal. Dawn was coming quickly and the light shining through the mist was becoming brighter with every minute. Sitting briefly on the pyramid steps, alone in the silence of that place, the sense a civilization long past again felt palpable. It was as though the modern world was somehow concealed behind the white fog which still covered the jungle. It was so, so peaceful but I couldn't linger. I soon reached Temple IV, the sunrise temple, and climbed to the summit where I emerged above the jungle canopy and mist to be greeted by a bath of warm orange rays. In the glorious colors of that sunrise the peaks of Tikal's other great temples stood as islands in a green sea while the problems of the world vanished, an effect I believe only the high and lonely places of the world can create. Right then, sitting there on that stone ledge with only a few inquisitive raccoons for company, nothing else mattered. Temporarily, at least, I was once more at peace.

That first hour in Tikal was as a dream. Eventually, though, the first intrepid tourists began filtering in and with their shouts and obligatory photo poses they facilitated Tikal's daily metamorphosis from an ancient mythical city into a tourist destination. The magic of that first hour faded and it was time for me to leave. Back at the dormitory I had a quick breakfast, changed my clothes and by 11.00am I was riding back to civilization, the modern version this time.

Leaving the park and entering the real world, at least as far as Guatemala is concerned, I zig-zagged alternately south and west through the lowlands hills towards a distant mountain plateau. The route I had chosen seemed rarely traveled by foreigners and much less by foreigners on a bicycle, the proof of which coming when I cycled past a small and remote school. From behind its weathered gates, with their chipped red paint peeling from rusting wrought iron bars, a great high-pitched cry went up in to the air. I stopped the bike and turned around to see a torrent of children streaming through the gates towards me. I was quickly surrounded by a mass of bright smiles and curious eyes. I said a few "Holas" but quickly began moving again, as though pushed by the flood of attention. The experience was too unexpected, too overwhelming. I felt like a film star walking into his first paparazzi ambush. The large group remained standing in the middle of the road and watched me depart with sadness. To this day, the image of distant dark storm clouds silhouetting these small figures in the road as their clean uniforms reflected the sunshine is one I will never forget.

Those dark clouds quickly arrived and brought rain that was both torrential and brief. I was instantly drenched but the sun soon returned and I continued riding. It was hard going, however, as the quarter inch of water the storm had dropped created a blinding reflection in the tropical sun. There was nothing unusual about that, until the road started to move. Almost imperceptible at first, I began to see tiny flashes of movement on the water's surface. Beginning at the edge of the road, they soon spread until the road flashed and flickered like a spitting cauldron. The cause was utterly mystifying so I stopped and bent down for a closer look. I followed a streak. Where it ended there seemed to be a tiny little spot which pulsed rapidly until creating another rapid short streak through the water. Only then did I see what it was. Each pulse was the breath of a miniscule baby frog! Zip. It hopped once more as the disturbed water behind it flashed in the sun. There were thousands and thousands of them covering the road. Not wanting to be known as The Frog Killer, I waited for a few minutes as the water dissipated, and in less than ten minutes both the water and the frogs had vanished without a trace. With no lakes, streams or rivers to be seen through the dense vegetation, where they came from or went remains a mystery.

By this point I was rapidly approaching the edge of a massive plateau which rose abruptly from the lowlands towards the mountains beyond, and on its flank I could see a strange grey line running straight up the side.

"Power lines?" I muttered to myself, unsure as I couldn't make out any of the pylons. "A pipeline, perhaps? But for what?" I had no idea. Capturing glimpses of this strange phenomenon through the jungle I eventually rounded a bend to arrive at the base of the plateau and the intersection with the object. I looked up and a cold dread mixed with anger shuddered through me. It was the same feeling I'm sure you've experienced when cresting a hill on the freeway only to see stationary red tail lights stretching to the distant horizon. Misery is coming and there is nothing you can do about it.

"Oh my god, it can't be," I muttered, "It just can't be. They *can't* have built it like that, they just *can't*. How can that be the road?"

A 30 degree incline of merciless pavement, as steep as the streets of San Francisco, rose unbroken for a vertical mile. With a bicycle weighing more than some adults this road was the very driveway of Satan.

It was moments like that when I almost gave up. Hopelessness is an emotion far worse than pain. These were the moments when I slumped over my bicycle and cried. I knew this climb would likely require more effort than I could summon, but with no other choice I was forced into the attempt. I lifted my head from my handlebars, took a drink of water, ate a snack, changed gears to the smallest cog and began the slow and agonizing grind upwards. As I rode I thought of my favorite advertising slogan. With a picture of Mohammed Ali on the poster it proclaimed a simple yet powerful idea:

Impossible Is Nothing.

That was the mindset I needed. Many hours later, as I stared back from the plateau's summit to watch the darkness creep across the lowland jungles, that wisdom was apparent to me. I was utterly spent but I'd conquered it, even though I had to push the bike for the last couple of miles. I have always felt, rightly or wrongly, that in many ways my trip wasn't all that impressive from a physical perspective, and that most people could replicate it. You could. The only question of any consequence is whether the individual has enough will and desire to do so. People can train to become fit, ardent planners can learn to tolerate improvisation, urbanites can learn to camp in the wilderness. To replicate my journey is therefore mostly a question not of "can do", but of "will do". A good friend of mine who is a former professional cyclist once told me what it was like, and I think it applies here.

"I might not be the best rider out there," he said, "but I know how to suffer."

Damn right.

# THIRTY ONE

# Colonial Magic

Continuing across the plateau I skirted around the capital, Guatemala City. With its dubious reputation and lack of attractions I had no desire to take a closer look. A long climb out of the valley then left me with a pleasant evening descent to the old colonial town of Antigua. The sight of three active volcanoes surrounding the town initially made me question the wisdom of building it there, but seeing the dramatic vista of these peaks rising into the sky at the end of every street in town made me extremely happy that they did. Antigua is a special place, much of it due not just to the setting, but also to the historical atmosphere that pervades the town. The streets are still cobbled in several places and many of the old buildings are constructed in the traditional Spanish hacienda style. The varying states of disrepair are charming and modernity is subdued; even McDonald's was forced to replaced its gaudy bright yellow plastic arches with a small golden plaque on the building's exterior wall.

I checked into a hostel located in a large crumbing building near the central plaza. Whitewashed walls and lichen-encroached terracotta tiles lent a certain charm and history to the building, both on the exterior and in the elegant central courtyard. On the floor of the courtyard was the open air common area, with hammocks and deck chairs interspersed with miniature trees and potted plants. It was lovely. I checked in with the young girl at reception, chained my bicycle to a pillar and was shown to my dormitory room on the first floor. The room lay through a set of heavy mahogany doors which had been decoratively carved in an age long past and they creaked noisily as they swung inwards on their elaborate iron hinges. As I entered I saw there was one other person was already there. He was young guy of perhaps 20, with a light brown mop of hair and a relaxed face. He looked up at me from the edge of his bed as I hauled my awkward handful of bike panniers into the room.

"Hey," he greeted me, "What's all that? You didn't cycle here, did you!?"

"Hey, how's it going," I replied, slightly out of breath from the exertion and altitude. "Yep, I sure did. And let me tell you, I'm pretty damn happy to be here. I'm knackered!"

I opened a couple of bags and pulled out some new clothes as we chatted.

"So where are you from?" I continued. "Oh, and my name's James, by the way," I said, and extended my hand.

"Great to meet you, eh," he replied, shaking it enthusiastically. "I'm Rob, from British Columbia up in Canada. Maybe you've heard of it?"

"Yep," I replied with a wry smile, "it does sound familiar."

We spend a couple of days hanging out in Antigua before heading together to Lago Atitlan, the deepest lake in Central America. We took a tiny boat to the tiny town on the opposing bank and spent a couple more days just hanging out. It was an odd little place, especially as it had a proper British pub right above the dock. It was about the strangest place I could think of to find a pub, but as it did a very passable fish and chips I was prepared to take it all at face value.

From Lago Atitlan it was time for me to head back out on my bicycle towards the Pacific coast and the border with El Salvador. From Antigua the road descends an uninterrupted 5,000ft from the mountains straight down to the Pacific in less than 30 miles, and what a glorious downhill that is. In the warm sunshine I saw meadows full of yellow flowers framed by smoking volcanoes and the bright greens of the lowland jungle. On the horizon beyond, the deepest pure blue of the ocean. I shouted for joy as I rode and hit the gas, breaking though 54mph and reaching the maximum speed of my whole trip. While that's not so fast for a road bicycle, on an overloaded mountain bike on a sketchy road it felt scarier than 150mph on the racetrack. The euphoric rush of adrenaline that thumped through my veins more than compensated for the climb of a week before and I was pumped for the next challenge. El Salvador watch out, here I come!

# THIRTY TWO

# Dominos

"Fly to El Salvador, I don't know why and I don't know what for," go the words of a song. Having been there, the main reason to fly there is to see what a civil war and imported gang violence can do to a country. Or to go surfing, it's a 50/50 split. Crossing the fortified border I was surrounded by a rough industrialized landscape, the main road lined unendingly with basic boxy buildings that housed scruffy machine shops and old warehouses, their fading paint and rough concrete walls creating an ubiquitous monotony broken only by the high metal fences and cracked pavement between them. It was lovely. The people and fashions also changed and everywhere I now saw the influence of US culture. Bright board shorts replaced the somber and conservative slacks worn by the men of El Salvador's neighbors, while baseball caps became the norm. In the pervasive coastal heat it felt like a rundown part of Los Angeles, which was perhaps more than a coincidence. One of the United States' most prevalent and unfortunate exports to El Salvador has been gang culture from Los Angeles and other border cities as Salvadorians who were deported after serving jail time brought their allegiances back with them. Stir that together with a weaponized population plus a familiarity with violence born from a 12 year civil war in the 1980s and '90s and you have all the ingredients for a problematic bicycle ride.

I was none too keen to discover the dark side of El Salvador so at the first available junction I turned away from the scenic but more dangerous costal route towards the mountainous interior. The road climbed up steeply from the ocean and I was soon surrounded by volcanoes once more, including a brand new one that was still smoking. Erupting continuously between 1770 and 1958 it lay immediately adjacent to a larger and now extinct volcano, along which they had built the road. I spent the night in the collapsed caldera of the old volcano and in the cold predawn air I dragged my bones out of my sleeping bag to begin descending the trail toward the younger volcano, intent on climbing it. The slopes of the old peak were covered in dense jungle but once I crossed onto its sibling the ground turned black and devoid of life, just a billion tons of treacherous loose stones and boulders rising steeply several thousand feet back into the sky.

The climb was a grueling progression. Each step forward was accompanied by a slide backwards that reduced my gain to mere inches. It was like climbing a sand dune soaked in honey while carrying some heavy shopping. With lungs and legs burning I crossed the lip of the crater and stood on another world. Planet Earth, two billion years ago. Fumes and steam hissed from holes dotted across the small crater and everywhere was a faint smell of sulfur. Fog from the ocean had moved inland as I climbed and I now stood there separated from the rest of the world, alone on this black island of fire in a sea of white nothing. The sense of loneliness and isolation is hard to describe. It was a feeling of insignificance and that there is no purpose to anything, as though I was the last man in history watching the death of our planet and the end of all things. I stood there for a long time, just watching and thinking about life in a greater context, and felt sad despite the wonders around me. In time the fog burned off and the world below slowly reappeared once more. It was time to leave.

I skated down the scree flanks and then up to the campsite. After a quick breakfast I was back on the bike, passing through the cloud forest within the caldera and then an alpine lake area which extended towards the border with Honduras. The crossing was very unmemorable and several days later I arrived late one afternoon at the coastal city of La Ceiba. I soon found a basic hotel in the old part of town near the harbor, and by the time I had sorted myself out it was dusk. Sunsets in the tropics are as quick as they are beautiful, and darkness fell as though a curtain of shadow had been drawn across the world. It was still warm and very humid, a typical Caribbean evening. As in Belize, walking onto the street was like stepping onto the set of Pirates of the Caribbean. Ramshackle old two-story wooden buildings faced a wide and dilapidated street illuminated by weak filament bulbs which hung from tangled wires between roadside poles. An atmosphere of piracy and danger seemed to hang thick in the salty air, as though I was being watched. A few buildings down I could see a small local bar where a couple of wooden tables were placed out on a long front veranda under a well-lit wooden awning. This looked like my best bet for some food, as well as saving me from further wandering in the darkness. I stealthily occupied at a table in one corner, ordering a large cold beer and some very forgettable food. Beer in hand I sat there and watched the other end of the veranda where sat four or five locals playing a game of dominos. It was fascinating. Along with cricket, dominos is *the* quintessential Caribbean game. It was like watching boule in a French village or chess in a Brooklyn park. This group was no exception to the stereotype of eclectic domino players. There was a young, heavily muscled man in a grubby green and white stripped vest, and an old man with short hair, rough white stubble and a wide smile, dressed in a pristine shirt and a hat. Next to him stood a smaller young guy dressed in a white wife-beater shirt, while several other people also sat and watched. The next game hadn't yet begun but the rivalry was in full swing, for the real magic of dominos is not in the tiles but in the gambling.

"You no can do it, man! Ha, can't beat me, man, I is the *king*!" shouted the stripy green shirt to the old man before pulling out a tightly wound cylinder of grubby Honduran currency from his pocket and placing it on the table beside the other bets.

"Eh young'un, I gonna show you how we play dis game!" came the response, and a wad of money appeared from the old man's shirt pocket from which he began peeling notes slowly onto the table, savoring the dramatic pause as each one fell.

"Hope you don't need dat roll!" he continued, and grouped the notes next to the roll into the center of the table. The stakes were set, the game primed and ready. The first dominos were laid.

"In your face!" yelled the old man to the stripy green shirt man, and with high swing of his thin arm slammed a wrinkled hand onto the table, the air resonating with a sharp crack from a 1|6 domino expertly slapped into its position from within his palm. The crowd howled as the old man revealed the tile and he smiled a wide toothy grin as a rapid burst of light hearted insults erupted from all sides. All part of this great game - the domino slap, the place-gently-and-slide-to-position technique, the good-natured abuse, the bluff and the call.

"Ay man, how are you?" came a voice from the group and I realized the green stripy shirt man was addressing me. Adrenaline surged; I was no longer going to be the invisible spectator, for better or worse. "Ay, come over, man! You wanna play?"

"Hey, um yeah, that sounds fun," I replied, "But ya know, I think I'm just going to watch you guys for a bit; I don't really know what I'm doing here!" While that was true, I also had a limited desire to get fleeced by these guys as the dumb money. I grabbed my beer and pulled up a white fold-up plastic chair next to the old man.

"Ay, how's everyone doing?" I said as I sat, shaking a couple of hands of the guys near me with a little false bravado as I dug deep into my tough-guy Caribbean vocabulary. I admit that my heart was pumping. I've never been one of those people who are just at ease with others no matter the situation. That only really comes from a deep internal confidence, a sense that you can talk your way into or out of anything, which is something I've never had. As with most things in life I have had to work at being comfortable with discomfort. Call me the unnatural traveler, perhaps.

I had nothing to worry about, though, as the old guy took me under his wing a little and pointed out what was happening in the game as the next domino came crashing into to place. Even with his help I didn't really understand how it worked but still got into the spirit of things and howled along with the crowd. It was a ton of fun.

"Ha, I almost had you, eh young'un!" shouted the old man, turning to the green stripy shirt man.

"No way old man, no way," came the vigorous reply, "Can't do nutin' to me, man! You getting too old, old man!" he continued, and without breaking their eye contact he slowly slid his last domino across the table and into place. It was a movement designed to draw out every ounce of drama as he removed his hand slowly to reveal the tile.

"Domino!" he cried, and the crowd erupted again, myself included. He'd won.

"Ha! Now in *your* face, old man!" he said, and rose out his chair through the claps of the crowd before extending a large hand to grab the pile of bank notes on the table. Ah, dominos. I don't remember any of the rules but I do remember that you can lose a lot of cash!

After a couple more beers and a lot more dominos I was feeling the pinch of tiredness and so said my farewells before retiring back to my authentic death-trap of a hotel. Having survived the night I checked out the next morning and headed to the ferry terminal to board the surprisingly modern catamaran for the trip to Utila, an island located about 30 miles offshore. By virtue of the island's reputation as the cheapest place in the world to learn to scuba dive, visiting was an opportunity I couldn't pass up. Stay for a week and learn to dive was the plan. I stayed for three months.

# THIRTY THREE

# Whale of a Time

The days I spent on Utila were some of the best of my life, although in truth, even if they weren't I would have stayed for a while. It was now February and I had cycled almost non-stop since June. Although my body had become stronger in that time I also felt stretched. Perhaps I needed an emotional pause as well as a physical one. Seven months of continuous mental struggle and uncertainty, seven months without a home. I needed time to again socialize myself to society, even if that society was a quixotic group of scuba divers and backpackers. In short, James needed some time away from James.

Luckily though, if one is going to stop for a few months Utila is about as good a place as any to do so. Small and relatively placid, the single town on the island surrounds a natural harbor facing the mainland located many miles in the distance. Protected from the elements, its bars, restaurants and dive shops have been built on long wooden decks suspended on stilts far out into the shallow water. Behind these, the remainder of the town's small wooden houses extend into the hills above through the lush vegetation of the tropical forest. Without resort-type buildings and expensive hotels, Utila still exudes a genuine Caribbean culture and a backpacker vibe, a place where the hardest decision of the day is whether to scuba dive in the morning or the afternoon.

While the south of the island faces shallow water towards the mainland, the north side drops precipitously into the Cayman trench, a vast fissure between Jamaica and Central America that reaches down to a ludicrous 25,217ft at its deepest point. The mineral-rich waters which well up from the depths make the ocean here a vibrant soup of life, and this life in turn attracts another, very special visitor. Utila is one of the few places in the world where you can swim with whale sharks. These rare monsters can reach 40ft long, but luckily they don't have normal teeth but rather feed more like whales, enabling divers and swimmers to join them in the water in relative safety. I had unintentionally arrived at the right time of year and I was looking forward to hopefully seeing one of these magnificent and elusive creatures.

After disembarking the ferry I headed up the main street in town, where, on the recommendation of a fellow traveler I'd met in Guatemala, I soon arrived at the Bay Islands College of Diving. Walking through the door of the shop I was greeted by a couple of the folks who worked there. First was Craig. To describe Craig is to describe the archetypal squaddie, the British army's rank and file. He was a sizable guy, a look developed carefully over the years through a regime of rigorous partying, and although he may not appear on the cover of GQ magazine any time soon (just like the rest of us!) it was irrelevant, as Craig has a larger-than-life charisma and an incredible sense of humor; the kind of guy people want to be around. Craig was a legend.

Also in the shop was Cat. She was also British, small and petite with blonde hair, and like Craig she came fully loaded with personality. Never afraid to state an opinion and always in control, Cat ran the shop and generally kept things from falling apart. She was also a scuba instructor but now spent more time in the shop after discovering a susceptibility to something called nitrogen narcosis, a curious physiological effect of diving deep. In most people, beyond a depth of 100ft or so the water pressure becomes high enough to force some of the nitrogen dissolved in your blood through the membranes that shields the neurons in your brain cells. Although this sounds pretty horrific, it is exactly what happens when you breathe laughing gas and it has a similar effect. In moderate doses it creates a sense of euphoria and a decoupling of reality; it's like being really drunk and really happy. Unfortunately, while nitrogen narcosis itself is broadly harmless, becoming unable to think properly underwater sometimes causes people to make dangerous or even fatal decisions. For example,

Cat had been known to try to share her air supply with the fish when she couldn't figure out how they were breathing underwater without air. She generally showed symptoms at quite shallow depths, which was a problem if you are leading a group and the only one who knows where the boat is.

I immediately signed myself up for the PADI Open Water diver course, the beginner scuba course, and began a happy time in my life. Once it was completed I figured I'd just keep going, and so signed up for the Advanced Open Water course, then Rescue Diver and eventually the Divemaster qualification. I had time so I took full advantage of the location and the pricing!

Along with Craig and Cat I also met another Divemaster trainee named Rowan. Originally from Canada, he was a good looking and well put together chap, the kind of easy going and fun guy that everyone likes. I couldn't have had a better study buddy. As well as the diving we used to work occasionally at the bar on the roof of the dive shop for a few hours on certain days, mostly for the free drinks but also to watch the sunset over the palm trees. We'd also help out with special events that the dive shop put on, one of which was called 'Sunday Funday'. This full day extravaganza was a great event for the customers, with four dives during the day and an attempt to find a whale shark in between. Once back on land there was a barbecue & beer party at the dive shop. These events were especially good for the trainee Divemasters like myself and Rowan as we got all this for free!

I had been learning to dive for several weeks when another Funday Sunday was due. At 6.00am Rowan and I left the small wooden shack we rented together on the hill and walked the five minutes down to the dive shop. It was a warm morning with a bright blue sky and one of the rarer days I'd woken up without some sort of hangover. I felt phenomenal, totally just high on life. It was going to be a good day. At the shop we met the regular staff and the other trainees, Brett and Sue, and went through the usual machinations of loading air tanks, ice water and other customary bits and bobs. Everyone was already having a good time. For the special event we also got to take my favorite dive boat, a modern 38 footer with a flying deck, which is a raised open platform where the controls are located. The deck enables the captain to see the ocean from a high vantage point; perfect for spotting whale sharks. Finishing our tasks with time to spare, we hung about in the shop and waited for the customers. First through the door was one of the hottest girls I saw during my entire time on the island. She was Guatemalan, young, fun, beautiful and with enviable proportions, shall we say. She was also wearing what must have been the smallest bikini I think I have ever seen. A good start, at least from my perspective, and things continued to improve when four young and very pretty Norwegian girls, also in small bikinis, walked in the front door. We handed around coffee and breakfast pastries while we got to know them, and once the final few customers had arrived we all boarded the boat. I untied the mooring and we chugged away from the dock in the sunshine and shimmering blue waters as Thomas, my fabulous Danish dive instructor, did the boat briefing. Before long we were lounging on deck as we zoomed across the calm ocean to our first dive spot. Totally epic.

Our first destination was my favorite dive site on Utila. 'Sea Mount' was the summit of a small undersea mountain that rose from the depths to peak a few yards below the surface. Ocean currents push nutrient rich waters up from the depths along its sloping sides to create a microcosm of rich marine life, and more fish could be seen here than anywhere else on the island. On this particular dive I wasn't chosen to lead the group, so with plenty of Divemasters to look after the customers I was able to sneak away from the pack and do one of my favorite things in the world. I descended to a sandy ledge about 60ft down on one side of the mount and lay down on it, looking up. Above me swam shoals of colorful tropical fish, brightly lit though crystal clear water as the surface reflections flashed high above. The only sounds were the hiss of my regulator as I breathed in and the gurgle of glistening silver bubbles as I breathed out. I was totally and utterly separated from the world and for 20 minutes I lay there in a deeply tranquil nirvana surrounded by the largest aquarium on Earth.

With my air running out I headed back to the boat. We helped the guests swap out their air tanks and then went back to sunbathing on the deck as the boat made the short journey to the next dive site, named 'CJ's Drop-Off'. As luck would have it, this was my second favorite on the island. CJ's Drop-Off was special in Utila as the only place where the undersea cliffs descended straight from the surface into the Cayman trench. There is no ocean floor visible beneath you and swimming along the wall can give you vertigo as you look down into the nothingness. As this sensation was the real magic of the dive site, today I had a new plan. Rather than hug the cliff as normal, when I reached 100ft below the surface I left the group once more and swam directly away from the wall and out into the open ocean.

Soon I had left the cliffs far behind and hovered with nothing below, nothing to the sides and only the faintest of sparkles visible on the surface far above. Dangerous, yes, but amazing. Electric blue ocean surrounded me on all sides, pure and translucent. It was like nothing else I have ever experienced, a floating weightlessness with no up, down, left or right, only infinity and beyond. It was a sensation that was both violently disorientating and serenely calm. It was how I imagine a spacewalk must be like. For the second time that day I had found a tranquil nirvana, although this time I kept one eye on the depth gauge to stop myself from sinking into trouble. I don't know how long I just hovered there, alone in the silence, but eventually I neared my time limit and ascended to 15ft for a brief safety stop.

As I waited I became aware of something small in front of me. Intrigued I moved towards it. A small jellyfish-like creature, two inches long and shaped like a football, hovered there, completely transparent apart from four thin lines which ran from top to bottom along its four rounded corners. Along those lines strobed a piercingly vivid rainbow of color. Reds, greens, yellows, blues and purples shone with an intense laser-like clarity and purity as the patterns traveled from the creature's top to its base. I was mesmerized, unable to tear myself away. I forgot where I was until reality reasserted itself as I ran out of air.

It is a strange feeling to run out of air underwater. It happens quickly, in the space of only one or two breaths, and then that's it. No more air. As we train for this in the scuba course I was surprised but not panicked, and actually held my breath to give me a few more precious seconds with the creature before looking up and swimming powerfully towards the surface. I emerged near the boat and my immediate uncontained enthusiasm for the tiny jellyfish and the infinite blue was greeted with bemusement by my fellow Divemasters, several of whom were already preparing to come and rescue me. Goodness knows what the guests must have thought!

With everyone now accounted for, it was time to find a whale shark. Captain Jose stood on the elevated deck and looked for the hints of a disturbance on the calm surface. Called boils, these are the tell-tale signs of an underwater feeding frenzy as carnivorous fish like jacks and tuna surround a shoal of small fish. Squeezing the shoal ever tighter until it forms a ball trapped against the surface, a feeding frenzy then begins. Darting like lightning bolts, jaws agape to snatch anything in their path, the surface literally boils as the prey fish try to escape. The meal becomes a free for all, with seagulls and dolphins often arriving to help themselves to the feast. Then sometimes, just sometimes, if you are very lucky and have been very good, a leviathan stirs in the deep. Unseen from those black depths, it rises from beneath the seething mass and a huge mouth opens. Up to a ton of fish are engulfed in a single bite as the whale shark feeds. Find a boil and you might find a shark.

"AAAYY!" cried our Captain suddenly, pointing into the distance, "There's one!" and slammed the boat into top gear as everyone rushed to the front. A few moments beforehand I had climbed up to join Jose and sure enough I could start to discern a disturbance on the water several hundred yards away.

"Get your snorkels on," shouted Jose as we tore along at top speed, "He's gonna be quick!" We were almost there when Jose killed the engines, and as we glided top of the shoal I looked down into the water. What I saw made my jaw drop. Beneath us was a shape almost as big as the boat, with the unmistakable mottled pattern of blue and white and the outline of a predator. It was our whale shark and it was magnificent. I turned to Jose and couldn't resist the quote.

"You're gonna need a bigger boat."

"Jump, jump! Go! Quick!" Jose shouted to everyone now sitting with legs over the sides, snorkels on. At deck level you can't what is in the water because of the surface reflections, so the unsuspecting meals sitting there just jumped in. Surrounded suddenly by a throng of snorkelers, the shark retreated back to the depths as the divers all resurfaced with huge smiles and effusive praise. Next time it was my turn to get in the water.

We soon saw another boil on the horizon and this time I was in prime position. The shock of seeing nothing below from the deck, only to jump in and see a huge shark right in front of you, swimming towards you with its mouth open, is quite something. It doesn't have any teeth, but right then that was hard to remember! The shark began to descend and I followed. I could hold my breath for five minutes at this point, a fortunate consequence of my cycling fitness, so I swam alongside the shark only a foot or two away at its eye level. It looked back at me and I felt like there was communication, a mutual puzzlement at what this other strange creature was doing. I was transfixed as we swam down together until I felt a tightness of breath and knew I could follow no longer. I hovered there as the shark slid gracefully past until it disappeared into the blue depths below. It was the serenest of visions.

Once the monster had disappeared I turned and looked up, and that was when I got scared. I was about 80ft deep and pretty much out of air. This was bad. Focusing on the surface I swam strongly but calmly upwards, trying to keep relaxed as the great fear and killer of free divers sprang to mind, the risk of what is known as shallow water blackout. At depth, the pressure in your lungs keeps the concentration of oxygen in your blood high enough to remain awake, but as you ascend and approach the surface the pressure quickly reduces and suddenly there isn't enough oxygen to keep you conscious. You pass out and drown just a few feet away from salvation. As I neared the surface the pain was intense and in the last few yards I could sense my vision beginning to tunnel. I was starting to pass out!

"Just a few more feet!" I thought, "Please please please!" I desperately stroked towards the light and as things started to go grey I burst through the surface. I gulped great slugs of air, hyperventilating until my breathing slowed. I had made it, barely. Looking back, to have experienced that connection with the whale shark, to watch it descend in silence back to the depths, that was more than worth the risk.

Back on the boat it was now lunch time so we sailed around the back of Utila and stopped at Water Caye, a tiny island outcrop just off the far western coast of Utila. Water Caye is a strange, strange place. The small island is only a few feet above sea level so every last inch of the island is covered with houses built on stilts and connected to each other by raised jetties and boardwalks. The inhabitants are similarly unusual, as by all accounts they don't get out much and are thus somewhat insular and unwelcoming. It is also rumored that they intermarry between themselves quite a lot so the genetic pool is as shallow as the surrounding sea. After walking around the caye it was hard to argue with the rumor. That said, the freshly cooked seafood lunch we ate while looking down at the coral reef beneath the window went a long way to endearing me to the island. It is a fascinating place to visit, but I wouldn't recommend living there.

After lunch we completed our circumnavigation of Utila and did our last two dives of the day at a wreck near the entrance of the harbor. A sizable cargo ship, the Halliburton, had been scuttled outside the harbor in 1998 and now sat on a sandy bottom at

120ft. Descending to the deck, Rowan and I swam beyond the light and into the darkness of the cargo hold. Silver bubbles from our regulators shimmered against the rusting metal roof above, lit by bright pinpricks of light penetrating from holes in the ceiling. It was a little dangerous, but that was the least of our worries. We were not alone. Something else was in there, waiting. I drifted towards a larger shaft of light, and as I reached it something else did too. Silver fangs appeared from the light barely a foot in front of my face as a large barracuda hovered into the light. For a long time I forgot to breathe as I faced this 6ft of wannabe shark, both of us motionless until I slowly reversed back out of the hold. The barracuda stared at us as we went and for the second time that day I communicated with a fish.

Returning to the open water outside the wreck we swam around the hull and settled on the yellow sand. We sat there, breathing slowly and waiting. Invisibly, the pressure of nitrogen in our blood was increasing and began to penetrate the membranes of our neurons. It was time to get nitrogen narcosis! It was brilliant as we got silly at 120ft. I must admit that there are few better ways to hang out with your buddy at the end an afternoon's scuba diving than pointing at fish and laughing hysterically for no reason at all. I was sad to return to the surface, although I was also excited for Phase II of the day – this was Funday Sunday after all!

Back at the dock we unloaded the boat and did our Divemaster errands of cleaning the gear and such, a short job made quicker by many hands and a crate of free beer. Once done we rejoined the guests in the back yard of the dive shop, where the music was blasting and more beer was flowing. It was time to call in a favor owed to me by Rowan, so I got in the hot tub along with Brett, the four Norwegian girls and the Guatemalan while Rowan brought me more beer and some of the chicken they were barbecuing as part of the event. Watching the colors of the setting sun illuminating the sky from the hot tub, beer in hand and music playing; well, it was a special moment. If I had died in that moment, I would have died happy. And Phase III was still to come.

Night time in Utila is a fun time, and that particular night was no exception. Two of my favorite bars on the island happened to be just down the street from the dive shop and right next to each other. They were both built on decks out into the lagoon, parallel to one another so that you could jump from one to the other if you were brave enough or very drunk. Many tried, most failed, some got hurt. One of the bars, Coco Loco, had another surprise in store. Above the dance floor was a thatched roof, open on both sides, and at the far end of the roof was a ladder. It led to a small platform suspended above the dance floor which was only big enough for three or four people. It was my favorite place to hang out, hidden in plain sight above the revelers. It also had the added bonus that you could jump off it into the ocean below, another bad idea but we used to do it anyway.

We met the whole dive shop crew, the customers and some other good friends from another dive shop at Coco Loco after folks had had a chance to shower and change. The partying was about to begin in earnest. Dancing, drinking with friends both old and new, laughing constantly and occasionally back-flipping into the ocean from the platform made for a perfect night, and I staggered back home after the bar closed with a huge smile on my face from the perfect end to a perfect day.

That was the best day of my life.

THIRTY FOUR

# Earthquake!

I spent 10 weeks on Utila and what a glorious 10 weeks they were. Apart from diving I also did the occasional fire spinning show on the deck of Coco Loco, for which they gave me free beer. Since my first ill-fated attempt in Mexico I'd made my own basic poi and spent a lot of time practicing, yet despite improving a fair bit I still had a high incidence of burning myself. No matter, it never really hurt that much and the burns usually healed after about a week, plus the bar patrons got a unique memory. My favorite occasion, if I can call it that, was when I was doing a night show and completely spaced out to the thumping beats of the music as the flames flew around my head in the darkness. I stopped 'doing' the poi and started watching them, a recipe for disaster, and zigged when I should have zagged. A millisecond after I moved I knew I'd made a mistake, but there was nothing to do except wait, a pause which lasted an eternity until the vision of my right eye was instantaneously filled with bright orange light. It must have only lasted a few hundredths of a second yet I still remember that visual in piercing detail. The orange light came, of course, from the flaming ball which was about to hit me in the eye, and when it did the fine mist of gasoline created in the impact flash-burned off the eyelashes and eyebrow on my right side. Fortunately, my face remained otherwise unscathed as it was so quick that the skin didn't burn. That said, no eyebrow or eyelashes on one side of my face did make me look pretty odd.

In my time there Utila became my home. I knew every bar, every cafe and every restaurant in town, as well as most of the people who worked in then. I knew which roadside shack made the best and cheapest baleadas, a Honduran specialty half way between a burrito and a gyro, and I knew how to get to the forest bar behind the town that only opened on Friday nights (and find the road back while drunk, a useful skill). I was part of the community. To complete that sense of belonging, my twin sister and my father both came to visit while I was there. It was wonderful to see them, especially as I hadn't seen my dad for nine months and my sister for nearly three years. She had been backpacking around the world and living in Australia, and was now travelling her way back to England via Central America. It was like being at home again, but much warmer, cheaper and sunnier. Indeed, the only downside was that eventually I had to leave them and continue my journey. Every day I spent on the island brought the difficulties of cycling through the Patagonian winter ever closer; a ticking bomb I needed to avoid. In late March I knew the time had come to buy that one way boat ticket back to the mainland and return to the road once more.

As my ferry pulled away from the concrete jetty I stood on the deck and watched as my sister waved me away. It was heart-wrenching in a way which I find difficult to convey; a feeling so intense that I found it physically hard to breathe, like a weight on my chest that forced short gasps between the tears. I never thought I could feel that sad; this goodbye was worse than when I had left for Alaska so many months beforehand. Departures have always been more intense for me than arrivals, yet those feelings were beyond anything I had experienced before. Maybe it was the wonderful time we had all had and the real bonds I had made in that tropical paradise with my family and friends. Maybe it was also because this time I understood the dangers ahead rather than merely trusting to optimistic naivety. I was weighed down by the enormity of the task still to tackle and by the knowledge that the good times were over and hard times were to come. Either way, the slow drawn-out departure of that boat was like pulling a band aid off a little at a time. I never want to feel that way again.

Two hours later we docked at the mainland harbor and I rolled my bike off the ferry. It took some effort to squeeze back into the saddle as I tried to remember how to do this cycling thing. On the plus side, for the first time in nine months I found the bike didn't hurt as my saddle sores had now healed - a gift from Zeus himself - but my legs were soft and powerless. As I rode slowly out of La Ceiba towards Nicaragua they were in for a shock and I gave them a merciless beating. Despite the rough reintroduction, four days and 300 miles later I found myself at the border. It was a confusing place, with a wide no-man's land trapped between high barbed wire fences. Just inside the first fence stood the Honduran border office, a long and low single story concrete box of a building with a line of basic counter windows along one side that faced the dusty road. As per usual there seemed to be no formal queuing or waiting procedure, but luckily it was quiet at that moment and I walked right up to a window.

A short man with combed tufts of black hair protruding from his balding head sat behind the glass. He looked up and gave me a distaining look, his crisp green army uniform complementing his position of authority. Great for a parade, not so encouraging when worn by a border official.

"Buenas Dias, Señor," I said politely, greeting him with a very deferential smile and a calm poise that I did not feel before placing my passport in the tray beneath the window.

"Buenos Dias," he replied without emotion and thrust his arm slowly forward to fish my passport from the tray. His arm moved with that peculiar motion unique to customs officials. It is a movement into which all the world's cruel ambivalence has been poured. There is no pause or recognition that your life may pivot at that very moment, scales balanced between wild adventures in a new land and the frustrating agony of denial, deportation or arrest. It is a motion repeated a million times a day across the world, a robotic and defeated motion by the dead soul inside the uniform before you. Time slowed as I watched him expertly sheaf through my passport as he looked for my Honduran entry stamp.

"Why have you overstayed?" came his stern question, eyes lifted and beginning to burn into mine. "You were expected to leave Honduras on the twelfth. Today is the twenty first."

Oh crap. I was in trouble and the panic rose inside. I hadn't even realized I had overstayed, let alone by nine days. This could be bad. I had no idea what the fine, bribe or penalty would be, but from the last three months as a white westerner living in Honduras I had learned that this was unlikely to be a cheap or hassle free experience.

"Oh, I am *very* sorry, Señor," I replied in my best Spanish. "I was delayed on Utila and had to ride my bicycle from La Ceiba. It took me many, many days." That was partly true, except I could of course have taken a bus had I known. "Your country is very beautiful," I added, piling on the sickly charm in the last ditch attempt of a man before the gallows who says what he thinks the executioner wants to hear. I stepped back slowly from the window and held up my fully-loaded bicycle for him to see while making it look very heavy, which it was. He gave a cursory glance without even moving and continued to zealously stamp a multitude of forms on his desk.

"There will be a penalty," he eventually replied. My shoulders sank. "Pay in Honduran Lempira at the window over there," he continued, pointing at another grey concrete building across the road. "The amount is written on this form. Here." In his hand was the dreaded citation, which he wedged firmly between the passport pages before deftly snapping it shut and returning it to the tray with the same rapid and ambivalent arm movement as before.

"Come back here when you have paid," he finished with a rhetorical command and continued with his paperwork, ignoring me as I thanked him for his mercy.

I moved slowly back from the window and unfolded the form. At the bottom of the page was the fine, and it was a number I could scarcely believe. In total for the nine days I had overstayed they had charged me the outrageous sum of 48 Lempira, which was about $2.50. I stood there grinning, obviously facing away from the man in the office to hide my joy. It was the most welcome fine I have ever received and I paid it willingly before quickly completing the paperwork and moving on to the

Nicaraguan side of this no man's land. At that office I was oddly forced to fill out a customs import form for my bicycle, and although a wholly unnecessary delay it was free and did get me a bizarre whole-page stamp in my passport for the effort. Forms stamped and fine paid I was now in Nicaragua, heading for the old colonial city of Granada.

Granada feels like a mini version of Antigua in Guatemala, only without a dramatic location and with less charm or historical purity. It was still worth visiting, though, and the great hostel I found, with its courtyard arboretum full of palm trees, made it a nice place to rest. Showered and with my gear locked in my room I was soon settled into a hammock in the courtyard to read 'Angels and Demons' by Dan Brown, the book that everyone seemed to be reading that summer. As I read I gently felt the hammock swing from side to side on its own accord, as if moved by an invisible hand. The trees in the courtyard were also swaying and I heard the clink of some small items rolling off a table in the corner. I smiled. It was an earthquake.

I really love earthquakes. No, seriously, I do. Coming from England where they are very small and exceedingly rare, I find them unique and mysterious. Exotic, even. In 2001 I was in a magnitude 8.4 earthquake in Peru and it was one hell of an event to put it mildly. It struck in early one afternoon while I was on a bus crossing a high altitude desert, so I barely noticed the initial quake above the normal bumps in the road. We learned about it a short time afterwards when we arrived at a section of the road which had been sheared in half. A two foot wide, one foot high trench zig-zagged across the desert at right angles to the road, just like in the movies. Unable to cross this fault line and still needing to return to the city, our bus joined a makeshift convoy that was now attempting a difficult off-road journey back home. For many hours we ground along dirt tracks, sandy paths and over smaller fissures on this quest, permanently worried about becoming stuck in the sand and occasionally towing out someone who already was. By the time we arrived in the city of Arequipa it was midnight and an eerie stillness hung across the carnage we now saw. Part of the central cathedral had collapsed and many other historic stone buildings had at least partially fallen into the street. Seeing the balcony of a restaurant lying in the main square was especially unnerving as I had taken breakfast on it only that very morning. That was a close call, but as I looked at the destruction I didn't get have the mental capacity to analyze just how lucky I had been. If I had nine lives I was now down to eight.

We arrived at my guest house, an old hacienda in the center of town, to find that the earthquake had split the entire building in two. A great crack had appeared in the walls and roof as though an ogre had cleaved the building with an axe. Beginning at the base of the ground floor it extended and widened up one side of the courtyard, crossed the open air and continued down the opposing wall. With half of the building leaning into the road it was unfortunate that the room I was sharing with a travel buddy that night was on the leaning side. We lay in our beds with a single bare light bulb glaring brightly from the ceiling and endured the aftershocks. The largest of these shocks was magnitude 6.8 and was devastatingly violent, shaking the floor horizontally at least eight inches each way. It was a feeling of unimaginable power, something completely different to the acceleration and deceleration you'd feel if someone just shook the bed. It was something more primeval and powerful, as though a giant had picked up the room and rattled it. For those 15 seconds we looked at each other and held onto our beds as we waited for the room to collapse. There was no panic though; the communication between our eyes said everything, a silent and shared recognition of our insignificance compared with these forces and of a sense of futility to save ourselves from it. We were pawns in a tectonic game.

After a few hours the aftershocks diminished and we both slept, waking next morning to an intact room. Descending to breakfast we then noticed that the crack in the building had widened a little more, which was not a good sign. I went through a strange set of emotions that morning, the sadness of this terrible disaster and tragedy offset by the happiness from our good fortune. I imagine it was a weak example of survivor's guilt, where good fortune is negated by the necessary suffering of others. In any case, we decided that sorting out these emotions would require a good breakfast and so off we wandered to book flights and find some coffee.

Remembering this event, I lay swinging in my hammock in Nicaragua and reflected on the few seconds of gentle shaking I had just experienced. Its very existence cemented how far I had ridden, although I also reflected that with more distance to cover before reaching Costa Rica I now needed to relax - my soft legs needed all the help I could give them. Time to get back to the book.

# THIRTY FIVE

# Fear in the Dark

Costa Rica is one of the safest, most beautiful, modern and endearing countries in Central America, with beaches, rainforests, volcanos and good, honest people all wrapped in a vibrant and stimulating culture. Apparently. In my short ride across the country I managed somehow to avoid every single one of those good things. Whereas Guatemala had been a trouble free journey quite against the odds, Costa Rica brought me back to my dangerous reality. It was here I found my fear in the dark.

From the Nicaraguan border the road had been surprisingly desolate. Whereas I perhaps expected rainforest and beauty I was instead subjected to an endless mix of plantations and surprisingly arid scenery, most of which devoid of any interesting features. The only redeeming attribute was the ridge of volcanoes I could see rising in the distance to my north which included Central America's most active volcano, Arenal. Erupting almost continuously since 1968, just a few months before I arrived it had significantly reduced its activity and dashed my dreams of seeing flowing lava up close, one of the big disappointments of my entire journey. To complete my poor luck, the weather in Costa Rica was endlessly stormy and cold, and as I turned towards the west and rode along the surprisingly rugged and remote coastal road both the sky and ocean were a leaden grey. No white sandy beaches here; it was as though someone had forgotten to finish this part of the country. Late one morning I reached a non-descript coastal village. Here the highway turned back inland so I searched for a smaller road which the map said should continue to hug the shoreline. There was no such road. This was tremendously annoying but not unexpected, as my map was the Lonely Planet guide book's one page continental-scale topography picture of

Central America. Not for the last time did I regret saving $2.00 and not buying a proper map.

With no coastal road I had but one choice, to climb into the mountains once more. Under the heavy sky it was a demoralizing prospect to ascend the high plateau from which I had descended only the previous day, but there was nothing else I could do. The road was ludicrous, rising 3,450ft in a little over 10 miles, and my tolerance for Central American road builders was reaching record lows. It was awful.

One thing did stand out about this climb, apart from the hideousness of it all, of course, which was that today I had company. At the very start of the climb I passed a small house when a shaggy yellow dog ran out of the yard to meet me. Rather than bite my ankles he was actually a mellow little guy who decided to come along for the entire trip to the top. Initially it was fun to have a furry companion alongside me, but for some inexplicable reason "alongside" very soon became "under" as he insisted on walking right in front of my bike and was continuously run into and over by my front wheel. This caused me either to stop, to swerve and then stop, or to run into him and then stop. For his efforts to be flattened beneath my bike I named him Tortilla.

There seemed to be nothing I could do to keep him away from the wheel. I was already standing up in the saddle and destroying myself to do 3 ½ miles an hour so this additional sabotage was unbelievably irritating. The only respite I could find was to wait until the little monster was right next to my front wheel and then swat him away via a sharp side-to-side snap of the handlebars. Forced to do this every few seconds for four hours evaporated my love for this dog, but when we finally reached the top and sat on a cafe deck looking back down to the distant ocean I couldn't stay mad for long. After all, he *was* still with me, panting by my feet under the table. He was lucky to have made it to the top, in more ways than one, but I kind of felt sorry for him. He had a long walk back home.

This re-climb was just the start of my troubles as I was now forced to ride through the capital city, San Jose, a place I had tried hard to avoid. Busy tangled streets made for dangerous riding, but after much stress and swearing at the traffic I emerged unscathed on its far side in the early afternoon of the next day. From there only one road was realistically available to me, a sparsely traveled highway which ascended from the city and over the central mountains to the south east. I managed another 20 miles before the sun drifted low in the overcast sky and a thick drizzle began to fall. I was tired, cold, wet and miserable. It was time to stop. Camp site choices thus far had been non-existent though the narrow mountains, so a small grassy area lying opposite a dead end turnoff at a bend in the road looked like a blessing. I set up my tent on the wet grass and huddled underneath the awning for shelter. Lighting my stove in the rain I heated a single can of refried beans for my evening's meal.

"Mmm, gourmet," I can hear you thinking. Believe me, after 100 miles of cold mountain riding with 60lbs of luggage, any hot food is a magnificent treat of delicious wonderfulness. Tonight was in fact more gourmet than usual as I actually bothered to heat the beans rather than just eat them cold, straight from the tin. In this condition I needed the heat for its psychological comfort.

With nowhere to lock my bicycle I resorted to my 'Plan B' method of security, which was to lock the bike to my pannier bags inside my tent with a long steel cable. My idea was that it was both a deterrent and early-warning system. With the heavy bags in my tent, to steal the bike you would have to pull the place apart, which although not a defense, *per se*, at least I would be awake enough to get really scared when it happened.

As I sat eating the warm bean paste I looked up to see a lone figure approach from the turn off. He looked to be a fairly young guy, short and thin, and dressed shabbily although not excessively so given where we were. His black hair was uncombed and tussled, but while his face was dirty he had evidently shaved recently. Certainly not the image of a well-to-do individual but also not quite that of a ruffian either. Even so, I felt my stomach sink as it always did when I was discovered. Without speaking a word he sat down in the drizzle on the wet grass just a few yards away from me and made the motion of his hand to his mouth, asking for food.

"Hola amigo," I said gently, "Que tal?" How are you? Silence. It was weird and immediately unsettling. I repeated the question.

"Hambre," he replied slowly. Hungry. He made the hand-to-mouth motion once more.

"Did you eat today?" I asked in Spanish. No response. I paused. This man was making me feel really quite uncomfortable and in my wet and tired state I didn't feel like suffering through this one-way conversation. On the other hand, I could see his need, plus we were alone and I was on his turf, so making a friend of him would not hurt.

"Would you like some beans and a tortilla?" I asked him, pointing to the can in my hand that I was now half empty. "I don't have anything else," which was true. Given what I had gone through in the last few days this was somewhat giving him the shirt off my back, even if he didn't realize it. I wiped the spoon, put it in the can and leaned out into the drizzle to hand it to this forlorn figure.

"Here. It's all I have, but I hope it helps." He reached for it and began eating while I sat and watched. It felt good to help.

"Is it OK?" I asked after some time. Again no response, just a pair of eyes staring at me. At length he finished and I recovered the can, primarily to rescue my only spoon. I'd disassembled the stove by this point and so with nothing else to do we just sat there and looked at each other in awkward silence until eventually I pulled the ripcord.

"OK, well, I'm very tired, so I am going to sleep now," I told him. "It was nice meeting you, have a good night," and with that I turned to start packing the rest of my things into the tent. It was still light outside but I couldn't take any more silent sitting in the rain while being stared at by a stranger. My new friend eventually got the message and climbed up out of his cross-legged position before wandering back to where he had come from, still without saying a word. With my karma newly improved I retired into my tent to read a little before falling into a deep sleep.

I learned a bit about Karma that day. I learned it is nonsense. It was the middle of the pitch black night when I woke with a start. Everything was silent, just the faint sound of the wind in the trees and grass, yet I felt a deep sense of unease. The realization of my solitude and potential exposure hit without warning, and with a hyper-awareness of my senses and with eyes wide open I lay there motionless, penetrating the silence with my ears.

A rustle outside the tent.

"Hello?" I called out loudly. "Hello, is anyone there?"

Nothing. For a long time not a single sound could be heard above the wind.

Another rustle.

Was it something? Was it nothing? A small critter poking around outside the tent, perhaps? I'd had these critter encounters before and things worked out fine, except this time felt different. Maybe it was my location or my prior evening's discovery. For what seemed like an age I lay there on my back, listening like a hawk and calling out occasionally as I stared at the tent ceiling and probed the depths of my helplessness. At length I decided it must have just been my imagination and drifted back to sleep.

It was still drizzling when I awoke in the early pale light. I pondered the night's events as I dressed before pulling out the stove and opening the tent flap to cook. As I set about moving by bike from its wedged position underneath the awning my heart began to pound. The clear plastic sheath of the steel security cable had been cut with a blade and a few strands of the cable itself had been severed. I then saw the bicycle tires, both flat from deep knife slashes. My cycle computer had been ripped off. Cold adrenaline surged and I looked quickly around. I was alone. As that feeling wore off it was replaced by a diabolical sensation of vulnerability. I knew a hostile knife had been wielded inches from my head as I lay sleeping and unprotected in the dark. And I knew how terribly things could have gone if this thief had been a little more desperate, or perhaps if I had instead decided to open the tent and investigate. Life can be cheap in Central America, especially when there are no witnesses.

I also felt betrayal and anger. I was certain the culprit was the same individual I'd helped in the evening, and who showed his gratitude by trying to rob me and then spitefully damage my equipment after his failure. Sometimes, when my faith in humanity reaches at a low point, something happens to restore it. This was the opposite. In that moment, all the people of the world could burn for all I cared. I would have watched it happen with a banal ambivalence as humanity received what it deserved. In my seething anger I had a strange vision, as though I could see inside the minds of the truly wicked and evil people that live in this world; those that feel no compassion, no empathy for the pain and suffering they cause in others. I understood the minds of dictators and warlords, those for whom the ends always justify the means. It was the sense that people got what they deserved. A sense that if they were stronger or had made 'better' choices they could have avoided whatever hideous fate was coming their way. Every action was fair game. The feeling of that moment soon passed, but I shall never forget it.

Breakfast could wait. The 'flight' part of 'fight or flight' kicked in and I repaired the tires and trash-packed my stuff as quickly as I could while bobbing like a gopher at every rustle of foliage. I was desperate to get away from that place. Once finished I jumped on the bike and sprinted away up the mountain. The climb was even worse than the ride from the coast, not helped by my lack of breakfast, only half a dinner the night before and this morning sprint. To put the final nail in the coffin, for some reason the Costa Ricans thought it would be fun to build this road to the very top of the mountain range rather than around it. From its start at 3,300ft the road climbed without interruption to a ridiculous 11,330ft, just 700 feet below the summit. I was in a pretty desperate situation when I eventually reached a deserted and isolated cafe at the top of the climb. Inside, protected from the cold clouds I had some food and coffee and tried to rest. I was doing better until I checked a map I found on a table and learned that the next part of road wound back down to sea level on the *same side* of the mountain range from where I had started. I couldn't believe it; the entire change in altitude was an epic waste of time and energy. Even the 20 miles of uninterrupted downhill in the emerging sunshine beyond the cafe wasn't able to improve my mood all that much; I was far too exhausted to really appreciate it. With Panama in my sights I was just relieved to be leaving Costa Rica behind.

# THIRTY SIX

# Sovereign Purgatory

I heard a funny story once about a man traveling in Africa. He was an older chap, one of those pioneer types that cut a path across the world in the 1970s, a time of real adventure before guide books and the internet made everything smaller, easier and a little less interesting. The person I'd heard this story from had met this fellow in a hostel in Nairobi many years before and listened to him tell the tale of his border crossing between two African nations. I now forget which ones they were so for the sake of convenience let's call them Kenya and Tanzania. It was a crossing that could have changed his life, at least for the short amount of it that would have remained.

After travelling through Kenya on a single entry visa, our man finally arrived at the border with Tanzania. After much paperwork he was stamped out of the country and free to pass through the gate in the barbed wire fence which marked the edge of Kenya. With a quarrelsome past, these two countries had decided to leave a mile wide no-man's land between them, a purgatory between sovereign states. Leaving Kenya, he crossed this stretch of barren land on foot and reached a similar fence and gate at the entrance to Tanzania, where he asked for his entry visa. Unfortunately, this was a visa he did not possess. Could they let him in without it, he asked?

"Not permitted, sir," was the reply. Could they issue one at the border?

"No, not possible, sir."

"So where can I get one," he asked.

"Kenya."

Somewhat perturbed by this news he turned heels and walked the mile back across no-man's land to the Kenyan border.

"I need to re-enter Kenya to get a visa for Tanzania," he told the Kenyan official, holding up his passport.

"Certainly, sir," replied the guard, "May I please see your entry visa for Kenya?" After showing his newly-canceled single entry visa to the official he was informed that, because it was invalid, he was not permitted to enter Kenya.

"So where can I get a new Kenyan entry visa from?" our man asked, I imagine with the sinking feeling of a man who knows that the answer he is about to receive will not be a good one.

"Tanzania."

Ah. He was now trapped in no-man's land, with neither side permitted to let him in and with no ability to get permission. The story goes that he spent a day and night trying to convince the Kenyans of his plight until he was eventually let back in, I expect after pointing out that his demise would look pretty bad on the international news. Another stark reminder of the idiocy at the world's borders.

Crossing between Costa Rica and Panama I remembered this tale with a smile, and for good reason, as I passed through the Costa Rica border controls and rode into another no-man's land. However, unlike the African tale, this no-man's land was far from a barren stretch of land but rather an entire town has sprung up in the middle. It doesn't seem to be in either Costa Rica or Panama. Costanama? Panarica? Your guess is as good as mine. Google Maps doesn't have a name for it either. At the far end of the town was a high metal fence and a sign indicating the border of Panama. It was without border guards or custom officials. In the bustling marketplace I asked about the border control and was eventually directed a few blocks along a side street to a tiny whitewashed building made of cinder blocks and concrete. It looked like a Mexican jail from the 1800s.

"Frontera de la Republica de Panama" read the plaque over the bare wooden door next to a tiny glassless window crossed with iron bars. Peering through the bars I saw a young woman in a

Panamanian army uniform sitting at a desk inside. I asked her about an entry visa.

"Of course. That will be one US dollar please," came her reply. I handed over my passport and paid, receiving a blue small postage stamp on one of the pages along with my entry date franked across the top. Job done. As I rejoined the main road and passed through the fence into Panama I wondered what you would do at night or at the weekend? Was the border open or shut? I had no idea.

Located between the coast and the mountains, the lowlands of Panama were scorching hot and the humidity ferocious. Riding was really quite unpleasant despite the soothing view across to the distant blue tinted mountains. I'd already been stopped once by the Panamanian army and told to put my cycling shirt back on, so I just had to suffer. Luckily, with Panama City less than 400 miles away, in a few days I would be back in the arms of air conditioning so I wasn't too concerned.

Bang!

I was jolted from my dreams of air conditioning and slammed on the brakes in a knee-jerk reaction. I'd been doing close to 35mph when I hit the pothole and the bike bucked underneath me as I slowed. I managed to hold it upright and was soon stationary, but not yet daring to move. As the shock slowly wore off I eased my white knuckle death-grip on the handlebars. I was OK but I was not looking forward to finding out what I had done to the bike. I gingerly dismounted and lay the bike on the ground before checking it over, staring in disbelief at the back wheel. What I'd done was impossible. The super strong wheel spokes were intact but I had instead torn a two inch long hole in the metal alloy of the rim itself between the tire and the spoke connections. I now had a twisted oval rear wheel rather than a circle, something which I'm sure is not recommended but there was nothing I could do about it until I reached Panama City, still over 300 miles away. The tire was unbelievably still inflated and otherwise the bike looked OK, but would it still hold my weight? Only one way to find out.

I admit to feeling quite worried at this moment. One of the things I dislike in life is hassle, and trying to get my bicycle repaired where I was would be an enormous one. It wasn't even the cost which worried me, although that was part of it. I just wanted most of life to be simple and stress free, which I am sure most people find hard to believe given the journey I undertook. And yet for me, I would rather sleep in a roadside ditch than fill in my tax forms or open my bills. Perhaps it is the worry about what might happen if I get it wrong which is what I dislike. Either way, a broken bicycle in the middle of Panama was unlikely to be stress free for a while.

Holding my breath in anticipation I climbed back over the frame and clicked my right shoe into the pedal. Moment of truth. I moved my weight onto the bike and pushed off, expecting the whole bloody thing to disintegrate beneath me and leave me stranded at the roadside in the middle of nowhere. It held. That was a relief and a good sign. I rode a few yards to test it further. Still holding. With each revolution I became a little bolder and a little faster, which was when I discovered the next problem. As the wheel was now an oval shape, each rotation wobbled the bike up and down by about an inch. It doesn't sound like much, but at 15mph it was like sitting on a jack hammer. It was intolerable. In the end I was forced to ride standing up in the saddle for hours on end while expecting it to catapult me into oncoming traffic at any moment. The next 330 miles were about as unpleasant as you can imagine, but against all my expectations the wheel continued to hold and four days later I reached the outskirts of the city.

Towering ahead was my last barrier on this continent, the Bridge of the Americas. It is a huge steel arch bridge which spans the Panama Canal as it exits into the Pacific Ocean, a bridge as beautiful as it is symbolic. Now if only it had a bicycle lane. Three lanes of pure freeway guided the high speed traffic, and squeezed between belching trucks and cars on one side and a precipitous drop to the ocean below past the low barrier on the other, my adrenaline surged. I had to be brave; trying to be invisible between the cars and the void was inviting disaster. I pulled out into the center of my lane and rode with desperation as the traffic behind me honked and swerved. Diabolical.

I reached the center of the bridge and despite the chaos I caught a glimpse of the canal below. To my right I could see huge container ships anchored offshore, waiting their turn to enter the canal, beyond which stretched the deep blue of the Pacific Ocean. To my left I saw the great estuary that leads to the canal locks a few miles inland. This was it, the crossover between the Americas. To me, this point was the border of North and South America, a physical break in the connection between those two vast land masses. As my speed increased on the descent from the bridge the traffic became less bothersome, so I put in my headphones, turned on my music in celebration and smiled the biggest of smiles. Through adversity, pain and against the odds I'd ridden a bicycle across a whole damn continent!

# THIRTY SEVEN

# A Man, a Plan, a Canal – Panama!*

## * READ BACKWARDS, LETTER BY LETTER

I checked into a hostel in Panama City near the city center. Located on the top floor of an apartment building it was fairly cramped but I got my stuff in OK. Once settled I emerged from the small dorm room and into the communal area, where I heard a brash and familiar voice.

"Aw this girl was beautiful, man. These Panamanian girls have got it *going on*, brother!"

I crept up behind him.

"They don't stand a chance, mate!" I remarked, and he whirled around, his curly blonde hair swinging out with the momentum.

"James!" he cried, "No way! Can't believe you made it, mate! Thought you'd be long gone past here by now. Or lying in a ditch somewhere! Ha!"

This was Stewart, who I'd met in San Cristobal some five months before. Stewart is one of the most charismatic people in this world. He'd used that gift to good effect, living a life that many of us only dream about as a successful DJ in Australia, touring the world and playing his decks alongside the ASP World Surf Championship. A professional partier, he was hedonistic in a way that most of us only see in the movies. I felt like he deserved it, a guy who was infectiously upbeat, charming, always fun. But also modest and disarmingly philosophical about the whole thing. I loved this guy.

"It's been quite the adventure since the New Year, I can tell you that much!" I replied, "But what about you? I didn't know you were heading down here."

"Yeah I guess it just kind of worked out that way. Bit of this, bit of that, you know," he replied. "I spent a bunch of time in

Guatemala and then in Costa Rica on the beach. Love that place, man."

"Nice!" I smiled. It was good to hear things were going well for him. "And it sounds like the ladies in Panama are happy you are here as well!"

"You could be right there, brother," he laughed, "Though I tell you what, for a 31 year old this life is getting harder!"

"31!" I exclaimed, "No way you are 31." I didn't believe it. I guess when you looked at him closely you could see a few years beginning to creep slowly up to him. His larger-than-life personality made it immaterial.

"Even if you are, you don't look it," I continued.

"It's not the age, mate, it's the miles!"

Damn right. I could see a side of him emerge then, the one that valued some stability and those deeper relationships he had built. I overheard him late one night in the hostel talking on the same topic to a calm and collected South African guy we both knew.

"I don't know if I want to keep doing all this moving around and that anymore, man," Stewart said as they sat in the common room. "I've been there, you know, done all there is to do. Part of me just wants to find that great girl and settle down. I always used to need to have the 'trophy girlfriend', but now I realize that's not what I need at all."

It seemed time for Stewart to move on to the next phase of his life. In my experience, it's not something you can put an age on, or force someone into, or even try to "get out of your system". The only timetable you can hope to be on is your own subconscious, a philosophy I have found difficult to understand over the years but I now know to be correct. Sure, it is hard to let go of the good ol' days, but at some point the past stops playing on repeat. There is always another chapter. Maybe that is why I wrote this book.

After a night of bar hopping with Stewart and a couple of the guys – man, those guys *know* how to party – I dragged my sorry carcass out of bed the next morning and hauled myself off to visit the Panama Canal. I took the bicycle as my head hurt too much to figure out the bus system. As I approached the great locks that mark the entrance and exit to the canal on the Pacific side I made a note of a huge white building that overlooked the area. Towering over trees it must have been 16 or 17 stories high. Only when I arrived did I see that the building wasn't a building at all. It was a ship. The scale was something to behold. You see photos and none of them have any impact until you stand next to a 900ft long ship loaded with over 3,000 containers. Both ship and canal were wonders of engineering.

My inner geek found the canal amazing. For example, every ship pays US dollars in cash for its passage, including the massive container ships. With fees more than $200,000 for single crossing, a man literally disembarks from these boats with a briefcase of money handcuffed to his wrist. Expensive as it is, this fee is a worthwhile investment because the alternative is to sail 8,000 miles around the entirety of South America. Canal fees account for a third of Panama's entire GDP, yet until relatively recently it wasn't even owned by Panama. In return for building it the United States annexed a four mile wide track of land on either side which, like an embassy, was officially American territory. In 1984 the leader of Panama, General Noriega, attempted to reclaim the canal by force and triggered a US invasion. The canal stayed in US ownership until it was at last transferred Panama in 1999, and so far so good. Indeed, one of the world's biggest engineering projects is widening the canal at a cost of $6 billion because it now too small to fit the next generation of oil tankers and container ships.

Crikey.

# THIRTY EIGHT

# Do I Stay or Do I Go?

During last few days of my ride across Panama I'd reflected deeply on the 10 amazing months I had just had. I'd seen things I could never have imagined and had unique experiences, both good and bad. I had also nearly got myself killed in a whole range of new and exciting ways and suffered to a degree in both intensity and duration that I had barely been able to overcome. As I crossed this Rubicon between continents two questions became my only thoughts. Had it been worth it, and should I continue? Yes, I knew I would remember those moments for the rest of my life. But as I suffered through the stifling heat of Panama those good memories felt spread out like an abstract concept. I realized that what had kept me going for through such hardship was not my desire to conquer the magnificent but rather to avoid the pain of failure. I thought about my sendoff party at a bar in London. One of my best friends, nicknamed Buddha, bounced energetically around the bar as he pointed me out to random people in the crowd.

"Hey look at that guy!" he would cry out, "He's going to ride a bicycle from Alaska to ARGENTINA!" After that, how could I stop? Stopping was defeat. More than that, it was regret. I knew I would forever think "what if" or wonder whether I could have stuck it out. Memories of pain fade with time. Regrets gnaw at you for a lifetime, a splinter in your mind. In Panama, however, I had a partial get-out clause. I'd ridden across a whole continent so could I stop now and call it victory? Was I really prepared to miss the rich wonders of South America, a critical reason for my trip in the first place? I didn't know. I pondered that for a long, long time, eventually phoning my parents and asking what they thought. My father reminded once again of the marathon story he'd told me in Alaska. I guess I needed reminding. He was right, of course.

Knowing myself, if I quit I would never have been able to remove
that mental splinter, even if others didn't mind or care. I couldn't
do that to myself. It was time for death or glory. I was going to
South America.

I now faced another difficult decision. I had told myself I
would never cheat on my trip, with no buses, no boats and no
planes if I could possibly or reasonably avoid them. Now I had
committed to South America I faced the infamous Darien Gap. To
slow the passage of narcotics and rebel guerillas across the border,
no road exists between Panama and Colombia. Instead there lies
100 miles of inhospitable jungle, rugged mountains and crocodile-
infested swamp. The region also comes with an unhealthy dose of
nefarious characters highly unlikely to welcome an English-
speaking, DEA-looking, young white male. My research suggested
I had a 98% chance of making the trip without serious incident.
Good odds until you consider the implications of the other 2%.
That made the Darien Gap one of the world's most dangerous
crossings. I have no desire to be murdered for no good reason in a
swamp by a Colombian drug lord. Plus my mother would never
forgive me if that happened. With a heavy heart I decided to fly.

The easiest flight was to the beach town of Cartagena on the
Colombian coast. However, that then meant traveling overland
across the Colombia / Venezuela border which was at that time
having a small-scale semi-official armed conflict. The information
I'd gathered from people entering Panama indicated that to cross
into Venezuela required a precise and ever-changing navigation
between villages to avoid being caught in the action. For a guy
constrained by the worst getaway mode of transportation invented
that didn't sound like a good idea. With a heavier heart I chose life
once again and took a rain check on Colombia. From Panama, the
land of socialist revolutionaries and black gold was now my next
stop. I was going to Venezuela.

# THIRTY NINE

# Cons and Kidnappings

Travelling the world can be a dangerous pastime. Even when you aren't getting sick or being bitten by unpleasant things there are always your fellow human beings to keep you on your toes. Scammers, con artists, pickpockets and thieves can be found in all corners of the world, from Afghanistan to Zimbabwe, and infinite are the ways in which these men and women will separate you, the unsuspecting traveler, from your money and belongings. Some of these ways are forceful and blunt, some are subtle and cunning, others are common and easily avoided. A few are new and novel. The only universal truth about travelling is that if you travel for long enough you will eventually be on the receiving end.

I was always puzzled about the ubiquitous nature of the most common scams. Variations on the same themes can be found from Peru to India, so I wonder if they have developed independently or if there is some secret underworld book distributed in a thousand cities across the world. I guess I'll never know. In any case, some scams are encountered everywhere and all travelers should learn about them. For example, one such scam is the classic "Hey look Mister, there is something on your jacket" distraction. Here, a "helpful local" interrupts you as you walk down the road to point out something on your shoulder, usually ketchup or mustard that an accomplice squirted there moments before. In the ensuing commotion this "helpful local" assists you with cleaning it off while the accomplice steals your stuff. This was one I personally experienced at a bus station in Peru, but luckily I had my wits about me. In the end it was almost comical.

"Señor, I am sorry but I must tell you," said a voice behind me as I approached the main station entrance. I turned around to see a short, middle aged man dressed in an ill-fitting suit jacket and beige pants walking towards me. He smiled a toothy grin.

"Señor, you have a terrible mess on your shoulder. Perhaps a bird, Señor, it happens here often," he continued in a suitably grave voice, conveying his deep sadness at my misfortune. Now, I'm no expert but that particular kind of mess isn't identical to the cheap mustard used in every Peruvian street cafe.

"Please, let me help you clean it, Señor," he continued, and with that pulled a convenient piece of rag from his pocket and started to rub at the stain. After a moment of disorientation I was now firing on all cylinders and back in the game. I quickly swung off my main backpack and jammed it in front of my legs, wedged my small rucksack on top and clutched my pockets like my soul was kept inside. I was locked down like a human Fort Knox, my eyes darting with a vigilant paranoia at anything that moved.

"Thank you," I replied with little warmth. Without shifting my gaze from my belongings I waited until the man had cleaned the stain as several evil-looking children right out of a Charles Dickens orphanage swirled around and tried to distract me per the scam's usual operating procedure. I didn't even blink as they pulled my pants and loudly pointed to things in our surroundings. Their growing and obvious despondency at this scam's impending failure was heartwarming and a feeling of minor triumph brewed inside. Perhaps I shouldn't have been so happy given their circumstances, but this was immoral any way you cut it. Eventually the man was finished and as I repeated my thank you we shared a momentary look. His failure and surrender to me was clear in his eyes, my icy stare met his look of vindictive defeat, as though he thought I was the bad guy for not playing along. I was not sorry to disappoint. Traveler 1: Scammer 0.

Many such scams can usually be avoided and so ultimately are merely irritants. Most of the time I ducked and weaved to emerge unscathed, but occasionally, when the stars aligned to conspire against me I was not so lucky. Such as the day I was kidnapped for the first time.

It occurred a few weeks after the Peruvian incident on the same backpacking trip. I was now in Bolivia, a landlocked South American country barricaded into the center of the continent by Peru, Chile and Brazil. While it is a stunningly beautiful country it has a dark and disturbing side. Public transport is preposterously bad and the bus stations are dangerous places. Heading across the country on an overnight bus I had one of the worst nights of my life, an agonizing and soul-destroying 15 hour ride jammed into a tiny seat as we hammered over endless bumps. At 5.30am it was still cold but already light as our bus spluttered into the Santa Cruz bus station, the rising tropical sun starting to illuminate the grimy melee of humanity gathered on the bare concrete of the open air concourse. Santa Cruz is the largest city in Bolivia and the most dangerous; it was at the time the only city in Bolivia to receive a 'high risk' rating by the US State Department. Which is saying a lot. I was overjoyed to see the sun that morning, for it represented the end of my nightmare. An endless hell of sleepless suffering. Every pothole was a ferocious lurch, a misery compounded by the multitude of bodies pressed against me in the over-capacity crush. Everything was permeated by a nauseating envelope of body odor, diesel fumes and worse. Children cried incessantly. Although we set off trapped in a sauna of festering humidity, for much of the journey I shivered in the intense cold of the high altitude night. Disembarking from that bus I have scarcely felt happier to be free and scarcely more disorientated or mentally drained. After walking aimlessly around on the station concourse to find a map to get my bearings I finally pulled out my lonely planet guide book. That was an error. For scammers that book is a burning flare illuminating their target. A red rag to a bull.

"Señor!" commanded a voice behind me. I spun around to see a short, thick set man with neat black hair and a tidy moustache striding authoritatively towards me. Dressed in a pristine light brown uniform and shiny black shoes, his brown hat perched erect on his head. He was the archetypal stereotype of the overzealous Latin American policeman.

"Señor, I must verify your documents," he began. "I am lieutenant Calderon of the Santa Cruz police department." He flashed an official-looking badge at me. "You have your documents?"

"Um, yes, of course," I replied politely, wary enough not to delve into my concealed money belt in the middle of a station. Opting to keep my valuables hidden and their contents concealed from this man, in itself minor triviality of choice, may well have been the best decision of my life.

"Very good. Now you must come with me. All foreign people in Santa Cruz are required to register at the police station. It is close, come this way," he commanded and directed me in front of him.

"Sir, I do not think that is necessary," I replied, to which he unleashed a torrent of abuse at me. The police in Bolivia are not to be trifled with and I thought only about getting arrested. In my dazed stated I felt I could not now refuse; I'd been in the city for less than five minutes and things were rapidly spiraling downwards. Maybe this registering thing really was just one of those rules, I thought. I'd heard of things like this in other countries, perhaps it was here also. As the path of least resistance I reluctantly agreed.

We walked past several empty buses and wove through the substantial crowd which occupied the terminal despite the early hour. As we reached the far end of the concourse he pointed at a car parked a few yards away at the curbside.

"We will take this car. It is a short distance but we cannot walk. The main road is very dangerous. Get in."

At this point I was slowly starting to come out of my daze. This definitely looked a bit sketchy. The beige car was old, with worn seats of cracked fake leather and a shabby plastic interior in 1970s brown. Parts of the door lining were peeling away and the carpets were either worn or missing. It certainly didn't look official. Another man stood next to it, dressed in a similar uniform. He appeared uncomfortable, almost twitchy. I started to protest once more whether all this was really necessary when I saw another man sitting on the back seat.

"Who's that?" I asked, pointing at the man, who sat facing straight ahead with a dazed far-away look.

"He is Ecuadorian," replied the stocky uniformed man. "He must also come to the police station. Get in the car, you do not want me to make you trouble."

Next thing I knew I was sitting in the back seat with my small rucksack hung on my chest and my large backpack awkwardly in my lap. The stocky man climbed into the front passenger seat, his uniformed companion behind the wheel. As their doors clanged shut my right hand door unexpectedly opened and another man forcefully clambered in beside me. I was now trapped on the back seat between this new man and the Ecuadorian. Before my brain could compute this event and react, the car lurched forward and we sped out of the bus station. Now suddenly I became hyper-aware, my daze broken by a flood of adrenaline as I realized I might actually be in some very serious and very real trouble if this guy wasn't a cop. I was alone in an unmarked car with four unknown men, being driven to an unknown destination against my will. No-one knew where I was. Not good.

We drove quickly along the busy main road through the light early morning traffic. After several minutes the stocky man turned in his seat to face me.

"Show me your documents," he demanded aggressively. "Show me your passport."

"I would like to wait until the police station, Señor. We must be there very soon, yes?" I replied calmly as I hid the rising storm of panic brewing inside. Under no circumstances was I going to show this guy my passport or anything else; that action would have unilaterally bad consequences. I was also certainly not going to reveal my money belt either.

"You have money?" he questioned next, visibly agitated by my calm refusal. Perhaps he realized that I had come to my senses and he had lost his advantage, not that this helped my situation very much.

"How much money?" he continued. "We have rules on money in Bolivia. Maybe you use it to buy drugs. Show me how much money!"

"I cannot show you now, Señor. I have only a small amount and it is very hard to find in my luggage. I cannot reach it here, we must wait until the police station." I stalled with another excuse. We had been on the main road for some time and were now in a rough industrial neighborhood towards the outskirts of the city. I forced myself to ignore the possibilities.

"Show me your documents!" he now shouted. "Show me your money!" He turned around further, almost climbing into the back seat.

"No."

"Show me! Ah, you must be hiding pornography! That is why you refuse!"

That was his justification for an imminent search, I kid you not. With that accusation any doubt about my situation and his phony policeman credentials evaporated. He had overplayed his hand. I had been kidnapped, no doubt about it now, and as the situation was deteriorating rapidly I needed to get out of there. Like, right now.

I looked for an escape route, however desperate it might be. Looking at the door to my right I saw my chance. A beige plastic knob was sticking up above interior panel's surface. It was unlocked! The sight of that plastic knob is now an image burned into my soul, forever a vision of salvation. We were still on a main road and approaching a set of traffic lights. Our car slowed momentarily as we reached the vehicles in front and this was it. Now or never. As we began accelerating again I wrapped my left arm tightly around my backpack while simultaneously lunging across the man to my right. Grasping the door handle I pulled, hoping beyond hope that the door would unlatch. It did. Before the man could react I rolled across him and hurled myself at the opening.

I hit the ground hard. Fortunately I landed at a good angle and rolled several times on impact while missing the curb. It took a second after stopping to regain my bearings, but then I leapt to my feet. A massive surge of adrenaline pumped through my veins like an amphetamine, and the minor scrapes I sustained in the fall didn't even register. I grabbed my bags and sprinted away from the car like a man on fire. After a few moments I glanced back as I ran to see the men standing outside of their car a little way down the road. They got back in and sped off. For the time being I was free.

I ran long and hard through the industrial area, fearful of being followed. The adrenaline eventually began to wear off and I slowed to a jog as my fear and paranoia subsided. I was now completely lost in the deserted streets but at least safe, so I guessed the rough direction of the city center and kept jogging. Periodically I checked the lonely planet map until after an hour my location appeared on its edge. Now I knew where I was, and two hours after arriving in Santa Cruz I reached the main plaza. It was 8.00am. So far that morning I had been kidnapped, jumped out of a moving car and run five miles through the slums of Bolivia's most dangerous city. That felt like a lot of work before breakfast.

With the memory of that story in mind, I landed in Venezuela late in the afternoon after the short flight from Panama City.

"Be careful there," my fellow travelers in Panama had warned me, "it can be pretty sketchy. Look after your stuff!" With this heightened awareness I disembarked from the plane and walked towards the baggage claim, steeling myself for my first problem, which was how to get some currency. Due to their economic woes, the black market exchange rate in Venezuela had decoupled from the official rate, so while the ATM gave you 600 Bolivars for every US dollar, your friendly money changer on the street gave you something closer to 2,600 Bolivars; a big difference which made Venezuela either very expensive or very cheap. Fortunately I had learned this in Panama where they use US dollars, so I arrived with a thick wedge of US bills, enough for my time there and more. My problem was the necessity of finding an unofficial money changer at the airport; I still needed to pay for a taxi to the nearby town. This was prime scamming territory but I was ready.

As any economist will tell you, where there is demand there is supply. I hadn't even reached the baggage carousel before a money changer appeared from the crowd. He was a young guy, shorter than me and with a shaved head. Innocuous he was not, and if harmless he definitely didn't look it.

"Buenos dias, Señor. Would you like to change some money?" he asked.

"Uhhh…," I replied, glancing around to check that no officials were watching. We were invisible in a throng of people.

"Sure," I replied. "What is the rate?"

"For US dollars, 800 Bolivars, Señor. A very good rate, it is the market rate." No it wasn't, and I told him so.

"That is a terrible rate! Don't try to con me, I know it is 2,800 Bolivars. I've spoken with people. So what is your *real* rate?" 2,800 was an exaggeration but this was a negotiation. Either way at least I knew this guy was trying to con me.

"Señor, you bargain very hard with me. Most is this," he said, and tapped out 2,400 onto his calculator. "It is the best, I cannot go higher."

That was more like it. "Surely you can do 2,700 Bolivars for me? I have brand new dollar bills with me, right here."

"Señor, I cannot go so high. Final offer is 2,550, no more." He began somewhat obviously scanning the baggage area for new tourists. I managed to get another 25 out of him and figured it was good enough. I told him I wanted to change 140 US dollars.

"Si. Come with me," he said, and led me towards the men's bathroom. Not a great sign but I guess that illegal currency dealing on the concourse was an even less good idea. In a corner of the white-tiled room he quickly began the transaction, pulling a brick-sized stack of bills from his jacket pocket. He seemed nervous and in a hurry to be done, no doubt a combination of the illegality of what we were doing and a keen desire to get back to price gouging my fellow tourists before they left the arrivals area.

"OK, Señor. Here are the Bolivars," he continued, "Show me your dollars." I pulled out two crisp $50 bills and two $20s. At the agreed rate I was expecting 360,500 Bolivars to grace my presence. He began counting out 10,000 Bolivar denomination notes in stacks of 10.

"One hundred thousand. Two hundred thousand. Three hundred thousand," he counted. So far so good.

"Four hundred thousand," he continued. Hmmm. At 460,000 he switched to a different part of the stack and counted out some small denomination bills.

"OK, 460,500 Bolivars. We are good, yes?" he asked, and held out the stack of notes in his right hand. I couldn't believe my luck. I had found a money changer who couldn't count!

Now I was faced with an ethical dilemma. Do I highlight his error and return the excess, or keep quiet and pocket the extra? Not a simple decision. In favor of returning the excess was that it would perhaps be the "honest man's" decision, the moral high road. And yet, in front of me stood a man who five minutes ago had blatantly attempted to price gouge me. Would returning the excess merely create moral hazard by showing him that by acting dishonestly with tourists he had a no-lose situation; in a successful attempt he wins, if unsuccessful the tourist will pay him back the excess anyway? By returning the money was I encouraging and rewarding future dishonest behavior? Returning the excess was thus a moral decision in one sense but immoral in another. Tricky. I'd occasionally been burned a little by dishonest money changers in the past, so might this be an opportunity to rebalance my Karma. An offset against past misfortunes, if you like. Was keeping the excess in fact the fairest outcome? I soon made up my mind.

I kept the money. I checked the Bolivars and handed over my dollars before making a rapid exit.

I must admit I felt a warm glow as I walked out of the airport towards a cab, my conscience clear. Rightly or wrongly I had scammed a scammer. There was no denying it felt surprisingly good. Perhaps two wrongs don't make a right, but two wrongs and a bit of revenge can sure do wonders for your sense of self-satisfaction.

The airport was situated near a small town called Catia Del Mar. It was located on the Caribbean coast while the capital city Caracas was around 30 miles away over the mountains. By staying in Catia and travelling the coastal back roads I could avoid Caracas, which was a good idea. I arrived in town after the short cab ride and found a room in a surprisingly nice motel before wandering into the town center around dusk. It was fairly busy with people, with the main throng congregating outside a bar around a group of plastic tables on the sidewalk. What caught my eye was that no-one was allowed to enter the bar itself. The entire front of the building was barricaded with wall to wall iron bars. It looked like a prison cell, thick metal rods, painted black and welded together, behind which were high piles of beer crates. Bottles were passed by the attendant to the crowd through a small opening in exchange for their cash. I ordered myself a bottle of Polar beer in the same fashion and sat on the curbside as I wondered what Venezuela was going to be like. Apparently, the bars here were so rough that they needed to keep their own customers out.

In the morning I took the wild coastal road. The weather was initially quite tempestuous with the road pinned between a dark sky and grey waves on one side and the man-made cliffs on the other. Not exactly what I had expected or hoped for, but as the road turned inland the weather brightened and despite some viciously steep hills the ride became far more pleasant. After staying the night in a picturesque village I emerged the next afternoon from the jungle covered hills onto a vast and arid plain. It was featureless apart from a modern freeway snaking to the horizon, dividing the landscape in two. The oil wealth of Venezuela now became more apparent as refineries appeared in the distance, fed by a haphazard network of small, rusting pipelines that occasionally crossed the road. Oil derricks peppered the landscape, which looked more

Saudi Arabia than South America. However, it was only when I stopped at a gas station that this infrastructure made a tangible impact.

I needed to refill my stove fuel bottle after I'd emptied it for the flight. The station still used the old fashioned pump-then-pay method, so I filled up the 32oz, or one liter, bottle right to the top and went to pay the attendant. It was then I discovered a problem. The fuel cost 70 Bolivars but the smallest currency denomination commonly in circulation was 50 Bolivars; the problem was that fuel in Venezuela was too cheap to buy! I even had an amusing discussion with the attendant about whether we should round up or round down. In the end that bottle of gasoline cost me less than two US cents.

The rest of north-central Venezuela was uneventful. A single carriageway now turned south from the highway across the dry scrubland, delineated with occasional roadside rest stops along the deserted road. The few locals I met at these stops were friendly and almost always surprised to see this lone and unarmed cyclist riding through the countryside. What was most fascinating for me about these meetings, however, were the customer's cars. Huge V12 American muscle cars from the 1960s or '70s were commonplace; gasoline prices made them economical to drive as well as cheap and easy to fix. In many ways this part of Venezuela felt like a journey back to the Southwest states of the US, circa 1970. This flashback vista continued for several days until the arid landscape gave way to greener hills until I finally arrived at the great Orinoco River.

Ah, the Orinoco. The fabled river, a place I never expected to see with my own eyes. It was nothing special to look at; rather it was what the river represented that was important. I felt I was now trespassing through deepest Venezuela, a sensation that made me tingle with anticipation. What also made me tingle was being stopped by the Venezuelan police as I began to ride over the river on their brand new suspension bridge. After some negotiation and a lot of pleading they eventually agreed to allow my passage, but only on the condition that they would chaperon me. I am now one of the few foreigners to have crossed the Orinoco River with a police escort, with lights flashing and sirens wailing, the full deal. It was awesome and it was weird.

The other bank of the river marked the start of the city of Ciudad Bolivar, a surprisingly pleasant and historic place. It was only the second real city I'd visited since arriving in the country so after checking into a hostel I went exploring. As luck would have it the first thing I found was a bakery and coffee shop. And what a coffee shop it was.

It came as a surprise to me, but in contrast to their Central American cousins who don't really seem to care for them, Venezuelans can't get enough of both espresso and delicious baked goods. They have a Venezuelan spin as you might expect, so here coffee is only really served one of two ways, either as an astoundingly strong double espresso, or as a "marron", which is an astoundingly strong double espresso with the tiniest splash of milk. The latte and Americano are strange concepts in this place. As a guy who drinks 10 or more cups of coffee a day, the plethora of coffee shops and bakeries found on every corner was heaven. The local pastries were equally delicious, the best of which was a local specialty called a cachito, essentially a ham and cheese croissant. What more could a guy ask for!

While this was clearly fantastic, I had come to Ciudad Bolivar for an altogether different reason. For 15 years I had desired to see one particular thing on planet Earth, and in Ciudad Bolivar it was now within my reach. It is a place so special, so unique and so hard to visit that only a few have seen it. After such a long wait I was about to join the list.

# FORTY

# The Fall of Angels

In contrast to the blandness of north-central Venezuela, the south of the country is a magical place. Here, amongst the jungles and grasslands of this complex landscape, hidden in an inaccessible lost world, stand the mysterious plateaus called Tepuis. Towering for three thousand vertical feet above the valley floor, they rise isolated from one another and the jungle below as islands above the forest. Created from some of the planet's most ancient rocks, they are remnants of the Earth's molten surface that solidified almost two and a half billion years ago. Once level with the valley floor, these plateaus gradually stayed solid as three thousand feet of surrounding rock was eroded by ice and a hundred trillion tons of rain. They are incomprehensibly old. After so many millions of years of isolation every Tepuis has become unique. Some harbor species which are found nowhere else on Earth, not even on adjacent plateaus. They are quite literally other worldly, an enigmatic vision completed by their rare and fleeting appearances through the dense fogs which hide them from view. Indeed, riding through this place I remember looking up to briefly glimpse the corner of Roraima, the inspiration for Arthur Conan Doyle's "The Lost World", as it emerged from its shroud of fog. It was visible only for a few minutes before disappearing into the clouds once more, when only the end of a bright rainbow showed evidence of its existence. Bathed in a tempestuous landscape of thunderclouds and dark skies, this splash of vibrant color was intensely spiritual to witness; it was as though I had seen the magical island of Laputa itself, floating in the sky.

In this land of the Tepuis, two plateaus stand above the others as special. Roraima is one, and the other is Auyantepuis, whose very name means "The Devil's Mountain" to the Pemon tribe which lives in its shadow. From space it would look like a great heart, whose inner apex has become tightly surrounded by immense cliffs to create the infamous Devil's Canyon.

Auyantepuis is one of the wettest places on the planet, as rising tropical clouds condense as they are pushed above the plateau. There is a downpour here almost every day of the year. These rains in turn feed a great river, tinged red by tannins, which flows across its hard and impermeable surface. Winding across the Tepuis it reaches the plateau's terminus at the Devil's Canyon and cascades over the edge, down into the oblivion of the void. This is Angel Falls, the highest waterfall on Earth.

I was eight years old when I first saw this waterfall on a BBC documentary and it left me amazed. Now, 15 year later, with the tour booked and my fingers crossed I left the hostel and headed for Ciudad Bolivar's microscopic airport. To visit the Tepuis by land one must first fly to the village of Canaima, a settlement at the edge of the Tepuis region. It is a place so isolated that it has no permanent access by road. After bemusedly exiting through the Arrivals door in the departure lounge just for the hell of it, I carried my luggage to the tiny six seater Cessna parked on the tarmac. There were five passengers, myself and two young couples, one of which was on the same tour as I was. They were on their round-the-world adventure tour and coincidentally were also both British. Both were pleasant travel companions. The girl was adventurous and athletic, although sometimes a little stern and hard to read. Her boyfriend was a nice fellow who complemented and matched her perfectly, one of those lucky couples that managed to find each other. This quest was shaping up just fine.

We piled up our bags for sorting, as the staff had to balance the airplane between the front and back luggage compartments to enable it to fly. I looked with a wry smile at my fellow passengers, who I think were just as amused, bemused, excited and terrified about the situation as I was. We were eventually given permission to board and I ran for the co-pilot's seat, which was available for one of us. From the faces of my fellow passengers I needn't have rushed; no one else was even close to wanting it. I'd never been in the co-pilot seat before, and watching the plane accelerate down the runway and climb into the air from the front was a wonderfully new and exhilarating experience. Flying above the brush and into the fluffy clouds, we were on our way.

It was at this point that things got really interesting; never a dull moment in Venezuela! Firstly, I noticed that one of my knees kept banging a very large and very red lever on the center console. I assumed that activating it during the flight was a bad thing; no-one paints a lever red for fun, so I regarded it suspiciously while wedging my knees to one side. With my attention focused on the lever I was slow to respond when the pilot leaned over, uttered a cursory "Pardon" and reached past my face to open the window. Maybe that is something you do in a car, but I wasn't expecting it on a plane. As I re-checked my seatbelt the pilot leaned back into his seat and typed a couple of things into his GPS before reaching down into the briefcase by his feet and withdrawing some papers. I thought it would be some navigation charts or a flight manual, but instead it was the morning's newspaper. He summarily unfolded the broadsheet across his side of the cabin and began reading, unperturbed that his view of where we were going was now fully obscured. Now I realize that at 12,000ft there isn't much to see, and even less so to collide with, but if it ever happens to you you'll agree when I say that it is not confidence inspiring. Thus I found myself two miles above the ground in a rickety South American airplane that may - or may not - have been correctly balanced, wondering what the big red lever did while I watched our blinded pilot read his newspaper as it fluttered in the breeze from my open window. There was plenty of remote jungle terrain below to crash into, so this situation got a 'Very High' on my what-the-hell-is-going-on scale.

After some time the pilot lowered his paper and glanced at the GPS.

"Ah, we are making good progress," he exclaimed in good English. "We are early in fact!" and with that he spun around in his seat to gauge each passenger. His eyes rested on me.

"You look like a young group, I think. Some fun, perhaps?" he asked, giving no hint of what that might mean. I turned and exchanged glances with my fellow passengers, who were as perplexed as I was. However, as I was feeling adventurous and as I didn't see anyone starting to cry I quickly jumped in to preemptively reply.

"Yes, sure, why not! I think we are ready for anything," I exclaimed. We weren't.

After carefully folding away his newspaper our pilot tapped a few more buttons on the GPS before gently pushing on the control pillar to begin our descent into Canaima. As we flew out from between the fluffy clouds and towards the jungle-covered hills I caught my first view of the Tepuis, standing like sentinels at the border of their realm. They were everything I had hoped for and more. I stared transfixed, until eventually noticing that we were now quite low. Despite my co-pilot's viewpoint, the village and its all-important runway were nowhere in sight. I glanced at the pilot's instrument panel. Altitude was 3,000ft and falling. Soon we were at 2,000ft with still only jungle where the runway should be. At 1,000ft and still nothing I was starting to worry. From skydiving I knew that at 1,000ft you are almost on top of your landing area, yet here we weren't even close. And then I saw it, except that "it" wasn't a runway. It was a river. And our airplane wasn't a river plane! Tinged brown and red, and maybe 120ft across, we were heading right for it. I tensed up and grabbed the door handle in preparation for an impact that never came, for at the last second our pilot leveled out, right above its placid surface. We couldn't have been more than 15ft above the water with the rainforest along the river's edge a mere 50ft away on both sides. The tree tops were above us. It was utterly exhilarating and utterly terrifying as we swooped through the curves of the tropical river with the jungle on both sides and the sun's reflection shimmering on the surface. I felt like we were escaping a secret tomb with a sacred golden idol in some implausible movie adventure; a genuine Indiana Jones moment which was almost too surreal to believe.

After a couple of minutes we rounded a large bend, whereupon the river not only widened substantially but up ahead it also disappeared. In my adrenalized state that just didn't compute. The visual was as though we were flying across an infinity swimming pool. I was still confused when we reached the far edge and once again I instinctively braced for impact...

The ground dropped as though it had been sucked away. Like crossing the edge of the world we flew over the 90ft waterfall that thundered into Canaima Lagoon below. My adrenaline spiked and I shouted out a wild "Yee Haa!" above the noise of the engines. What a rush! A fly-by past the waterfall once more and it was all over as we quickly touched down on the runway in Canaima village only a few hundred yards away. It was such an incredible buzz that my jaw hurt from smiling, and to his surprise I hugged the pilot on the tarmac when we disembarked. Not bad for a commercial flight, after all. Flying British Airways has never felt the same again.

We spent the following day in Canaima where we explored the surroundings and took a trip to walk behind Hacha Falls, the waterfall we had flown over. What a unique place to visit; the torrent of water gushing just feet away as we walked along the thin path against the rock face. The next day we left Canaima and travelled by motorized canoe into the heart of this land that time forgot. The isolation was palpable as we navigated the narrow rivers, our slim boat carving through the mirrored surface like fresh tracks in snow. The overhanging jungle at the water's edge was full of life, untouched and untroubled by human influence. Monkeys played in the trees and birds flew overhead. At every turn I half expected to see a dinosaur emerge from the forest. We journeyed for many hours until, at a curve in the river perhaps an hour before dark, we reached our destination for the night. On the outside edge of the curve, a little way back from the jungle-covered banks, rose towering cliffs that surrounded us on three sides. On the inside edge the river became shallow and formed a small beach onto which we dragged the boat. A long narrow meadow sloped up from the beach. At its top, some way back from the river, stood what looked like a large barn but without walls. Under this shelter sat a couple of other tourists on some benches, while in the corner two guides busily tended pots hanging over a small fire. From metal beams underneath the roof hung the hammocks which were to be our beds for the night. As the sun began to set and the others drank hot coffee under the shelter I took my cup and walked back down to the river, where a mist had slowly risen from the water. A soft and eerie light shone with incredible depth from the orange of the sunset and the greens of the jungle. I stood there watching two small waterfalls cascade through wisps of cloud down the 1,000ft cliffs that encompassed us. A flock of bright green parrots, shining in the light as beacons, broke the gentle sound of burbling water and the hum of insects as they squawked overhead to roost nearby. The dampening foliage gave everything a smell of pure freshness; the smell of rain mixed with cut grass. A surge of happiness welled inside and I laughed out loud, helpless to contain my emotions. It was just so spectacularly fresh, just so stunningly beautiful. It was an ecstatic joy to be alive.

As I watched, the darkness of night came swiftly. The mist rose and the scene slowly became hidden from view by this ghostly veil, replaced by the twilight buzz of the jungle. I waited there until nothing more could be seen before returning slowly across the meadow towards the lights of the shelter above. It was time for bed.

At sunrise we crammed into a smaller boat than the prior day and headed up a narrower tributary towards the Devil's Canyon itself. The sky was clear and a very thin layer of translucent mist hovered over the placid river's surface, glowing in the early sun as we carved our way like explorers. After several hours we were in the canyon and the walls slowly converged as we approached its apex. Eventually we were nearly surrounded by cliffs. I stared along the wall as the river followed a wide curve, and as we progressed far enough to see around the overlapping cliff ahead my jaw fell agape. As if by magic a giant waterfall had emerged from its hiding place between these two faces. There it was, Angel Falls. I was dumbfounded. It was so utterly, utterly breathtakingly majestic.

We continued closer and soon disembarked at a small beach for the hike to a viewpoint at the base of the falls. Perched on a rock still 1,000ft from falls you get covered with spray, even at that distance. It helps you better comprehend the incredible size of the waterfall, something that is almost impossible to do unless you see it with your own eyes. Water drops unbroken for more than three thousand feet, the height of 20 Niagara Falls stacked one on top of the other. It is so unfathomably high that your brain compensates, making it appear as though the water is falling in slow motion. It takes nearly a minute to descend the entire drop, falling at the bottom as rain. Unfathomable scale, stunning beauty, immeasurable power. To see Angel Falls was worth my bicycle trip in its entirety, and it remains the greatest natural wonder I have ever witnessed. I feel privileged to have seen it.

# FORTY ONE

# The Giant of Brazil

The beautiful long boat ride back from the falls and the return flight from Canaima were uneventful, and after a day's rest I left Ciudad Bolivar to continue on towards Brazil. The road took me back through the land of the Tepuis, although on a more easterly trajectory than the flight to Canaima. The land here was more grassland than jungle, but the area had lost none of its wonder, culminating in my afternoon glimpse of Roraima through the fog. Its disappearance and replacement by the rainbow added a final touch of mystery and surrealism to this place, a most fitting end to my journey in Venezuela. It is a remarkable land of remarkable contrasts. After two nights in the town of Santa Elena, beyond the Tepuis at the furthest tip of the country, I continued the short distance to the edge of the plateau and enjoyed an exhilarating ride down to the lowlands and the border of Brazil.

Ah, Brazil. Of all the countries on my trip none evoked for me such strong feelings of apprehension and anticipation. I hoped it to be all the things you probably do as well. Hedonism and carefree freedoms, beautiful people in body and mind, a passion for life and lifestyle. Yet I had no illusion that this was all to anticipate; the sinister edge of crime and danger were expectations also. Nothing is done by halves in Brazil. It is all or nothing, and yet even with such bright lines Brazil remains the paradox of South America, a vibrant juxtaposition of itself. It is a deeply catholic country that popularized the G-string bikini. It has ostentatious wealth within a stone's throw of despairing poverty. Mud huts with dirt floors have satellite dishes in the yard (something I saw more than once). These things seem to make no sense but in Brazil it somehow works. Perhaps because its people are a bit like that too. As unique as they are colorful, everyone seems just a little bit crazy, for the most part in a good way. The country is fascinating, terrifying, electrifying, exhilarating and maddening all at once. Buckle your seatbelt and hang on for the ride.

Descending from the plateau I was greeted by a vast rolling grassland stretching as far as the eye could see. Call me clichéd, but in my stereotyped view of the Amazon Basin I was expecting rainforest. However, having passed the world's smallest sandy desert in northern Canada of all places I was now taking scenery at face value. This bland vista was broken only by a few isolated trees, great behemoths that stood as a great chain of ancient sentinels, the last of their kind, as they watched my passage through their dominion.

At length I crested a ridge along the straight yet undulating road to see bright orange dots far ahead. As I approached, the dots resolved into the high-viz orange jackets of a road repair crew working in the middle of nowhere. I was about to ride past when the foreman spotted me and strode into the empty road to flag me down. He was perhaps the first Brazilian I'd ever met and against my stereotypes he did not disappoint. He was a monster of a man, the physical equivalent of Apollo Creed from the Rocky movies. Afro-Brazilian by descent, his massive ripped muscles tore across his body like a body builder as the hi-viz jacket stretched in vain to close across his chest. His biceps glistened in the sunshine from the sweat of hard labor in the humid air. I named him the Giant.

"Hey, hey, my friend!" he cried out to me in Portuguese as I cycled towards him. He smiled a great warm smile. "Hey, stop here and have a chat! Where are you from?"

"Bon Dia!" I replied as I came to a stop in front of him and shook his great bear paw of a hand. "Good morning!" Now, sometimes I would keep riding past when someone blocked my path if that person looked threatening, but even with his intimidating size the Giant somehow gave me a feeling of reassurance. It was a sense of both humor and respect, perhaps. Plus, I'd been teaching myself Brazilian Portuguese for the last month and here was my first chance to practice. The first thing I discovered? Brazilian Portuguese is tough!

"Where are you going?!" he asked.

"I'm going to Rio de Janeiro," I answered to quizzical expressions from the Giant and his nearby crew. Did they not know Rio, I thought?

"Rio de Janeiro," I repeated.

"Rio?" Nothing.

"Um, copacobana? Ipanema? Carnival?" I tried. Suddenly a wave of understanding swept across my new friend.

"AAAAAH!" he cried, turning to the others with a great grin, "He-oo dje shan-ay-roo!"

That was apparently how to pronounce the name in Brazilian Portuguese, a language I now seemed to be learning the hard way. In Brazilian Portuguese, 'r' is pronounced as an 'h' when at the start of a word, but as an 'r' if in the middle, unless of course it is a double 'rr', in which case it's back to an 'h' pronunciation. 'h' itself is silent if at the front of a word, whereas 'o' is an 'ooo' at the end of word and an 'o' elsewhere. 'j' is a 'shhh' sound at the beginning but elsewhere a 'j', unless it is then followed by a vowel, when it becomes an 'h'. Got that? These are the easy letters. I won't even go into 't' and 's'.

"OK!" I replied, smiling and bewildered. "Let me try. He-oo dje Shan-ay-roo?"

They laughed. "No no! Hee-ooo dje Shan-ay-roo!"

"Hee-ooo dje Shan-ay-roo?" I tried once more.

"Haha!" The amusement continued at my apparent inability to pronounce these simple words. In my head I was mimicking them perfectly, but I guess I wasn't. Finally, on my fifth identical attempt they erupted in proud laughter as I somehow got it right. This easy mispronunciation never left me in the six months I was there, even when I became nearly fluent. My favorite example was when I once asked a man in the street for directions to the bank, the "Banco do Brasil". There is a branch in every town. Finally on my seventh exasperated attempt he nodded.

"Ah!" he replied, turning to point down a side street, "Banco do Brasil!"

I mean, what else could I possibly have been asking for! What could even sound close? Maddening.

"So where are you from?" continued the Giant as he gave me and the bike the once over.

"I'm from England."

"England!" he shouted, looking back to his fellow workers as though making a great discovery. "He's from England! That is a very long way!" he said, turning back to me. "You rode from England?"

"No, no!" I replied, "From Panama. It is a very long journey! And Brazil is the best so far," I said, to wide smiles all around. In Mexico I'd given up saying I'd ridden all the way from Alaska. It was far too hard to explain and no one believed me anyway. I'm sure none of them even believed I was heading to Rio.

"So, where are you all from" I asked, trying out plural words for the first time.

"We are from Sao Paulo! It's very far away, in the South. Do you know it?"

"Yes I know it!" I replied. "Many people."

Knowing of Sao Paulo caused another great stir. As it has 30 million people and is the largest city in South America I think I got too much credit. That said, knowing a little about someone's home is travelling gold dust. Maybe it's a bridge to common ground.

Then I tried something more difficult.

"Was this all forest?" I asked. Lots of trial and error, mostly error, but we got there. The Giant nodded vigorously. With the help of arm waving I learned that it was all once rainforest which has now been cut down. Those great sentinel trees were the last remnants. I was shocked. You read statistics about the deforestation of the Amazon, but those numbers mean nothing until you stand there and see just grassland to the horizon in every direction. How is it possible to cut down so many trees? It scared me. At current deforestation rates my great-great-great-great-great-

great grandchildren won't be able to visit the Amazon rainforest because most of it won't exist anymore. For something that took 500 million years to evolve, humanity could erase it in less than 500. That ratio is equal to how long it took you to read the last two chapters compared with your entire lifetime.

The Giant and I talked a little more until it was time to say goodbye. It had been a good encounter and a perfect introduction to Brazil. As I continued south, the complete deforestation slowly receded to leave small patches of forest as more of the Amazon appeared. Otherwise it was fairly uneventful riding with the exception of a slight error I made one evening when it was time to remove my contact lenses. I was dehydrated from the humidity and had forgotten to remove my lenses the night before, so they were now firmly stuck to my eyeballs. They were beginning to sting and needed to come out whether I liked it or not. Now, if you have ever used a bare fingernail to physically scratch something off the surface of your eyeball you will understand how that process felt. Eventually I managed to strip out both lenses while my eyes burned and fell asleep, in pain but safe in the knowledge that there was no damage done.

Wrong.

If you want to scare yourself, I highly recommend damaging the surface of both corneas while alone in the Amazon. I had torn the top layer of cells from both eyes, creating both pain and blurry vision. Indeed, the excruciating pain made putting in new contact lenses impossible and I was forced to cycle wearing my glasses. That sucks. The next few days were thus spent looking at a blurry road through fogging glass, all the while wondering if my sight would ever return. Slowly, fortunately, the pain did subside and my sight returned, and a very relieved James went back to business as usual.

Through this part of the ride I'd been carefully tracking my position by GPS and late one afternoon I finally saw it. A small grassy area with a few parking spots appeared on the roadside and in the middle of the area stood a large sculpture. A bronze line ran through its center and along the ground. I dismounted my bicycle and stood there with my feet either side of the line. One foot was in the northern hemisphere, and the other in the southern. I straddled the equator! Feelings of triumph and pride surged as strongly as when I crossed the bridge in Panama. I had reached the southern half of the world!

# FORTY TWO

# Hostage Crisis. Again.

Later that day, as the sun slid low over the trees I arrived in a tiny village occupying a small hollow amongst the jungle. With a small unkempt meadow on one side of the road it gave the same impression as a village green in some hamlet in rural England. The village boasted a tiny hotel and a small open air bar where 50% of the floor area was taken up by huge speakers. What was notable in this particular place though was the choice of music rather than the volume. This deep in a Brazil I expected traditional folk music or perhaps forro, northern Brazil's equivalent of samba. Watching the parrots fly through the sunset colors and mist creeping across the grass I instead had the surreal experience of going for a walk along the lonely road while listening to "Take my breath away" from the Top Gun soundtrack as it echoed across the landscape. Top Gun meets Gorillas in the Mist. Top Gorilla? It was weird but I must admit it was also supremely relaxing. Perhaps it was the combination of exotic landscape and familiar music. It is moments like these which make travelling so special.

The next section road had a special significance, unfortunately not for good reasons. The BR-174 wound through the territories of several Amazonian tribes who were none too happy at this invasion into their lands. Initial animosity with gold prospectors and truckers descended into a guerilla war, and during the 1980s several hundred people are said to have met an untimely demise at the hands of the tribes, often through poison darts or being hacked with machetes. In the 1990s a truce was finally negotiated, whereby the violence was halted. The road was to remain and sections paved, and in return the Waimiri-Atroari tribal reserve was established, approximately 150 miles wide and 80 miles top to bottom. Strict conditions on the road's use through the reserve were also introduced, including no stopping, no driving at night, no getting out of the vehicle and no photos - only driving from one side to the other in daylight between 6.00am and 6.00pm. Signs frequently remind you along the entire stretch and the tribe takes it seriously even now. So seriously, as I was told by some locals in Manaus, that when someone breaks the rules or their vehicle breaks down, in the morning all that can be found is the vehicle. No people. I was a little concerned as it is hard not to stop or 'get out of the vehicle' when that vehicle is a bicycle.

A tall metal fence marked the boundary of the reserve. I miscalculated where the reserve began and just before midday arrived at the entrance after having already riding a little over 30 miles. With 76 miles across the reserve still to go my day was thus extended to about 110 miles, a long ride indeed over the hills of the Amazon. I passed through the gate and my race against the clock began. Six hours and the opposing gate would be shut, trapping me inside. Despite these concerns I put them to the back of my mind as I reveled in the glory of the experience. Here, the pristine rainforest came right up to the very edge of the road. It is loud and alive. The calls of birds, monkeys and macaws are heard all around, sopranos over the buzzing and zinging of unseen things. I rode around things which scurried onto the road and back, including at one point a large python. It was an interesting place to be.

I had already learned that the Amazon is anything but flat and this road was no exception. About half way across the reserve I reached the top of a hill and looked into the next small valley, where to my surprise I saw a large group of people walking in my direction along the road on the opposite side of the valley. I was incredulous.

"What the hell are these people doing?" I thought, marveling at the rashness of their decision. "If they're not careful they'll get caught by the Amazonians!' It was only as I rode closer that I realized my mistake. The people walking towards me *were* the Amazonians. And they were not happy to see me.

To meet the tribe was to step out of reality and into a copy of National Geographic. This was the real deal. Women were fully tattooed and topless. Some had earlobes stretched down to their shoulders. Small children in their mother's arms wore head bands of exotic feathers and held small bows and arrows. A number of the men wore animal skins, although there were western fabrics as well. Their sleek, taut torsos evidenced their lives within the forest. At their front walked a shirtless young man in his late 20s or early 30s, dressed in beige knee length khaki pants which had been battered by hard use. In one hand he carried a machete and in the other a rusting rifle with a worn wooden stock. As I approached he strode into the middle of the road and held up his hand up for me to halt. I did so, unclicking from the pedals and then offering my hand to shake his. He ignored it and the group surrounded me in a ring. Maybe he didn't know what a handshake was.

"Niway piwanmi purinki!" he shouted at me in an unknown language.

"Um, yes. Hi. I am a friend! Friend!" I answered once he paused, which I assumed was meant for my response. Plenty of slow and predictable arm waving accompanied my reply, especially of pedal motions and pointing in the direction I was going.

"Ama anchata rimay chu! Mana muns'paqa," he continued, this time with some vigorous machete waving thrown in for good measure. Most definitely not encouraging. Beyond repeating my "I'm cycling to the exit" mime I wasn't sure what else to do.

"I'm going that way," I repeated. "That… way…!" More arm rotating and pointing.

"Pisin muns'aqpaqqa!"

He turned to consult with several of the other tribesmen and a heated discussion ensued. For 20 long minutes I stood there against my will, a prisoner in this human courtroom. I tried to look harmless while intensely scrutinizing the tone of the discussion, the consequences of which I could only image. Was I to be let free or… not? Whatever 'not' was, it was bad. Either way, for the time being I was a hostage.

I'd overcome some challenges on this journey so far, to say the least. I'd escaped from a forest fire, battled extreme heat and cold, and avoided a knife in the dark, to say nothing of my encounters with the money changer and the conspiracy theorist. But nothing quite prepares you for the moment you are kidnapped. And in my case, for the second time. Once is unlucky, twice is starting to sound like carelessness.

At length the group reached a consensus. The leader began shouting at me once again, but finally, with a grunt and a flourish of his machete, he stepped back and the tribesmen blocking my path parted like the Red Sea. I could see my exit to freedom and I didn't need to be asked twice. With a quick snap onto my pedals I was on away, grinding slowly out of the valley bottom away from the tribe.

"Why are my getaways always uphill?" I wondered as I climbed on pure adrenaline. Eventually I reached the crest and stopped to look back for a final glimpse of the tribe. They had continued to walk away along the road as before and I considered taking a photo before deciding not to push my luck. The guy had a rifle, after all. With a sigh of relief I pushed over the summit and I was free once more.

I now had to focus on my other problem. I was in a race against the clock, the stakes vividly raised by my close encounter. I had to make it. Those last 35 miles nearly destroyed me, not only from the effort but also because the authorities had painted numbers on the road. Every 10 yards they ticked down by one, an unavoidable countdown to the exit. From 5,000! There is nothing like riding up a difficult hill to find you only passed 28 numbers and have another 2,134 to go. Most of that section was appalling apart from the last few miles, which were worse; a frantic torture as my success stood upon a knife edge. As twilight fell I reached the gates with less than 10 minutes to spare. Exhausted I pulled up at the only nearby house, a small wooden shack with a covered veranda illuminated by a single bare incandescent bulb. Below the insects that swarmed around it sat a family watching an old TV set, its twin aerials sticking out like alien antennae. Somewhat surprised to see me, they were very kind and let me pitch my tent next to the veranda and join them, which I did after wolfing down some food and my anti-malarial pills. Tiredness soon descended and I bid them goodnight, crawling to bed like a vampire to a coffin.

Something strange happened that night. I dreamed. But not just everyday dreams. Hyper-real, ultra-aware, awake dreaming dreams. It was a warm welcome to the wonderful world of Lariam, your favorite hallucinogenic anti-malarial and mine.

Lariam is the brand name of the anti-malarial drug Mefloquine Hydrochloride. Once offering 98% protection against malaria it has become one of the world's most popular prophylactics. As well as protecting you against malaria it can also have some side effects, some of which aren't all that 'side'. Most common is nausea and vomiting, which affects 20% of takers, followed by dizziness and insomnia. Unpleasant but tolerable. Then we reach the less common but far more worrisome 'severe and permanent side effects'. Their words, not mine. Severe depression, anxiety and paranoia start the list, not ideal things to read about when you are already on month three of the course as I was. Paranoid about being paranoid, now there's a vicious circle if ever I saw one. Beyond these effects you might also experience seizures and the less than encouraging 'peripheral motor-sensory neuropathy'. I have no idea what that is but it sounds bad. I like my peripheral parts just the way they are. Lariam can also create birth defects, make you blind if you take it for a few years and can in rare cases ignite psychotic suicidal tendencies in certain vulnerable people. Not awesome.

Fortunately, Lariam does have two very redeeming benefits. Firstly, it does help prevent you from getting malaria. A friend of mine contracted it while growing up in Kenya and described the headache as like having your head squeezed in a bench vice. In comparison, a bit of nausea doesn't seem so bad. Secondly, for whatever strange reason, Lariam can give you hyper-vivid dreams. These are quite something. Your senses are as keen as when you are awake but it is as though you are a passenger in your own body in some parallel universe. Unfortunately, in my experience it was always an uncontrolled parallel universe that never had any bikini models or hot tubs in it.

On the veranda that night, my error was to watch a game show on TV before going to bed. It was one of those shows where the contestants get a demonstration of some skill or other and then have a few minutes to attempt it themselves. Unfortunately for me, the skill they were demonstrating was how to do horror movie makeup. Could my timing have been any worse? I think not. In a hyper-real nightmare of my own creation I sat face to face with a zombie and watched a black scorpion emerge slowly from a hole in his face. It was as realistic, grotesque, terrifying and vivid as though I was awake and this was actually happening. Still in the dream I then glanced down and saw a scorpion coming out of my face as well! I woke with a shout in the darkness, drenched in sweat. The memory is still so vivid it makes me shudder. Lesson learned - next time I'm going to watch "Baywatch" before I take my pill.

The next few hundred miles traversed rural but increasingly populated and deforested areas of the rainforest as I headed towards Manaus, the famed city in the middle of the Amazon. Lying at the juncture of two great rivers, the Solimos and Amazonas, it is an unlikely metropolis of a million souls that was founded during the great rubber boom which began in 1879. Before the discovery of vulcanization, the process which turns oil into rubber for things like car tires, natural rubber tapped from rubber trees was used instead. As the world industrialized and demand rose, the main growing regions of these tropical trees became increasingly important. As a center for the rubber trade, Manaus flourished and grew rich. It became so wealthy, in fact, that a great opera house was built in the city center to replicate the 'civilized society' many of the Nuevo Riche had left behind in Europe and the United States. Marble was imported from Italy, exquisite wrought iron banisters from France, all across the Atlantic and then by river boat up the Amazon. The floors were made from solid mahogany and teak, and the large domed exterior roof glistens from gold leaf shining between the colorful glass panels. For some forgotten reason I had wanted to see the opera house for many years, which like Angel Falls was impossibly remote for an eight year old boy. I never dreamed I would ever stand on its steps, and doing so was another special moment. Another lifelong ambition box checked!

# FORTY THREE

# Messing About on the River

I sat in a cafe and pondered a fundamental decision I now needed to make. From Manaus there were two possible route choices, each offering an entirely different experience. The first was along the Trans-Amazonian highway, a 3,000 mile marvel of engineering built to connect east with west through the rainforest and open up the interior of Brazil for 'development', to use a charitable word. It was likely a route of pain and suffering, with utter remoteness and purity as its compensation. Travelling the highway was not an unachievable challenge on its own, but getting to the start of it was close to one. An 800 mile mud track stretched from Manaus to the highway, a track so remote and badly maintained that it doesn't even show up on maps printed since 1991. As I considered this path I got word from Alvaro, the Spanish titan with whom I had traveled through Baja. He had blazed a trail across Brazil ahead of me and in fact chosen this very route. He described it as "almost impossible". Given the truly epic challenges Alvaro has completed with relative ease, that meant "fully impossible" for mere mortals like myself. In addition, I estimated it would take four months to navigate these two roads alone, leaving just two months to cross the rest of this vast country. Not encouraging.

The alternative option was to take a boat down the Amazon River to the city of Belem, from which could ride along the coast to Argentina. Checking on the GPS I discovered that I would disembark the boat in Belem further away from the tip of South America than Manaus - at least in a straight line - so I wouldn't be cheating within my own criteria. The four months I saved with this option would then allow enough time to explore the coast and perhaps even enjoy Brazil a little along the way. This was clearly the better choice.

I was excited. This would be my first time on the Amazon River and my mind was full of ideas about swashbuckling and adventure. And yet also solace. Five days in which to watch the world go by, five days to think about the journey ahead.

On a hot and steamy afternoon a few days later I found myself navigating a cacophony of people, bags and belongings strewn along Dock 5 as I tried to locate my ship though the chaos. Looking like a cross between an old Mississippi paddle steamer and a container ship it was fortunately moored a little away from the greatest of the activity, and in any case I had arrived early enough to avoid the crush. Walking up the gang plank I could see that along most of the boat's length and its entire width was a flat deck area floating only a few feet above the river. The deck was covered by a long low roof and open on both sides apart from an iron guard railing. The roof also acted as the floor of an open air upper deck, which was covered in deck chairs. At the bow and stern were cabins – air conditioning! – and a raised structure stood at one end of the roof fed by stairs on the outside of the boat. This structure was the bar.

With so many passengers and so few cabins it was necessary to use that indispensable item of Brazilian travel equipment - the hammock. Similar to "The Hitchhikers Guide to the Galaxy", where all one needs to facilitate intergalactic travel is a towel, in Brazil all one needs is a sturdy hammock. Hanging from the underside of the roof for the length of the deck were scaffolding poles. To create a bed for the next five days I merely tied my hammock between two of them at an appropriate distance. The boat was packed and they were hung at very close quarters, close enough to be touching even before their owners lay in them. Luckily, they are magical and to my surprise it was still possible to get comfortable, notwithstanding the occasional unintentional kick in the head one occasionally gives and receives.

When traveling in a hammock along the Amazon I learned three secrets. These are special secrets that can save you, the savvy traveler, from a large bag of misery.

*Secret Number 1* – Lie Diagonally. If you lie diagonally on a big enough hammock you can actually lay completely flat. Yep, it really works, but only if you have a big enough hammock, which brings us to Secret Number 2.

*Secret Number 2* – Buy a Big Enough Hammock to Use Secret Number 1. Bigger is better, as with most things. When you are in the hammock shop then use Secret Number 3.

*Secret Number 3* – Get a Cloth Hammock. They are infinitely better than those stringy mesh things, which have two big disadvantages. Getting stuck in the mesh is the first. A travelling companion then discovered the second as we sailed through a swarm of mosquitoes. You can wrap a cloth hammock around you into a warm protective shield. If you are in a mesh hammock you can only look at other people wrapping their cloth hammocks into warm protective shields while the mosquitos devour you.

After hanging my hammock above some fine deck real estate I adjourned upstairs to the bar with some locals while the rest of the passengers arrived. As the boat got underway so did the party. The roof deck was soon humming with people in their beach wear drinking cold beer and cocktails. We soon sailed past the Meeting of the Waters, a strange phenomenon where the two huge tributary rivers meet just downstream of Manaus but don't mix. Rather, they simply flow next to each other for several miles with a distinct line delineating them. Something to do with them being at different temperatures, densities and acidities, I think. One is dark and somewhat transparent, the other milky and opaque, so the line is very apparent. We followed it for a while before turning towards the middle of the river where the current was strongest. Our 2,000 mile river odyssey had begun.

These boat trips are quite an experience, and mealtimes are no exception. A loud bell rings, triggering a commotion at one end of the hammocks where a set of long wooden tables and benches are attached to the ceiling with a pulley system. Every mealtime these are lowered to the floor, evicting the poor souls who suspended their hammocks at that end of the deck. Which brings me to secret number 4.

*Secret Number 4*: Don't arrive late or get a spot below the tables.

In true Brazilian fashion, i.e. for no apparent reason at all, their inconvenience is compounded by the absurdly early breakfast time of 5.30am. Why the need for this inexplicably early start? It is still dark and it is not like the passengers then rush into their daily commutes to beat the traffic. After breakfast everyone simply returns to their hammocks and goes back to sleep. Another mealtime oddity is farofa. I remember my first dinner on the boat, sitting down to a surprisingly good and hearty meal of stewed meat, rice and beans, when I was handed a large semi-transparent Tupperware container. Inside were small light brown grains that looked a bit like birdseed. This is farofa. Glancing at the plates of my neighbors I saw they had liberally poured it all over their food; 'sprinkled' doesn't capture the sheer volume that most added. I figured it must be good so I scattered a little over my rice and took a good bite. It may have looked similar to birdseed, but birdseed is almost certainly softer and more flavorful. This stuff had all the texture and chewability of sand. I also couldn't tell if it had any taste because it is also utterly insoluble.

"How on earth can they eat this?" I wondered as I gulped down most of the meal without chewing for fear of chipping a tooth. Made from dried and ground cassava, something similar to a potato, it is an important source of carbohydrates in Northern Brazil. Like most things when travelling you get used to it, and despite that first stumble I grew to love it. By the time I left Brazil a meal wasn't a proper meal without a generous helping liberally added to the plate.

I spent the days reading in my hammock, or sunbathing and drinking on the deck. Laying there in the afternoon of the second day with some new Brazilian friends (who wore the obligatory speedos and string bikinis) we drank beer and sunned ourselves in the warm tropical heat. Suddenly a shout went up from the deck below and several passengers rushed to the rail. My fellow drinkers were more relaxed. Mauro turned to me as he slowly rose from his chair.

"You want chocolate?" he asked, motioning for me to look over the side.

"Sure... uh, what?" I replied in answer to this odd question, and with a blank shrug got up and walked with him to the railing. Below us, hooked onto the side of our boat and buffeted by our wake we saw two large dugout canoes, inside of which precariously sat several Amazonian tribesmen. They were naked apart from loin cloths and held up what looked like misshapen oranges. A pile of them rolled around at their feet inside the canoes. A negotiation was already underway and after a few minutes several packets of potato chips from the bar were thrown down to the tribesmen, upon which several fruit were thrown back in return. This being Brazil, however, the continuing negotiation was both hilarious and complex, a game of cat and mouse as each side attempted to out-hustle the other.

"We have potato chips! Throw up three fruit!" shouted my friends.

"No, no! First the potato chips. Five packets for two fruit!" replied a tribesman using fingers to count each item and waving his arms vigorously, nearly falling out of his canoe in the process.

"No, no! First you throw up the fruit. Three for three!" came our response. This would continue until finally someone actually threw something. Just not necessarily to the customer or vendor though. Sometimes the tribesman would throw the fruit too high on purpose and miss the boat - the fruit floated so they could be retrieved later - or not throw them at all if we had already thrown the packets, which of course also floated. Sometimes it was the other way around, the crisps we threw down missing their boat completely. I admit I was outfoxed in my only negotiation with the tribe, but figured that a tipsy sunburnt British tourist is probably their staple dumb money. And in any case, the entertainment alone was worth far more than a packet of potato chips.

Finally catching a fruit of my own as it whistled overhead, my friend took it from my hand and broke it open on the railing. He returned the halves.

"Chocolate," he reiterated, and to my surprise it was, although not like you might expect. It was a fresh cocoa pod, with a sweet white fleshy goodness surrounding the hard, bitter chocolate seeds that are the actual chocolate. Ironically it is the white bit you eat and discard the seeds. It was delicious.

The days bled into each other, a succession of mealtimes and sunbathing, napping, scenery watching and casual drinking. On day five I awoke as dawn began to break across the lower reaches of the Amazon, ushering in the last spectacle of this pioneer's journey. The river was like glass, and having risen unusually early I sat alone in the cool air at the bow of the boat to watch one of the greatest sunrises on Earth. Reflected from mirrored waters, a thousand burning shades of golden fire shone against the darkness, the river so vast that the far shore disappeared into shadow at the dark purple horizon. Waves from the bow rolled soundlessly across the surface to create perfectly smooth curves of reflected fire which undulated to infinity. The only break in their symmetry was from pink river dolphins surfacing as they swam with our boat. The light slowly grew until an atomic fire from the first rays of sunshine torched from the horizon to mark the arrival of the sun. It was a marvel, the power and majesty of nature in that moment made me feel insignificant, a passenger on Earth instead of a participant. All too soon though the colors faded and the rustles and sounds of humanity's waking could be heard over the faint drone of the engine. The breakfast bell rang out and I returned to the main deck to join the emerging masses. One last communal meal and we were packing our stuff as the boat navigated its way through endless narrow channels towards the city. Around one final corner the buildings and harbor of Belem emerged on the distant far shore and soon we arrived at the dock.

We were back in civilization once again. I was relaxed and happy, yet sad I would never experience such a unique boat ride again.

# FORTY FOUR

# The Greatest Show on Earth

I arrived at the hostel in Belem at around 8.30am and had to wait a few hours until some current guests checked out and my room became available. I chained my bicycle to the stairs in the central common area and wandered about the building. It was old, a curious mix of colonial architecture overlaid with a distinctive tropical ambience. Worn hardwood floors and high vaulted ceilings contrasted with its peeling paint and the sound of creaking heavy doors. Having spent the last five days in the open air I looked forward to some indoor relaxation on terra firma, so while my fellow travelers also checked in I poured myself into an old armchair in the common area and slurped on a tropical juice I'd picked up on the walk. The lounge saw a slow trickle of people at that time of day, and after a while I struck up a conversation with a young chap from South Africa who was on a half work, half play trip though South America; the advantages of being a professional photographer I suppose. I warmed to Evan immediately and was disappointed to learn he was leaving that very day.

"Ah, that's unlucky timing, I just got here!" I exclaimed as he took a seat next to me. "So where are you heading to next, then?"

"I'm actually heading up the river to a festival on an island in the middle of the Amazon. It's supposed to be like carnival in Rio, but better, so I thought I'd go and check it out," he replied. "I don't suppose you've heard about it? It's in a place called Parintins; there isn't much info out there about it."

"I haven't heard anything I'm afraid. It sounds pretty awesome though!" I responded. "I kind of wish I was going, especially as I'm going to miss Carnival in February." I had already reflected that my timing was wrong to visit carnival in Rio. Disappointing. But now there was this Parintins thing not too far away.

"Yeah bro, I heard this festival is pretty wild," Evan continued, his enthusiasm building. "Apparently the little town on the island normally has 50,000 people living there, but between a quarter and half a million people show up for this festival. It's one of the largest in Brazil, I think. And then I hear they put on this amazing show for three days, like the big samba celebrations in Rio but in a stadium. I'm going up there to see if I can photograph it," he said, pointing towards his camera. "Bro, you should come along. This could be wild!"

"Urgh I'm torn," I replied. "I super want to go, but I've been on a boat for the last five days and I literally just got off it an hour ago." I really was torn.

"How far up the river is it?" I asked.

"It's about five days! But you should come anyway! Is there a schedule you have to be on with that bicycle?"

"Uh, yeah, good point. No, not really. I mean, I suppose I have enough time," I replied. I could feel myself talking my own subconscious into it. I'm often quite a 'maybe' kind of guy, but at the same time I'm capable of making quite irrationally spontaneous decisions. Was this going to be one of those, I wondered.

"So when does the boat leave?" I asked.

"1.45 this afternoon. I'm sure they still have tickets. There are a couple of us going and we only got them yesterday. You should do it."

"Yep, Yep." Now I was pondering. "You know, I think I could make this work. In fact, screw it. I'm coming!"

Generally I don't believe in "once in a lifetime" opportunities, but this felt like one. Time to spring into action. A quick shopping trip to get some essentials, and five hours after arriving in Belem I lay in a brand new hammock and watched the city recede into the distance as our boat glided upstream, back towards Manaus. Never let it be said I can't be impulsive!

We sailed far closer to the shore in this direction than on the downstream journey to avoid the current, often taking narrow channels as shortcuts. Traveling next to the shoreline brought us much closer to the river's wildlife than before, which was both good and bad. Seeing crocodiles on the bank was good, but our proximity also brought us much closer to the bugs. Great swarms of bugs. On one occasion we steamed through a cloud of odd-looking, half inch long flying beetles which seemed to like the lights of the boat. By the time we had passed through, the entire deck, every single square inch, was covered in them. On several other occasions we would pass through a swarm of mosquitos and have to run downstairs to seek refuge in our hammocks. I was very happy I'd bought a new and very thick cloth hammock in Belem. I'm telling you, Secret Number 3!

Evan and I were joined by a couple of other intrepid travelers for the festival. Alina was from Israel, where incidentally she is now a policewoman of all things. I introduced myself.

"Hi, great to meet you," I offered, taking her hand in mine. "My name is James. Like James Bond, but not quite as cool." I sometimes used this line to make myself a little more memorable in the sea of non-descript backpackers.

"I can see that," she replied, "Definitely not quite as cool - not a Double 'O' Seven for sure."

"I'll give you that one," I agreed, "Not as cool, but close enough?" I playfully suggested. "Maybe Double 'O' Six?"

"No, not that close. Perhaps more like Double 'O' Nothing," she replied, slicing into me. And that was it, my Brazilian nickname had been born. Tough crowd. Alina still refers to me by that name, although I always secretly hope that I have since graduated to Double 'O' One. She would probably say I hadn't.

At dusk on the fifth day we pulled up to a small town at the river's edge, squeezing into the long line of similar boats which were moored side by side along the dock. We had reached Parintins. With no accommodation available on the island, our hammocks would continue to be our homes for the four day stay, so we tied up our stuff as best we could and climbed across three or four adjacent boats to reach the shore. After walking up the short gangway to dry land we were instantly met by the pre-festival party. And what a party! Tens of thousands of people reveled in the town's central plaza and the surrounding streets. The whole area was cocooned in an envelope of music and conversation. Samba and forro blasted from huge speakers at earthquake-inducing volumes, the fast beats driving the crowd's fervor ever higher as they danced and drank, absorbing the electrically happy atmosphere. Food stalls competed to sell you fried mini catfish and other Amazonian treats, while street sellers sold cold beer from polystyrene boxes. There were also makeshift drinks stalls in the road which specialized in serving Caipirinha cocktails, the national drink of Brazil. Made from ice, sugar, crushed lime and sugar cane liquor they are delicious and lethal. We grabbed a couple of these to get us going, setting us back just $0.20 apiece. Knowing I was about to get very happy for about $1.60 I plunged into the chaos. In the tropical warmth the women all wore bikinis (which was great) and many of the guys wore speedos (which was less great). No-one cared. It was Brazilian hedonism at its finest and this was just the pre-party. No western influence here; in four days we met exactly six other western tourists.

At 6.00am we surrendered. With the party still raging we staggered back to the boat where I fell into my hammock like a dead man, yearning for sleep. But this was Brazil. At 7.30am a wailing sound from the very depths of hell itself tore through the air. A banshee of the underworld had been released. I was so startled I literally fell out of my hammock and onto the deck. Initially unable to process what catastrophe was occurring, it took me a few seconds to notice that this demon was accompanied by bongo drums and someone over-enthusiastically playing a triangle. Then reality dawned. It was 150 decibel karaoke from next door's boat. Climbing back into the hammock I tried to stop the screeches from penetrating my skull but it was futile. As the saying goes, if you can't beat 'em, join 'em, so I rolled out of my hammock once more, this time with a thud of capitulation, and greeted the others who were now also awake. And also traumatized. I cracked open a tepid beer and before long we were crawling into town on a mission kill our emerging hangovers. The party was still going, albeit with fewer people and at a more subdued pace, so we also grabbed some more beer and breakfast from a stall by the dock. Barbecued catfish for breakfast was a strange but necessary choice. With the hangover gone I was back in action, dancing in the streets as the day warmed up and the remainder of the masses returned to play.

The festival in Parintins is officially known as 'Boi Bumba', boi being the Brazilian word for an ox, the essential work animal of the river tribes. The festival is centered around a contest between two teams, Caprichoso and Garantido, who for three nights vie with each other to tell an ancient Amazonian folklore story of an ox brought back to life by celebration. The winner is basically the team which can celebrate most spectacularly through song and dance. Held in a stadium called the Bumbodromo, the one built in Parintins was used only for this three day event. It was huge, holding some 20,000 people, but even at that size it was too small and a 35,000 capacity replacement was under construction. For a sense of scale, this new stadium will hold as many spectators as some venues used in the English Premier League.

At around 4.00pm we wandered across town to get into the stadium ahead of the evening's show (for free, I might add). I had no idea of what to expect other than that we were in for something a bit special. Arriving randomly on one side of the stadium we found ourselves as supporters of Caprichoso by default. Our side was in blue and Garantido, on the other side of the stadium, was in red. A wide tunnel led to the terraces and at its entrance was a long table manned by an army of blue T-shirted volunteers. The table was overflowing with blue plastic bags, several of which were thrust at us by an attractive young woman as we walked past. I took mine gladly. Once we'd found a good spot on the terraces I turned and faced Alina.

"How do I look?" she asked, a blue feather boa draped around her neck while the open blue bag swung from her hand.

"Definitely Caprichoso," I replied, now fishing into mine with a level of expectation normally reserved for Christmas mornings. What a haul! A blue feather boa, a blue foam "big hand", a small blue flag and numerous other treats. The crowd filled in around us and our side of the stadium became an ocean of blue. The stands across the stadium were simultaneously turning red, and the fierce yet friendly rivalry had begun. For this festival you can't avoid picking a side; there are no spectators here, only participants. It was a microcosm of Brazil - encompassing, enveloping and interactive. Your side and hence color is therefore important in Parintins. So important, in fact, that it was originally the only place in the world where you could buy Coca Cola in a blue can.

With the stadium full and night falling the show began. A small stage on one side of the stadium between the two sets of supporters became brightly illuminated and a band burst into song. Small band, enormous sound system. The music reverberated through every bone in your body as it dragged you off the sidelines and into the game. Below us, at the bottom of the stand and repeated at intervals around the stadium, were small platforms that were visible to the crowd above. On each of these platforms stood a dancer holding the same props we had, and as the music began they coordinated the dancing in their sections. Choreography is a very odd, very fun and very Brazilian obsession. 25,000 people moving in unison to the same synchronized beat was an electric experience as we waved our boas to the right, and now the left, and then back again to the music. The crowd was one.

After a while the music stopped and the crowd hushed a little as huge doors at one end of the stadium were opened. Through them were rolled six enormous carnival floats, each float carrying a gigantic statue of an animal, perhaps 50ft high. Arranged like a movie set in the stadium's center they were swarmed by hundreds of dancers dressed in those fabulous costumes you see in pictures of Carnival. The crowd cheered. Behind the dancers emerged the drummers, thumping out a rhythm to the music. I lost count of them at around the 200 mark. The band played, the dancers danced, the drummers drummed and we all moved in rhythm as one vast human consciousness. I could not imagine how this could get better, except then it did. The statues came alive! Mechanized from inside, the 50ft high jaguar pawed the air, the wings on the huge bird flapped, and the python writhed. It was mind blowing. 25,000 people went completely crazy.

The night continued and the story was told. The huge models were changed for each scene in an endless parade. Such effort, such creativity! The absolute highlight, though, took things to the next level. It was something I barely believed was possible. One of the models which was brought into the arena was a house, life sized but perhaps a little dull compared to some of the previous wonders. Abruptly though the sloping sides of the roof opened, like the doors to a secret lair of some James Bond villain, and a deafening noise burst from within. It crescendoed rapidly to a screaming howl, so loud that you had to hold your hands over your ears. Then, as everyone looked on in collective amazement, out from the model flew a man wearing a jet pack! He circled around inside the stadium scarcely above our heads as the noise ripped the sky apart. 20 seconds later he landed deftly back into the house and it was over. Those seconds were so enthralling that if Elvis had returned at that moment he would have been asked to stop blocking the view. I still have a hard time believing it.

For two more days and nights we continued with this glorious madness. Some of the locals went out wearing a camelback full of whiskey so that they didn't have to go home for all three days. By the end everyone looked like they had seen better days, including us. A lot of better days. It was mercifully time to leave. As the last passengers boarded our boat and we reversed from the dock in the early morning, I realized why most of the festivals in Brazil last for three days. Brazilians don't seem to have an off switch and go until they drop, which is on day four. With no boundaries everything is taken to the limit, and in that sense this place really is the last bastion of hedonism. Party 'til you drop, worry about the consequences later. Or if you are Brazilian, don't worry about them then, either.

The festival continued aboard the boat for the 24 hour journey upstream to Manaus, albeit at a more subdued sunbathing pace. When I arrived I immediately boarded yet another boat back down the river to Belem. The wonderful non-stop hedonism of those days slowly ebbed away and the pace of life returned to normal.

# FORTY FIVE

# Map of Lies

I arrived back in Belem just in time; apparently I had forgotten to tell the woman who owned the hostel that I would be leaving my bike chained up in the lounge for two weeks. She was about to have someone come in and cut the lock. Lucky escape. After a few days relaxing it was time to painfully remount my bicycle and head out of the city, now following the coastline east towards a national park called Lencois Maranhenses. Translating to 'The sheets of Maranhenses', the park's 580 square miles are covered exclusively by pure white sand dunes. Walking across these dunes is to walk on another world, with blue tinged pools of crystal rainwater shimmering between the folds of white. Only the occasional lone palm tree stands there to remind you that this is still planet Earth.

On the banks of a small river at the edge of the dunes lies the small town of Barrarinhas. The Brazilian Rastafarians who hawk a living there give the place a tropical and hippy atmosphere, and I liked it a lot. I sat on the veranda of a local cafe in the evening warmth and watched kids playing in the river as I pondered a problem. Barrarinhas was potentially a dead end. I needed to reach the coast in order to eventually reconnect with the main road and my map showed a route which could do this, a 40 mile dirt road from Barrarinhas that traversed the edge of the dunes through just a single small village, Paulino Neves. It was either take this road or do several hundred miles of backtracking. It looked doable. However, I had asked the hotel manager the previous evening where that road began and was told some troubling news.

"Oh no, Senhor, there is no road from here to Paulino Neves," came the reply.

"Yeah, but look, it's right here on the map," I said, pointing.

"I am afraid not, Senhor. There is no road."

"No road? But it's right there."

"There is no road, Senhor."

"OK, you already said that. But if I wanted to go that way, how would I do it?"

"But there is no road, Senhor."

"Right, yes, OK, I understand the concept. But if I *really* wanted to do it?" Persistence here was the key. In many places in the world it is considered impolite for someone to answer with an "I don't know", so they just say yes instead. It is an infuriating human condition. As rule of thumb I would ask three or four people the same question and go with consensus. Or with none.

"Well, you *could* try alongside the airport runway," he finally capitulated, "Maybe a track begins from there. Maybe."

He was not convinced, though, not at all. Sitting on the cafe veranda I figured that given my circumstances it was worth a try anyway, so next morning found myself feeling the roughly graded dirt road deteriorate into sandy ruts as the runway on my right ended and the scrubland began in earnest. The sand soon became too soft to support both my weight and the bicycle and I had no option but to drag it. It felt like that "World's Strongest Man" competition where they pull the airplane. As in Utah, backbreaking effort was needed to heave it a foot at a time and I could only manage 40 or 50 yards before having to briefly stop for a rest. For 10 miles I did this, all performed in heat and humidity with minimal water and food. As with Utah, I was also lost for most of the time. Each drag became mere inches, and after 11 solid hours I was physically exhausted at an unexplored level. If you've ever been on such a hard run or bike ride that you had to physically crawl upstairs to reach the shower, and then fell downstairs afterwards when your quads gave out, it was like that but about three times worse. I could barely stand, so when the buildings of a tiny village appeared around a corner the knowledge of my salvation was overwhelming. The last 30 yards up the final sandy slope took 15 minutes, enough time for the whole village to come and see this nutter pushing a bicycle into town. One friendly fellow in the crowd came forward, though, and offered me a bed for the night, beckoning me to his house a few yards away behind a low picket fence. Eduardo was my hero and my savior.

Eduardo lived with his family and seven kids in a spartan little brick house adjacent to a small cassava plantation. Attached to the house was a large shelter made of worn wooden beams, beneath which was some equipment. There, busily grinding and steaming, drying and mashing the raw cassava in the heat was Eduardo's old grandmother. She was a tiny woman with deep age lines weathered across her face. It looked like one hell of a job for a little old lady. Past the plantation at the foot of the hill was a small patch of dense scrubland, and beyond that a small stream covered by a dense tree canopy that only a constant water source can sustain. Leaving my stuff in the house, Eduardo beckoned me to follow him and we walked down through the undergrowth to a large and deep pool at a bend in the stream. It was wash time, and boy did I need it. The deep cool water reflected vibrant greens in the waning sunlight, and I floated in that afternoon warmth with the water easing away my soreness. I absorbed the fresh smell of the lush foliage and the background of gentle chirps from the many birds that flittered around in the trees. It was more relaxing than any spa could ever be, a paradise lagoon hidden from the world. As the light faded to purples and reds it was time to return to the house, where Eduardo's mother was preparing dinner. As she was finishing I sat in the front yard with his seven children and taught them how to write their names. Jailson was the bravest and quickest to learn, even when dealing with my pretty appalling Portuguese. I occasionally wonder what happened to this young man. I felt he deserved an opportunity to do more with his life than spend it in a tiny village. He will have to work for those opportunities, though, such is the unfortunate inequity of life. It is not that some have more than others, but that some have less opportunity. I hope he is doing well.

Suspended in my hammock between hooks in the walls of Eduardo's tiny living room I had one of the best night's sleep of my life. I woke refreshed, despite now facing another day of suffering. With a stroke of good fortune, the track did harden a little to allow me to ride some short sections, and in the early afternoon I crested another sand dune to see the top of a TV antenna jutting into the horizon. It was Paulino Neves! I have rarely been that happy to reach a village, whereupon my joy was compounded by the discovery that the only guesthouse in town was also one of the friendliest in all of Brazil. The accommodations were in a small building at the side of a garden, a beautiful area overflowing with flowers and hummingbirds, and managed by the sweetest old lady you could ever meet. She was so nice that when I went into the village the following evening to watch Brazil play in the South American football cup finals she came looking for me at the end of the night, just to make sure I was OK! I'd been randomly invited into someone's house to watch the game on their TV so she joined us for the last 10 minutes before walking back with me. She knew the family, of course, so we all had a grand old time. Ever had that kind of service at a Hilton? No, neither have I.

# FORTY SIX

# Deathly Dangerous Driving

I was back on the main road and back on track. Next stop was the nearly unpronounceable village of Jericoacoa, but to get there I first had to pass through Parnaiba, the main town in the region. It was on that long straight road that I was confronted with one of my best examples of the Brazilian psyche. During my time in the country I'd failed to really understand the reasons behind some of the things I'd seen people do, and this chance encounter only compounded my confusion.

Brazil's roads are ludicrously dangerous, with around 100,000 people killed each year. After spending six months cycling there and witnessing some driver's absurdly fatalistic regard of the road I'm surprised the figure isn't higher. Small white crosses are often seen by the roadside to mark where some poor soul met an untimely demise. They were a stark reminder of the dangers I faced. These crosses aren't just seen on blind corners either, they are seen everywhere, even on dead straight roads where overly ambitious overtaking maneuvers went tragically wrong. It was on one such road on the way to Parnaiba that I saw in the far distance a small group of people who had gathered at the roadside. Several held flowers as they stood by two white crosses. A sad scene indeed, no doubt they were relatives mourning the two unlucky people killed in that very spot. In itself this was not so unusual, but what *was* unusual was the behavior of the two young men in the group. As the family grieved, these two stood in the middle of the road a few yards away and played a game of chicken with the oncoming trucks. Each was trying to push the other in front of the traffic. Big trucks here stop for no man, ever, so this was a game with real consequences. As I rode past, one was holding the other in a headlock, pulling him into the path of a large truck and only letting go at the very last second as it tore past at full speed just inches away. On a good day this was exceptionally idiotic, but to do it while visiting the grave of a relative killed in a traffic accident it is quite mind blowing. As I saw often in Brazil, it seemed as though the mental connection between cause and effect was missing. I think perhaps it is a kind of deep fatalism, of which I once saw an even more shocking example.

This other incident happened early one morning at some small rest stop, also in northern Brazil. I'd stayed in the accommodation annex the previous night and was finishing up breakfast in the cafe when a couple of truckers came in. They were dressed in grubby work clothes that matched the run down state of their overladen trucks parked outside. Pulling up two worn stools they sat at the counter.

"Morning, brother," one addressed the server standing behind the counter. "Two glasses of vodka, please."

By "glass" I mean half a pint. The barman didn't miss a step, and pulling a bottle from the shelf he poured out two full glasses of neat vodka. I watched in awe as both men downed their glasses in one slug, glancing at my watch as they paid and walked out. It was 7.18am. Through the window I saw them climb up into their respective vehicles, crank the engines and pull onto the highway. To most of us, this behavior is moronically irresponsible and grossly negligent, but if you subscribe to the fatalistic belief that if it's your time it's your time, this approach becomes a logical way to get through the monotony of long distance driving. As I said, 100,000 fatalities a year seems low.

From Parnaiba my next destination was Camocim, the last main town before Jericoacoa. Colloquially known as Jeri, part of its appeal is that it is not connected to the world by real roads, only a 4x4 track across the dunes. And the start of the track is already miles from anywhere! It is this isolation which makes it a cult retreat for back packers and wind surfers. My problem was how to get there with a bicycle. I was rapidly falling out of love with sand as you might imagine. Luckily, at a guest house in Camocim, I met Tom.

"Oh, I'm heading to Jeri as well," he said in answer to my semi-rhetorical question. "Actually I heard you can walk there on the beach from here. It's like 40 miles or something after you take the ferry over the river. I'm going tomorrow, you should totally come along. Would be way more fun with two."

So much for avoiding sand. Early next morning we found ourselves on a tiny rundown old car ferry making the short trip across the wide mouth of the estuary to the opposing bank. Camocim is a large town, but on the other bank there were just a few buildings and then nothing. From the dock the sandy beach began almost immediately and we quickly left the world behind. Walking and riding alongside the ocean's edge was a dream, just the blue ocean, hot sun, sand and the continual sound of gently breaking waves. No people at all. Only Tom and I were on this endless beach as far as the eye could see. It was purest tranquility; two calm and merry days that lifted the spirits and relaxed the soul. I pushed the bike along the hard sand at the water's edge, so progress was surprisingly easy. Small streams flowing into the ocean were admittedly an occasional challenge, and one larger stream could have blocked our path. However, it was conveniently manned by a pair of entrepreneurial locals with a small wooden raft. Other than those minor inconveniences it was just golden sand all the way. In the afternoon of the second day we saw a large dune on the horizon that we knew marked the edge of Jeri, and as the sunset approached we finally arrived.

Jericoacoa was a great little place, its sandy streets and small buildings offering the opportunity to eat, drink and relax. The mix of other tourists was eclectic; an amalgamation of backpackers, windsurfers and Brazilian tourists which created exactly the right combination for an interesting and 'authentic' experience. Indeed, I had my first taste of Brazilian authenticity the moment I arrived. Heading to the guesthouse I pushed my bicycle along a narrow sandy lane only wide enough for a single car, and as I reached the middle a car pulled in ahead of me. Simultaneously I heard another purring engine and turned to see a second pull into the lane behind me. Both advancing, when the cars reached the center they just stopped and faced each other. It was obvious that one would now have to back out, so rather than try to squeeze past I simply stopped and waited for this impasse to end. A minute passed with no movement, and then another. After four minutes one of the drivers got out of his vehicle and gestured at the other, who then got out and returned the insult. This debate of who should reverse lasted an incredible 10 minutes, as neither driver was prepared to retreat less than 20 yards back to their respective street. Finally, 15 minutes after they had first pulled into the lane, another car drove in and made it two against one. The losing driver was now forced to reverse out and allow the others passage, an action which took less than 15 seconds. I couldn't believe it. Three cheers for South American machismo.

After the trials of the dunes I needed a proper rest, and so I spent a week in Jeri. It was as refreshing as I hoped it would be. Early on the eighth day I rode 10 miles across the sand to reach the main road, a section which to my surprise wasn't as bad as I had feared. I now turned east and headed towards Fortaleza, an unremarkable city in my view with the exception of one oddity. It is famous for having the 'wildest' Monday night in the world. Here in Fortaleza, Monday is the new Friday. As luck would have it, I arrived on a Monday, so despite that day's grueling 90 mile ride I went to check it out. It was total carnage, with the main street full of revelers and a Saturday night party atmosphere in the numerous bars. I was out with a couple of Irish lads I had just met in the hostel, and true to the reputation of both Brazilians and the Irish the night was a blast. We went to a huge bar called Piratas, or Pirates, which is the epicenter of the festivities. It is amazing, with a full sized wooden pirate ship in the back. With cheap rum, a stage full of scantily clad dancers and a happy crowd, what more could you ask for? I was still bopping away on the dance floor at 6.30am before staggering back home. Although I didn't know it right then, I was celebrating the end of the good times. Fortaleza was to mark the start of the most traumatic and dangerous leg of my journey.

# FORTY SEVEN

# Russian Roulette

My laissez faire attitude to planning prior to the start of my trip had resulted in quite a few difficulties, as you have by now probably noticed. One of my greatest errors, which I was now discovering, was my ignorance of the trade winds. These are consistent winds which blow across parts of the world, always in same direction as they are driven by the land masses and the rotation of the Earth from what's called the Coriolis effect. Across the north of Brazil, just south of the equator, one of these trade winds blows from east to west; the main reason why Jeri is such a mecca for windsurfing. Unfortunately for me, this resulted in a permanent headwind for thousands and thousands of miles. The suffering it created was brutal, requiring a near superhuman effort to ride at just 8mph. This alone this would be challenge enough, but the road out of Fortaleza then added the next layer of hell. Connecting Fortaleza's population of three million to Natal, a city of one million at the north east corner of the continent, it has just a single lane in each direction. This road has a soul, an inner demon bent on inflicting great suffering on those who dared travel across its dominion. This spirit sits on the shoulders of drivers and whispers subversive ideas until bad decisions are made, multiplying towards tragic results. It is a death trap for cyclists. Even the local villagers would ride their bicycles over large rocks along the shoulder rather than brave the flat pavement a few feet away on the road itself. Drivers here never try to avoid hitting bicycles. Ever. Instead, they *are* kind enough to honk the horn a second or so before impact to warn you, so if you are quick enough you can steer off the road into whatever happens to be there, whether a fence, an 12 inch drop to the shoulder or perhaps some thorny bushes. I experienced all of those the hard way. If you aren't quick enough you briefly get to see the underside of a truck as it rolls over you. To say that riding along this road is stressful is an understatement. In the nine days it took to complete this segment I was run off the road something like a hundred times every day, that's nearly one thousand times in total. Mess up just once in those 1,000 events, just once, and I wouldn't be here to write this. Indeed, it was so stressful that a doctor I met a few years later informally diagnosed me with mild post-traumatic stress disorder after I described the symptoms I subsequently suffered.

You might think that over time you'd get used to these close calls, but as I instead discovered, quite the opposite happens. You subconsciously start counting down to the moment you meet the bullet (or truck) with your name on it. It could arrive in a second, an hour, a year, or never. It was like playing Russian roulette with the traffic, each incident another spin of the barrel and pull on the trigger. Each time I became a little more scared until I eventually found myself standing at the side of the road with my head on my handlebars, the tears running down my cheeks as I begged for it to end.

I still didn't cheat and catch a ride to Natal, though. I probably should have. The thought of looking back at that moment for the rest of my life and knowing that I failed to tough it out would have been more painful than to continue, no matter what the cost or risk. I am sure many people would think me foolish to make such a choice, but that was just how I felt right then and how strong the drive inside me had become. I have always been a bit of a 'strange one' when it comes to making sacrifices. It is ludicrous what I have done over the years in order to strive for goals which I have cared about, whether they seemed to make sense or not. Inflicting such mental anguish to avoid future thoughts of 'cheating' is just one example. In my banking jobs and even in my university studies over the years I have worked so hard that I reached the point of mental exhaustion; in one case actually hallucinating after working 131 hours in a single week. I think it is from my upbringing, where I was taught that if you work hard enough, someone will notice and you will be rewarded. It is deeply ingrained into who I am, despite some contrary evidence that this philosophy is perhaps only partially right. Maybe that is why I like physical challenges – the rules are set and hard work is all that is required. No-one can steal the results from you or take the credit, ignore your hard work or give you the minimum necessary according to their own agenda. Physical challenges are pure, universal, and above all, fair.

I was fortunate on that road. I avoided every one of those trucks but arrived in Natal an emotional wreck. After a few days of intensive recovery I decided that I needed some serious beach time to continue my rehabilitation. Fortunately, a short day's ride down the coast was the village of Praia de Pipa. Tucked away amongst pink tropical cliffs, Pipa is something of a gem. Developed enough to have some cute little shops on its well-groomed main street, it nevertheless maintains a backpacker-chic vibe, with plenty of guest houses supplying patrons for the small restaurants just above the beach. I stayed in a small guest house a short way up the hill from the main road. The rickety bright blue doors of the dorm rooms surrounded an open courtyard full of flowers and greenery. It was the very essence of tropical and a lovely place to relax. When I wasn't reading The Da Vinci Code I was hanging out at one of the beach restaurants, chatting to the owner while drinking ice cold beers and looking out across the Atlantic Ocean. Of note was the occasion we were told, right around sunset, that we needed to leave the bar because we were about to get cut off from dry land. With its back to the cliff, the bar was raised slightly on stilts, and looking down to see the ocean waves lapping underneath the floor boards of the open air deck was an interesting moment! Only a well-timed dash to the stairs leading up from the beach kept us safe.

Having turned the corner of the continent in Natal I was now heading south east. Battling on against the road for another few days I reached the outskirts of the next city along the coast, Joao Pessoa. Oddly enough, here I discovered the most easterly point of the entire South American continent. It was remarkable only in its unremarkableness. There was barely a sign to celebrate this fact. Unremarkable was a theme here; the only thing of real use to me in town seemed to be the consulate, where I was able to extend my visa for a further three months. If you can't get it extended you are required to exit and re-enter the country, and as Joao Pessoa is about the furthest place in Brazil from a border this requirement had the potential to become a titanic pain in the backside. With this potential outcome in mind I readied myself for this renewal visit. I dressed in my cleanest and most conservative clothes, i.e. my one remaining pair of pants which I had laundered just for the occasion, and arrived promptly at 9.00am with a smile and every piece of paperwork I could find. The front door opened and I was ushered into a waiting area which exuded the customary institutional blandness. Soon I was sitting next to another British guy as well as several locals on other businesses. Before we had spoken more than pleasantries I was summoned to the counter by a stern official dressed in an impeccable uniform. In Portuguese I told him what I needed and he snatched my passport across the counter and went into the back office, returning momentarily with a small slip of paper.

"You must pay the fee at the Banco do Brasil," he said, and left me standing halfway through a question as he called up his next victim. I looked at the slip and the fee. 8.08 Brazilian Real, about $3.00 at the time.

"Can I pay this here, it's only a small amount?" I asked him through his other conversation. No. So off I traipsed to the bank. It took nearly two hours to pay the damn thing, but eventually I returned with the receipt in hand. The same officer took it and returned shortly with my passport, the visa updated and good for three more months. Painful but successful.

Back at the hotel I unexpectedly ran into the same British guy I'd briefly met in the waiting room earlier that day. His spikey blond hair, tattooed arms, nose and eyebrow rings hadn't inspired complete confidence regarding his chances of success. Combining that with the shabby singlet top, shorts and flip flops he'd chosen to wear to the consulate I was not expecting good news.

"Mate! Can you believe it! They wouldn't extend my visa!" he exploded after I asked him how he had fared.

"What?! Um, no way!" I replied, not all that surprised, of course, but still concerned about what he was now going to do. This was the disaster scenario I myself had tried to avoid.

"So what happens now then?" I asked. "You don't have to leave and come back, do you?"

"Mate, I bloody well do! Can't believe it. I had to get a flight this afternoon, I have to go to *Peru*, man!" he ranted.

I felt for this guy. He obviously hadn't helped himself, but at the same time there didn't seem to be a legitimate reason that I knew about for why he had been declined an extension. It sucked and there was nothing he could do. Things only got awkward when he asked me how I had got on.

"Yeah, must have been because of the whole bicycle thing, you know, maybe he was into that or something," I suggested, trying not to make this guy feel worse. "It's all pretty random. I've been on your side of the fence more than once, believe me. I know how you feel."

We commiserated his bad fortune and cursed our common enemy. I never saw him after that but I hope he enjoyed Peru and eventually made his way back.

# FORTY EIGHT

# Things that go Bump in the Night

It was early the next morning, perhaps 5.00am. I lay asleep on the bed in my gloomy cell-like room as a shaft of warm dawn glow shone through a small high window to illuminate a patch of peeling light blue paint on the wall. It was my only connection to the silent city outside. The day was already hot and I lay on my back wearing just my underwear, the sheets discarded at the end of the bed. I was motionless and oblivious to reality, gently sweating in the humid heat of that room as my mind dreamed in a vivid luxury of Lariam enhancement. I dreamed of the beach. I lay on the sand in that dream and talked to a girl while I listened to the waves and watched the tips of her fingers touch my chest. It was lovely, and yet the feelings from those touches were most curious. If you've ever had an alarm clock ringing in your dream that matched a real one ringing in your bedroom, you will know what I mean. The alarm is in your dream, but even asleep you know that something isn't quite right. The sensation is too vivid, but at the same time so familiar and so 'in step' that it doesn't wake you. I felt a similar level of integration as I lay there, my subconscious confusion growing until finally I was gently stirred awake. As my eyes grew accustomed to the faint light they glanced down towards my chest and the source of the sensations. That was an error.

The tingling was not caused by fingers, but by legs. Thick, black legs. In the center of my chest walked a tarantula the size of my hand. It moved slowly, tasting the air as it crept towards my face just inches away. Trying to reconcile between the touches of the dream and what I now saw, my brain could not comprehend what was happening. And then all of a sudden, it did.

"WAARRGHH!!"

No man in history has moved faster than I did right then. I let out a yelp, and defying the law of gravity I took off, levitating about two feet off the bed as my hand shot out and swiped the spider from my chest. It flew across the room and into the wall on the far side, landing dazed but quickly regaining itself and scuttling off under the dresser. I landed back on the bed, heart pounding like a jackhammer, eyes frozen and transfixed on where it had gone. I stopped breathing. Nothing moved. I fully stripped the bed and jammed the sheets against the wall so I could both block it from behind and see it coming from the front, and for over an hour I sat there and waited. Eventually it was late enough to go out for breakfast, at which point I had mustered enough courage look for it. It was gone, but not knowing where it had crawled to was nearly as bad as finding it. It never returned, but neither did my ambivalence towards tarantulas.

That animal experience was my scariest in the Amazon but it wasn't the worst. A few weeks prior I had bought a small bag of Brazil nuts from a street vendor and in my tent that night I munched on them until it was time to sleep. The next morning I awoke, relaxed in the warm glow, and in my half-asleep state glanced over and wondered where the big shiny red ball next to me had come from. And why it was moving. A fist-sized nest of red fire ants now swarmed over the bag of nuts. Fire ants are vicious stinging little guys which inject concentrated acid into your skin. While one sting is painful, searing like a cigarette burn, a hundred are like being burned with a blow torch. In this case, things were even worse as they were also accompanied by soldier ants, much bigger ants with sharp biting jaws. I lay there completely motionless. Moving just my eyes I followed the ant trail down the side of the tent and watched them walking over both my bare thighs before exiting at my feet next to another nest in the corner. As long as I stayed still they ignored me completely, but of course I couldn't stay like that forever. The plan was to get out of the tent and the ants off me before I could get too badly stung. Dreading what was coming next I eventually gave myself the good old

3…2…1… countdown and made a dash for it. The moment I moved they stopped ignoring me and went completely berserk, even wiggling into my shoes through the lace holes to sting my feet. Lots and lots of stings later I had finally removed most of them from my stuff. It seemed impossible to eradicate them all, though, and I was still being stung by stowaways for the next week.

In contrast to these tiny invaders, an animal I encountered on a backpacking trip to Bolivia was very much the opposite. In the lowlands of Bolivia, trapped between the Andes and the Amazon rainforest, lies the Pampas, a vast swamp packed with mosquitoes, crocodiles, piranha and various other delights. I took a three day boat camping tour into the swamp to really experience it. To get to our base camp we were taken by narrow boat for many hours along the marshy waterways, at one point rounding a bend to see two pink river dolphins surface right next to the boat. The guide slowed us to a stop.

"Hey, do you guys want to swim with the dolphins?" he asked.

"Oh for sure!" I replied. "But what about the crocodiles?"

Lining the banks of the river almost nose to tail were hundreds of large crocodiles, all of which were now staring right at us. I'm no scaredy-cat, but I still think twice when crocodiles are sitting there, hoping against hope that you are stupid enough to actually get into the water. They were in luck.

"You'll be fine!" was our guide's reply, which also came with a complete lack of volunteering to swim with us. Still, I figured it would be bad form to lose a paying customer so early in the trip, and giving him the benefit of the doubt I jumped in. There is something to be said for swimming in murky water with a curious pink dolphin surfacing 3ft away while you stare at the crocodiles less than 10 yards away. Gets the blood flowing, that's for sure. After a few wonderful minutes I figured I shouldn't push my luck and got back into the boat. A mile or two upstream we arrived at our accommodation, and after settling in we returned at dusk to that very same spot… to go piranha fishing. Thanks, guide, for withholding that minor bit of information a few hours earlier. No crocodiles could be seen on the banks, and no dolphins either.

"Hey, can I go swimming again?" I asked him.

"I wouldn't recommend it," was the guide's reply. Good answer. I was happy to oblige.

The fun didn't stop there. Next day in the early dawn we took a smaller boat further up the river until stopping at the edge of a vast swamp. Soon I found myself walking in eight inch deep water, pushing through decomposing grass and mud as our group traversed between small grassy mounds of land scattered around the flooded landscape. We were looking for something, a fearsome yet elusive beast that was the top predator in these parts, above even the crocodiles of the day before. We were looking for an anaconda, the largest snake in the world.

"If you see one, grab it!" was the advice from our guide. I seriously doubted this was good advice, but what the hell, after the previous day I would believe anything from this guy. After several hours walking between and over these atolls in the swamp I glanced down as I stepped up onto the latest small mound. Barely a foot in front of me, almost hidden in the green-brown grass, moved the diamond-patterned body of a snake. A snake whose body was as thick as my arm. Grab it or don't grab it? I hesitated, wondering what would happen, but as it continued to slither away I was galvanized into action. I bent down and held it firmly but gently in my hands. It froze, and so did I. Neither of us knew what to do next.

I made the first move.

"Help! I've got one! Help!" I cried, startling not only the guide but probably also the snake. "Help! Help HELP HELP HELP!!!" My tone was rising and I was not kidding around. The guide ran over gleefully and took control, slowly reeling in the anaconda towards us. What a snake it was! 10 or 11ft long, its muscular body contrasted against its beautifully smooth and soft scales. The anaconda was for some reason relaxed about the whole situation and let itself be handled with contempt; at one point the guide opened its mouth and we saw a row of half inch long conical and razor sharp teeth grinning back. It was scary. That thing could have shredded my arm with ease. It eventually curled into a ball so we put it down and let it slither back into the swamp. It was an intense experience, a privilege to be so close to something so wild and so fearsome. I learned later though that it was still only a small one and that the local tribesmen hunt for the big ones by diving into murky creeks and feeling for them with their feet. I saw the head of a big one in a jar at a tiny remote nature reserve several weeks later; this snake had been 10 inches in diameter and almost 30ft long. Its pointed teeth were more than an inch long. This snake had apparently eaten a villager *whole* before they caught and killed it. Murky river, bare feet, anaconda hunting, swallowed whole? I decided to end my anaconda catching days while I was still ahead.

Not every close encounter of the animal kind is dangerous, however. Some are just hugely unpleasant. Every traveler has a creepy crawly story, but I think my self-inflicted experience on the South East Asian island of Borneo is still worthy of a mention. Hidden by mountains and rainforest deep in Borneo's interior is Mulu National Park, where limestone bedrock has been etched away for many millions of years to create some of the world's most spectacular and unique caves. One of these, the Deer Cave, has been carved through an entire mountain. It is so large that a jumbo jet could fly in one end and out the other. Mulu is truly a magical place. In the Deer Cave, hanging from the high ceiling and walls are Mulu's next wonder. Bats, all three million of them. Every night they leave the cave in an endless stream, with bat hawks and peregrine falcons diving into the swarm for prey. Such a huge number of bats living in the cave has created a unique ecosystem driven by what the bats leave behind. Huge mountains of bat droppings, known as guano, have accumulated on the cave floor, reaching hundreds of feet up the walls and into the darkness. The cool wet air stings with the scent of ammonia, and entering this cave is to enter another world.

Along the floor of the cave there is a small path along which you can traverse its length. Looking up the guano slopes rising on both sides into the shadows I couldn't see much, but had a strange urge to discover what might be hidden up there in the darkness. Had I heard about something to see there, or was I just curious; I can't now remember. What I do remember, though, is stepping tentatively from the path up onto the slope. It felt soft under foot, like freshly tilled soil but a little more pliant as the running shoes I was wearing sank an inch with each step. I continued stepping upwards as the smell of ammonia became stronger and more sickening. In the faint light from the cave entrance I began to see tiny bright spots scattered across the surface ahead, flickering in the darkness. The density of these bright spots grew as I climbed until I stood in a dense carpet of twinkling sequins. There was now a faint humming noise discernible in the dead air and a feeling of strangeness about where I was. Perhaps like Jonah realizing he was in the belly of the whale. As my eyes adjusted I stared at the sequins by my feet and began to realize the horror of my situation. In that putrid air I saw that the millions of sequins were twinkling because they were moving, and that were not sequins at all. They were cockroaches. Millions and millions of cockroaches crawling over the guano, and now my feet.

I stood in a place unique for its grotesqueness. I hate cockroaches, just hate them, and I was quickly jogging back down the guano mountain trying to keep my breakfast on the inside. Looking back I'm happy I did it, but it was one of the most nauseating experiences I can imagine. Key take-away: if you get the urge to climb a mountain of bat droppings in a dark and mysterious cave, don't. In fact you don't even have to - the Planet Earth documentary series features the very slope I walked up.

Even beyond the bats, Borneo was not yet out of surprises. Moving on from the caves of Mulu I headed for a wildlife sanctuary near the coast. It was here that I had an encounter more dangerous than the others, yet also magically irreplaceable. It was here I met the orangutan.

These majestic apes live only on the islands of Borneo and Sumatra, and are sadly now constrained to small areas as humanity encroaches upon their habitat. All too often their encounters with humanity have tragic results, so two orangutan sanctuaries have been set up on Borneo to care for the injured, displaced and constrained. On the long bus ride to reach one of them I was annoyed to read that it was closed, but as the bus dropped me off at a deserted roadside stop in the jungle it was too late to turn around. I went to take a look anyway and found it was very much open! Indeed, I was fortunate. Because of these rumors the sanctuary had just four other visitors.

The sanctuary was not a zoo but rather a protected forest where orangutans live in the wild and can visit for food. Like a buffet stop for great apes. Entering the grounds I saw small single story wooden buildings raised a short distance from the ground in a well-kept grass covered area, each with stairs leading to a veranda. Fading white paint and rustic looks gave the complex a feeling of dying colonial military grandeur; quaint and faded glory but with noble presence. Walking a few steps up to the veranda of the main building I paused to read the large sign hanging by the door.

> *Orangutans are wild animals!*
> *We work hard to keep them that way.*
> *Do not feed them! They can be dangerous.*
> *Orangutan sightings are not guaranteed!*

Well that sure took the wind out of my sails. Perhaps I might see one in a distant tree, I thought. That would at least make the journey worthwhile. Deflated, I turned around and almost fell over the small orangutan which was walking behind me, not three feet away. I stood there and watched it waddle across the grass and silently sneak up behind one of the other tourists, a woman who was carrying a large beach bag over her shoulder. The orangutan reached in and grabbed something before immediately making its getaway up a nearby tree as the woman shrieked and ran after it.

She was far too slow, so we all stood under the tree and watched this ape play with the shiny thing it had stolen. This was going to be a good day after all!

There was a short tour around the facility, which also included a number of huge cages where some animals were kept for their rehabilitation. Afterwards we were taken to an area on the opposite side of the complex where the forest began. A wheelbarrow full of bananas was waiting for us. It was orangutan feeding time! As we sat there we heard whooping noises in the trees above and a family of apes swung out of the branches and joined us. It was strange to be so close to these wild animals with no bars or barriers, watching them peel and eat the bananas just a few yards away. As we watched I talked to Alice, our young Californian guide, and asked her about the one orangutan we had seen in a cage earlier on the tour.

"Ah, that's Hassan. The poor thing drank some paint and went partially blind. He can't survive in the trees anymore so we keep him here," she replied.

"Oh no that's terrible," I responded, and of course it was. What a thing to happen.

"Hey, would you like to meet him?" she asked.

"Uh, what do you mean by 'meet him'? But yeah, sure, that would be great. Can we do that?"

"Well… normally no, but you are the only one left," she said, and looking around I saw the other three tourists had indeed wandered off. This was an opportunity I couldn't pass up.

"Ok! Let's do it!"

And with that she grabbed my hand and led me along the boardwalks through the compound. When we reached the cage we ducked under the railing by the path and sat cross-legged in front of the bars. Hassan was in there as before, swinging in his low-strung hammock like a sack of potatoes and periodically falling out of it just for fun. He was a very large and very bored male. Alice called to him, and after falling out of his hammock once more he swaggered over and sat right in front of us, putting his arms through the bars and holding out his hands, palms up and open.

"Put your hand in his," she told me. "He will close his hand slowly around yours; just make sure that you take your fingers out before he gets hold of it."

And so I did. Directly face to face with this orangutan I put my hand in his. It was a feeling that was almost indescribable. There was a connection. It was like holding hands with a Buddhist Master; such wisdom in the eyes and a thousand lifetimes etched into the rough yet surprisingly supple skin on his palms. I touched the orange hair on his arm; it was thicker and wirier than I expected. As his fingers closed you could sense an exceptional strength tempered with a supreme, human delicacy. Orangutan means "Old Man of the Forest" in the local language and right then I understood why.

As his hand closed I withdrew my fingers, and as soon as I did so Hassan opened his hand back up, waiting for me to replace them. This went on for a few minutes until I was distracted for a split second and let my fingers linger in his palm just the tiniest bit too long. As I felt his fingers close I tried to take them out but it was too late. Now I discovered what exceptional strength really means. With my fingers now held fast, I pulled harder to extract them. They didn't budge and the squeezing continued to build. I pulled a little harder and then harder still. Zero effect. They were in a vice grip now and as the pain began I grabbed the railings behind me for leverage and pulled as hard as I could. Alice was now pulling me as well but nothing moved. I was in deep doo-doo. There are plenty of stories about chimpanzees pulling the fingers off children at the zoo, but I wasn't panicking yet. Then I saw Hassan's other arm move, and in what seemed like slow-motion he grabbed my wrist with his other hand. OK, time to panic.

I clutched the railings for dear life until suddenly I felt a surge of relief in my fingers; Hassan had let go of them. Unfortunately he then grabbed my shirt sleeve. Given the situation that was still a big improvement. He pulled my shirt and I pulled back as hard as I could until with a tearing noise the shirt arm ripped right off at the shoulder. Hassan let go of my wrist and pulled the sleeve off my arm, retreating back into his cage where he began playing with it. I'd worn a bright shirt that day and I guess he just liked the color. If I'd known that was what he wanted I'd have given him the whole shirt!

I still look back on this as a fabulous experience which I wouldn't trade for anything, especially as I still have my fingers. The connection we shared for that brief moment was incredible, plus I'm now the fellow who wrestled an orangutan, lost, and lived to tell the tale!

# FORTY NINE

# Pickpockets and Posers

After my visa renewal in Joao Pessoa I could now continue onwards. I cycled through Maceio, currently the murder capital of Brazil (I actually thought it was nice), spent few nights in the old colonial city of Olinda and then rode through the city of Recife. I found the city somewhat dull apart from the warning signs along the beach about the 'High Risk of Shark Attack!'. Despite the beautiful beach and warm blue waters there wasn't a single person in the ocean. Several years later I saw that exact beach featured on Discovery Channel's Shark Week as part of a segment on the most dangerous beaches in the world. I guess the signs weren't joking.

From Recife I rode to the city of Salvador, capital of the state of Bahia. The old part of the city, Pelourinho, is beautiful. It is also intensely sketchy. It was here I saw a guy getting beaten up by the police. In fairness, the guy deserved it; a few minutes beforehand he had stolen a can of beer from me, snatching it right out of my hand. He then went and immediately started an argument with a local shop owner, a short but solid looking guy who wasn't in the mood for such antics. At all. The police eventually wandered over to "break up" the argument. The thief was made stand in the center of the cobbled pedestrian area and one of the policemen took a huge open-hand swing at him, knocking him down. Fair? Fairness has nothing to do with anything in this place.

If something bad happens to you in other parts of Brazil you can occasionally stand your ground. In Salvador you let them win. The troublemakers and weirdoes hanging around the tourist area are both psychotic and dangerous. Getting stabbed isn't worth a $0.30 can of beer. As another example, one afternoon I was walking through the tourist area, minding my own business, when a guy high on crack cocaine wearing only a black trash bag and with his face and mouth all covered in blood, tried to pick a fight with me. He was aggressive and in my face, screaming at me that he was going to give me AIDS. That really wasn't fun in the slightest. I knew people that lasted less than a day in Salvador before running away, and I certainly don't blame them.

I figured that as I was in the tourist crime epicenter of Brazil I might as well make the most of it, so I purposefully set myself up to be pick-pocketed at a street festival. You know, just to understand what it feels like. It worked. I stashed a R1.00 note, about $0.20 at the time, in my back pocket and waded into the festival crowd. The rest was in my shoe, which is the standard money carrying method in such places. Sure enough, after a while I felt a tug on the side of my shorts and when I reached down to check the note it was gone. I stared behind me, right into the eyes of the guy who had done it. He stared back at me and we both knew I'd caught him. We also both knew I wouldn't do anything. However, only I knew how little he'd stolen. Knowing the sensation of being pickpocketed was worth more than R1.00, and to disappoint the thief was worth a lot more.

Leaving Salvador on the ferry across the bay (with body and money blessedly intact) I continued south to a small beach town called Itacare, a very long day's ride south across bumpy dirt roads. It was a magnificent journey through rainforested hills and across rivers, and although I didn't know much about the place I figured I would stay a day, maybe two. It was only when I arrived that I realized I had discovered paradise. I stayed for a month.

Lots of things made Itacare special for me. It had a relaxed atmosphere. The food was great at the little restaurants and stalls along the main street, and amazing at a couple of places in particular, the Garden of Eden and Acai Point, where I bought a pint of acai sorbet and granola each afternoon. The surfing was fantastic and the women were beautiful and bikini clad. I also met a Ruth, a wonderful English girl who was staying at the same guest house, who became my best friend and partner in crime for the next few weeks.

And then there are the beaches. Itacare has five main beaches, four of which are in the Brazilian Top 20. Prainha is in the top two or three. Each has its own sheltered little bay of azure water fringed with palm trees and rainforest covering the cliffs and hills above. Everything is bathed in sunshine and the sound of waves gently barreling onto magical sand. Oh, the sand! I have seen nothing else like it. Made from the purest white sea shells, it has been ground so fine by the ocean that it squeaks as you walk on it.

It was during my stay in Itacare, sunbathing on Tiririca beach, that I experienced one of the favorite moments in my life. Without doubt a Magic Moment. For me, a lot of life is about collecting these; much of the rest is filler. I sat on my sarong on the white sand under the clear blue sky, relaxing after a morning surf session. I was surrounded by several beautiful young bikini-clad girls on the sparsely populated beach and I was already feeling amazing as I sipped the juice from a freshly macheted coconut. As I gazed out across the ocean I noticed what looked like an explosion a few hundred yards offshore. I sat up and now stared intently until I saw another one and discovered its cause. Humpback whales were jumping out of the water, rotating slowly in the air and falling back in; the great splash of their re-entry was the "explosion" I had seen. For the next 15 minutes I watched as whale after whale breached out of the blue water. People fly to Alaska to see this rare sight and I managed to witness it in paradise without lifting a finger. I was so happy that my jaw began to hurt from smiling. Boy oh boy, was life good.

# FIFTY

# It's Better to be Lucky than Good

From Itacare the road turned a little inland, skirting but rarely meeting the ocean. The terrain was hilly but pleasant, and sugar cane fields now separated the few small towns along the way. It was on such terrain I was reacquainted with punctures.

Punctures are a way of life for the long distance cyclist. They happen with infrequent consistency, but despite their ubiquitous nature the feeling of getting one never gets any better; that wobbly loss of control, the demoralizing squish of black rubber between metal and tarmac. Fortunately, with the right choice of equipment they aren't nearly as common as you might think. In 20,675 miles my wheels rotated 153 million times and yet I had only 34 punctures, three of which occurred in a single afternoon after several months without any. No matter, with an extra inner tube everything can be fixed, so a key rule of cycling adventures is thus to have one with you, along with your trusty puncture repair kit.

Armed with inner tubes and a repair kit I zipped down Brazil's central coast. Halfway through one particular day I had seen no signs of civilization for 40 miles and still had another 40 to go, but with the sun shining and the air warm the hard riding felt good. I crested a hill and descended at around 35 mph into a corner, only to find that most of the road was missing. Not good. I jammed on the front brake. With so much weight on the wheel my front tire actually slipped around the rim rather than skidding on the ground, but the effect was unfortunately the same and I was catapulted over the handlebars, rapidly followed by my bicycle and luggage as I was still clipped into the pedals. After everything had stopped I lay there motionless and did an internal mental check to see if I had broken anything important. Everything seemed more or less OK apart from my right arm. A chunk of skin and flesh about the diameter of a golf ball was missing from the outside of my elbow. With my fingers I could lift up part of the skin and see the bone and cartilage of the joint extend up my arm a little way, although most of the cavity was obscured with stones and dirt from the fall. I washed it out as best I could with some squirts of my water bottle, and after dosing it with iodine – boy did *that* sting – I wrapped it with a piece of bandage from my med kit. It was the best I could do with what I had.

I then assessed the damage to the bike. Apart from the front tire, things seemed OK.

"I'll be on my way in a jiffy," I said to myself, and dragged everything to the side of the road. I took out the front inner tube from the wheel to find it had been shredded into ribbons. No matter, after a quick rummage in my bags I found my four spares. I had lost track of how many were in good condition and the answer was none. They were all unusable, which now left me stranded in the middle of nowhere. What to do? I had seen no civilization in the prior 40 miles and I had no way of knowing what lay ahead in the next 40, if anything. The way I saw it I had three options. I could hitch a lift to the next town (cheating), go back to the start (annoying and time consuming) or cross my fingers and push. I chose option three.

I began pushing my crippled bicycle up the next hill, hoping to find salvation sooner rather than later, especially given the state of my arm. At the crest, about 200 yards from where I'd fallen, stood a roughly hewn picket fence surrounding a small wooden shack set back from the road. On a wooden bench by the gate sat an old man, with a weather worn face and a short white beard. He looked at me as I approached, but my attention was focused elsewhere. What caught my eye was the shack. In an inconceivable coincidence its exterior was completely covered with inner tubes! Salvation is *very* quick these days.

I walked up to the man and after showing him my puncture problem he beckoned me through the gate and into building. As my eyes adjusted to a dusty darkness tempered only by the light from the doorway and small bright shafts piercing through the slatted walls, I saw great piles of car tires and tubes on the floor. Many more hung from the walls. We rummaged around and finally, on the back wall near the far left corner, I saw the impossible. A 26 inch, Schrader valve mountain bike inner tube, exactly what I needed. It was old and starting to perish, but it would do the job! Inconceivable! As I've often said, it's much better to be lucky than good. A quick tire change and $2.00 later I was ready to go.

Life is oddly replete with such impossible coincidences. A girl I met travelling told me of a tour of Tibet she'd once been on, the kind where you are driven round for a week in a jeep with three or four other eager tourists. Real once-in-a-lifetime kind of stuff. One of her random jeep companions on this tour was an Irish fellow named Phil. They parted ways at the end of the trip and didn't stay in contact. Next year she decided to go on a jeep safari in Kenya. Same kind of deal, another once-in-a-lifetime trip. The jeep picked her up at her hotel, whereupon she got in and greeted the other passenger. It was Phil.

Time and distance are no barriers to coincidence. On my first trip to Thailand I met some random travelers at Heathrow airport before we even boarded the plane and ended up going to the island of Koh Tao with them. Amongst the group was a pair of English girls traveling together, Carrie and Emma. After a great week on the island we said our goodbyes and I spent the next two months beating a path across the wildest parts of Malaysia and Borneo. Returning back through Malaysia I once again found myself off the beaten path at a tiny guest house in the east of the country. The hostel had two computers in a tiny room, and after spending an hour checking my email I had a few minutes to kill at the end of my pre-paid time. On a whim I sent the girls a message, shamefully the first email I had sent them since leaving Koh Tao so long ago. I hit send, and as I was shutting down the computer I heard a voice behind me.

"Carrie! I just got a message from James!"

I spun around and saw Emma sitting back-to-back with me on the other computer. Inconceivable!

Fate? Destiny? Divine intervention? I choose to believe not. Personally I think impossible coincidences are unavoidable. With a billion combinations of possible events surely the chances are that *something* coincidental happens. Meeting one particular person in some far-flung place is always unlikely, but meeting *any one* of the many people you've met in your life is far, far more probable. Chances are you'll also remember the encounter. So next time you meet that high school friend on a faraway tropical beach, rather than exclaim "Oh my God, it's you!", instead ask what took them so long!

# FIFTY ONE

# Masked Men and Mangroves

Armed with a new tire I was flying, metaphorically speaking. The map I had of this part of the country was poor but I figured that the apparent break in the road ahead was an error. I arrived one afternoon at the town of Canavieiras at the edge of a river and discovered that the map was in fact correct. Beyond the river I could see the ocean and the mangrove forests on the distant bank, no road in sight. As I was not relishing a complex 300 mile detour I checked into a small hotel for the night and asked the woman at the reception desk about a boat to the next town.

"I don't think so," was her answer. Not encouraging. "But ask at the dock." With this glimmer of hope I wandered down to the small dock and started asking random people. It was times like this that I was extremely pleased that I had made the effort to learn Portuguese.

"Not tomorrow but maybe the day after tomorrow. Maybe. Come back and see," was the best response I could get. I returned the next morning to find a grumpy old man preparing a tiny beaten up boat with a thin aluminum skin and small outboard on the back. I asked about passage to the road on the other side, a journey he seemed exceptionally reluctant to undertake. He really couldn't be bothered to take me, but after an hour of arguing I eventually pestered him into submission and we set a price for me plus the bicycle. He then decided that departure time was in 30 minutes, so a mad scramble ensured as I rushed back to the hotel to pack and check out. Returning in the nick of time I threw my bicycle into the boat and we set off towards the mangroves. Impossibly narrow channels only a few yards across bisected the forest as the canopy closed around us, and for several hours we navigated the mangrove swamp as though we were in one of those adventure documentaries. Finally the channels opened up a little and we emerged into a small lagoon created by a barrier spit, behind which I could see the breaking ocean waves. On the opposite shore of the lagoon was a nearly deserted concrete dock, and this was our destination, the tiny village of Belmonte. It was a ramshackle place without so much as a drink stand. I could see why the boat didn't go all that often. In any case, the road now resumed its course south so I was happy.

For 50 miles I rode the arrow straight rode into the increasing presence of civilization, beginning with sparsely separated military outposts and ending with luxury beachside apartments. At a river crossing I reached Porto Seguro, a famous resort town, but merely passed through and took the picturesque ferry a short distance across the river. Here was another town called Arrial de Ajuda. Smaller and quainter than Porto Seguro, I liked it immediately. I checked into the local Hosteling International hostel for want of a better option, but quickly discovered this was a fortuitous lack of planning. The best HI hostel in the world? Quite possibly. It was beautifully appointed with a tropical open air courtyard integrated expertly into the building. It had palm trees, water features and a fantastic staff. What more could you want? The owners were also so impressed with my trip that they let me stay for free!

After a few relaxing days I decided take the recommendation of the hostel owners for the next leg of the journey - a 20 mile walk along the beach to the village of Trancoso. Carrying an 80lb bicycle across the numerous streams that flowed to the beach and into the ocean was a minor inconvenience; in comparison to my two day journey in Lencois Maranhenses this was a baby. The trip was a great idea and suitably spectacular, full of deserted beaches and crashing blue waves, and after 20 miles it was a vision of splendor to see the small white church of Trancoso perched atop the cliffs in its grassy plaza.

Here I remounted the bicycle and for the next several weeks rode through the Brazilian states of Vitoria and Espirito Santo. The environment became slowly more developed and industrial, and the ethnicity of the local people also changed from the African ancestry of the north to the European heritage of the south. Not as gradually as you might think, either. In the small town of Linhares the local's ethnicity seemed to flip flop, with European influence appearing and African declining as though a switch had been flicked; a switch that remained on that one setting for the next 5,000 miles until my encounters with the tribes of Southern Chile.

I was now within 70 miles of Rio de Janeiro. Stopping for the night at the coastal town of Saquarema, an unremarkable place backed by the vertiginous coastal mountains and surrounded by rolling fields of sugar cane, I sat atop the cliffs and watched the locals surf the beautifully pealing waves that broke on the glassy ocean beneath. My time there was placid and without incident, but not all of my acquaintances had been so fortunate. Fate is a fickle and cruel master, and Geert's tale is a tale of Brazil's dark side. It is a country of extremes, as I'm sure readers have discerned by now, and crime in Brazil is no exception. Either nothing bad at all happens, or something very bad happens. I was very fortunate in Brazil, almost to a fault. I'd leave my bicycle in the street outside a cafe with all the pannier bags still attached, unlocked and unguarded for an hour at a time, and yet not once, not once, in over six months was a single thing stolen, let alone the whole bike. On top of this I often rode or walked through slums or rough parts of town and nothing bad ever happened. Geert was not so lucky.

I met him in Itacare at the small guest house where we were both staying, and we would see each other almost every day for breakfast in the small building surrounded by palm trees in the courtyard. He would then either go surfing or to work, as he was being paid to be there by O'Neil, one of the world's largest surfing brands. He was a muscular, good looking guy from Holland, and exuded the relaxed easy-going confidence of the Dutch. After a few weeks he left Itacare and blazed a trail ahead of me with his surfboard. I lost contact with him after that, until I met another

Dutchman in Rio many weeks later who happened to be telling his story.

Stopping in Saquarema, Geert had seen the same beautiful waves as I had and spent several days surfing them along with our Dutch storyteller. Together they had met a couple of local guys on the waves, but from what I could tell from the story it was mellow out there, with little animosity or trouble to report. After a few days in town, however, Geert was woken up in the middle of the night by a strange sensation. It was the cold metallic taste of a gun barrel in his mouth. In the darkness of his room stood three or four masked men who proceeded to steal everything he owned while he lay there helpless, leaving him with nothing, not even his passport. By the time I'd heard this story Geert was already back in Holland after understandably getting the hell out of Brazil as fast as he could. It is a harrowing story and I am ecstatic that things worked out OK for him in the end. In a country where life is cheap, it could have been so much worse.

As yet unaware of this incident I had an uneventful afternoon in Saquarema, and next morning was motivated to leave for a different reason. I'd ridden for many thousands of miles to get to this point and now the fabled city of Rio de Janeiro was within my reach. I rode that last day to the city like a man with a plan, arriving early that afternoon in Niteroi, an industrial city which lies across the bay from Rio. With some difficulty I found the port and boarded the ferry to Rio itself, a magnificent way to enter this iconic city, with Sugarloaf mountain silhouetted beyond the blue water and the statue of Christ the Redeemer floating high above all. As I stood at the bow of the boat the enormity of my journey came into focus. I'd cycled to Rio de Janeiro from the damn Arctic! Feelings that I had suppressed as a survival mechanism for so long now welled up in a flood and burst briefly yet powerfully forward. I felt a wild joy at my triumph and a deep pride for the obstacles I'd overcome. And yet these emotions were tinged with despair. I felt the horror of how far was still to go and a fear of the foreboding unknown that I was yet to encounter. At the front of that boat, with the wind whipping my hair and peppered with the fine spray from the bow I felt tears on my cheeks. They were both tears of joy and sadness, a fitting tribute perhaps as I travelled through one of the most iconic views on Earth.

I arrived at the terminal in the business district and after disembarking I headed towards Copacabana beach a few miles away. It was during this ride that I quickly learned the number one rule of riding a bicycle in Rio. It is 'Don't'. Rule number two is under *no circumstances* ride through the tunnel which connects the business district with the beach. It is suicidal, and that is no exaggeration. With no shoulder or even lane lines on the road, the tunnel is 150 yards of dark thundering chaos. It was like riding to the Promised Land through the very fires of Hades itself, 150 yards of torment to reach glory. I rode in a manic burst of desperation as my adrenaline surged, desperate to get through without being hit by the buses and other traffic which tore along the road beside me. My heart was exploding through the red line as I reached the tunnel exit, and that moment of reaching the sun and the glorious views of the beach and ocean a few yards ahead was an explosive release. I had made it to Copacabana beach! And what a place it was!

The city beaches of Rio are special. I expected to see unkempt grey sand with bits of rubbish and cigarette butts scattered on the surface, but the reality was far different. Instead, there are wide areas of clean golden sand leading down to the gently crashing surf of the azure blue water. Copacabana, Ipanema and Leblon are worthy of most resort getaways, let alone to be found in a major metropolis. The same can be said for the mountains that are the skeleton of the city. These are not mere hills but towering peaks. On one of the highest stands the famous statue of Christ the Redeemer. When you see it for the first time you realize that is not the statue, *per se,* which makes it so special, but rather its ethereal effect as it hovers high above the city like Rio's guardian spirit. On the far side of the city, meeting the statue's gaze, stands another guardian, the vertical peak of Sugarloaf mountain at the entrance to the bay. From its summit at sunset, the elements of the city come spectacularly alive as you look down from this improbable natural tower at the million twinkling lights below. Reds and oranges of the burning sky and a deepening blue of the ocean spread across the landscape as dark shapes of the silhouetted mountains line the horizon. Christ the Redeemer floats above all, illuminated, a supernatural spirit. In that moment, Rio is the most beautiful city on Earth.

# FIFTY TWO

# The Wealth of Nations

Fabled place of beauty and tropical mystique, yet also of darkness and fear. Slums and shanty towns, called favelas, house a million people here. They are bastions of lawlessness and poverty which envelope the hills of the city and cast their ominous shadow across it. Their reputation is fearsome, the warnings stark, but I wanted to see and experience them for myself. And as luck would have it, I had more than one chance to do so.

Favela tours have grown in popularity in Rio. Sadly though, it seems that most of these tours are rarely for the benefit of either the locals or even the tourists. I heard of one expensive hotel's tour where guests are taken around the largest favela in Rio in an armored car. This struck me as preposterous. How can one understand the humanity and circumstance of the people who live there by visiting in some kind of human safari, protected from the 'animals' outside. Luckily not all tours are like this, and one in particular offered a very, very different proposition.

We were to visit Rocinha, the largest favela in Rio, which rises from the base of a mountain to cover every inch of the slopes up to the ridge at the very top. Early one morning a few of us were picked up in a nice SUV at the hostel and driven by the guide to the favela's entrance. One oddity of these favelas is that they are often self-contained, and in this case a main highway running past the bottom of the favela acted as an invisible and impermeable barrier. From the main highway a single paved road turned into the favela and wound up the mountainside. We parked opposite the turning, and to my surprise the guide walked us across the road towards a large group of young guys sitting on motorbikes. After a quick negotiation and a flurry of bank notes he turned back to us.

"Right, we're going to the top!" he said with a big grin, "Pick a bike and climb on!"

We each climbed onto a pillion seat of these motorbike taxis and shot off at ludicrous speed up the road. It was a chaotic ever-changing maze of traffic and people that was both exhilarating and nerve-wracking. We ducked and dived, James Bond style, through closing gaps between vehicles, wove around pedestrians and overtook around steep - and blind - hairpin corners. I loved every terrifying second. Miraculously we all reached the top in one piece and stood admiring the view over the rest of the city as our drivers careened recklessly back down the hill to collect their next victims.

The top of Rocinha is remarkable, not only for the view but also for the sense you get of one of Brazil's key problems, the great inequality between the Haves and Have Nots. The poverty of the favela pours down the hillside to its boundary at the main road, beyond which are situated the beautiful lush greens and landscaped fairways of an opulent golf course. If you live in Rocinha you see that view every day; every day you are confronted with privilege and wealth so close you can almost touch it. That can't help but foster a heightened sense of lack, a heightened sense of resentment, a heighted desire for power and money, perhaps. In the favela that means gangs, drugs and weapons.

"Do exactly what I tell you to, exactly when I tell you," our guide commanded before we began. Initially it did feel quite scary, all the stories of drug dealers and violence playing on my mind. What we saw though was for the most part quite different, just people going about their everyday business. Children happily playing in the alleyways, people selling things in ramshackle stores, women hanging out laundry on makeshift washing lines between the roofs. You have the realization that 98% of people here are just trying to make the best out of the cards they were dealt in life. It's the other 2% that cause most of the trouble.

Over the next several hours we walked down through Rocinha on our way back to the car. It was fascinating. Spider webs of wires leading away from each power line showed why no-one pays for electricity here. Everyone steals it, as apparently you can pay a guy to illegally connect you up for a one-time fee. Stores and bars poke out into the complex sprawl of alleyways and staircases. We stopped for a beer in one and I had a chat with the friendly owner. He was a great guy, and coincidentally it was the cheapest beer I bought during my entire time in Brazil.

Slowly we started to loosen up and relax. Relax, that is, until our guide rounded a corner in the alleyway just before the exit to the favela and suddenly stopped, commanding us to do the same. Adrenaline surged. What was happening? I crept up to the corner and peered around like a sniper. 20 yards down the alleyway sat a small group of young men, guns hanging loosely from the hands of several of them. The younger ones, only 13 or 14 years old, had fireworks in small backpacks. They were fortunately looking away from us towards the other end of the alley, where I could make out a couple of cars with lights flashing and several men looking back up the alley towards us. It was the police. We had walked into an armed stand-off. The young men were part of Amigos dos Amigos, the gang that ran this particular favela at the time, and the fireworks were to warn the gang leaders of a police raid. Our guide quickly and quietly barked some orders to us and we followed him back along the alley and took a different route to finally exit the favela a hundred yards or so away from the original path. Having a proper guide who knew the streets was worth its weight in gold right then. Along the road we could see perhaps 10 policemen wearing bullet proof vests and holding machine guns. This was serious stuff, so as we jumped into our parked car and drove away our guide tuned his radio into the police band. You have to love Brazil. To my surprise we could hear a radio conversation between the gang and the police.

"It's normal," explained the guide. "Both sides trash talk, mostly about what cops will do when they catch the gang and what the gang will do to the police if they try. It's kind of funny." Funny would not be my description, but listening to the conversation was strange indeed, a surreal insight into a game that was both real and deadly. A few days later I read that four policemen were killed in a raid in Rosinha. No game indeed.

# FIFTY THREE

# The City of God

Night time in the favelas is to enter another world, and no less so than in the most famous of all of Rio's slums, the Cidade de Deus. The City of God. I'd found out about an organized visit to a nightclub there, and as it was chaperoned by the same people who'd done the favela tour I knew this was going to be interesting.

"I don't care if you meet the man or woman of your dreams," explained our chaperone as we hurtled through the hot night in our minibus towards the club. "You *are*, absolutely, 100%, definitely, coming back to the hostel with us on this bus," he commanded, and he wasn't joking. "We will see you again at 3.30am, so try to stick together. And be here!"

Given where we were going our group decided to actually heed the warning. At around 11.00pm we pulled up in front of a huge warehouse-like building a short distance inside the favela. A crowd, dressed up and drinking, thronged in the lights outside. They were most definitely looking for a party. Muted bass beats from the club washed over everything as the backdrop to the laughter and shouts. Amongst the masses we could make out a line of people backed up against the concrete wall leading to a non-descript entrance at one corner of the building. Instead of joining it our chaperone walked up to the front and had words with the bouncer, a huge man wearing a bullet proof vest. With our chaperone remaining outside the eight of us were soon granted passage through the double doors and frisked by men with guns and bullet proof vests, before being escorted through another set of black double doors to the interior of the building. Music burst out as they opened and I felt fantastically alive as I walked towards the flashing lights. Great anticipation mixed with the alertness of slight trepidation. What a sight greeted me.

A stage on the far side of the space was raised as in a theatre, on which stood the DJ and his decks isolated in the center. Great banks of speakers stood at either side. The far left wall was taken up by the bar, and the dance floor in front filled half the club. Lights and lasers flashed through the hazy darkness to end their brief travels on the black interior walls. To my immediate left stretched a wide walkway, along which stood a line of young men partially concealed in the shadows. And what men. They were without doubt the scariest group of people I have ever seen in one place; dark skin contrasting against the sparkle of crazy, coked-up white eyes. Partially unbuttoned shirts and tank tops revealed thick gold chains and medallions hanging across bare chests, while ubiquitous tattoos complemented the occasional broken front tooth. This was the local drug dealer elite, a group not to be trifled with, so we kept a wide berth as we walked to the bar. The long Formica counter top was manned by a large number of extremely pretty female bar tenders who were busy exchanging blue tokens for cans of beer, which they retrieved from a line of freezer chests behind them. That was it. Not only were there no spirits or mixers, but also no glasses or even plastic cups. Just cans of beer. The first problem was figuring out the blue tokens. Adjacent to the bar we could see three short lines of people queuing in front of three six inch square holes in the concrete wall. I took a spot in the line and at my turn I peered through the hole to see a young woman staring up at me from her desk in a small office. Apparently the concrete is needed to reduce incidents of armed robbery, which was not encouraging.

"How many?!" came her urgent question.

"Six please," I replied, and passed some notes through the small hole which were rapidly exchanged for tokens. We were in business.

The night that followed was one of the best of my life. We were soon a couple of beers in and the club was packed, the dance music pumping and the crowd happy. I was amazed at how welcoming people were towards us, these strange tourist interlopers in their midst. As always in Brazil, even in the clubs as I now discovered, it was important to dance in line-dancing synchronization with the crowd to avoid disapproving looks. Luckily a group of lovely young girls took pity on us and endeavored to teach us the latest moves. Being where we were I first made sure they weren't girlfriends of the guys we'd seen earlier, you know, just to avoid a potential diplomatic incident. They weren't, thankfully for us and probably for the girls also. Everyone danced amongst the many discarded beer cans that eventually lay scattered across the dance floor; weird but manageable. At the end of the night, with all eight of us accounted for and still mostly standing we said our goodbyes and met our chaperone outside. Tired and happy, we were soon hurtling back home through the dark as our bus chased the oncoming light of a new day. After we reached the hostel, myself and Nathalie, a beautiful French girl from Reunion Island, inadvisably walked down to Copacabana beach as the dawn began to break. Another big no-no in Rio. We sat at the water's edge on the cool sand as we watched the sun rise over the ocean. It was a lovely end to a perfect night.

# FIFTY FOUR

# Paradise Lost

Later that morning I took a bus to the statue of Christ, high on Corcovado Mountain. From the bus stop I ascended to the platform below the statue, where the marvel of this iconic sculpture becomes apparent. Standing beneath such a recognizable symbol really cemented my sense of being in Rio, the same feeling which I experienced on the boat ride across the bay. To complete the picture I had brought Tolly along for this excursion, as he had been hiding from bandits for some time and needed the air. With paws outstretched and legs dangling, he mirrored the statue perfectly and became the Savior of all bears and the patron soft toy of Rio. I stood on the terrace and looked down at the strips of golden sand far below, Tolly sitting on my shoulder for company, and once again admired the city. It was a wonderful moment.

After the excursion I needed some more beach time. As well as being beautiful and picturesque, Copacabana and Ipanema are fascinating because of the people. I hung out on Copacabana and it became a sport to watch unsuspecting tourists wade into the water without knowing that the waves broke with surprisingly force right at the shoreline.

'Crash!' Another pale tourist would get completely taken out by a wave and scurry back onto the beach like a drowned rat. A few minutes after they had gone another unsuspecting tourist would try, creating endless hours of depraved amusement. The locals offered equally bizarre and hilarious entertainment. On Ipanema beach, for some reason the 'Post 9' lifeguard station has become *the* place to see and be seen in the Rio beach scene. While hanging out there I once saw a young guy strutting past the sunbathing crowd. In fairness, he was physically very impressive; bronzed, muscular and exceptionally ripped. However, he then ruined it all by wearing the smallest red speedos available without a license, the ubiquitous habit of the Brazilian male. On his walk he passed three very pretty young women who were sunbathing on the sand a few yards away from me and stopped in front of them. They rolled over to face him. Without warning, not even a "hello", he proceeded to flex his muscles into bodybuilder poses! It was so funny I almost wet myself. After several different positions he stopped and waited for their response, which was to merely roll back over and continue their sunbathing. Rejected! This, of course, made no difference to our friend, who simply continued his strut along the sand. Only in Rio.

That week was a special time for me. From the favelas to the beach, the statue of Christ, partying in the club or at the weekly Lapa street festival, Rio de Janeiro had surpassed the expectations I had tried so hard not to ascribe to the city before my arrival. It was with a heavy heart that I rode away, the only placation being that my next stop was perhaps to be equally special. In stark contrast to the city, the ride was surprisingly bland, ugly even, as the mountains gave way to miles of flat and humid coastal plain and a road lined with continuous semi-industrialized urbanization. After 70 miles the mountains blessedly swung back to the coast and at nightfall I arrived in the port town of Angra Dos Reis. Nathalie was waiting for me as she had taken the bus during the day, and I have rarely been happier to see someone after a ride. We had dinner at a restaurant by the small harbor and spent the night at a nearby hotel before boarding a ferry early the next morning to the island of Ilha Grande, located 10 or so miles off the coast.

It was a fun journey. On the boat we met two young Norwegian lads, a genuine rarity in this part of the world. While sitting in front of us they began to make light-hearted fun in Norwegian of a nearby elderly couple. It was their secret language that no one understood so they were quite obvious about it. Unfortunately, after 10 minutes the elderly couple began talking to each other, also in Norwegian. Oops. Small world.

We arrived on the island at the small harbor village of Vila do Abraao. The ferry maneuvered to dock between beautiful white sail boats in a sandy cove of luscious blue water. We walked for five minutes through the village and then back onto the beach to reach the eastern point of the cove and one of the greatest hostels in the world. 'Aquarius' means aquarium in Portuguese, and this place had that name for good reason. As well as the spectacular views across the cove and the coast, the hostel has created an artificial enclosure the size of a small swimming pool that flooded at each tide. Sea creatures found their way into the sandy aquarium but not as quickly out, creating a tropical fish tank full of strange and wonderful animals. Corals, parrot fish, urchins, even a rare bat fish. Looking back across the water to the jagged blue coastal mountains in the distance, you listened to the sound of wavelets lapping against the low sea wall by your deck chair, the picturesque harbor in front and the rainforest covered hills behind. Paradise is really quite something. Add to this the inexpensive and well-kept rooms, the family owners who were friendly and fun, the scuba diving trips and the famous Lopez Mendez beach on the island, and this place might be the world's best holiday destination.

Lopez Mendez, a beach on the far side of the island of Ilha Grande, has been consistently voted one of the top five beaches in the world. It can be reached only along a rough mountain trail from the main village, so intrepid beach lovers must walk for two hours over the hills and through rainforest to experience its glory. It is well worth the effort, as ultra-clear waters lap onto a half mile crescent of the purest white sand fringed with palm trees, devoid of humanity. Indeed when I arrived it was completely deserted, my own private utopia. I took in as much of the rest and relaxation as I could, as not only was the next stretch long but I also had to leave Nathalie, one of the harder things I have had to do. We knew not whether out paths would cross again and I will look back on those days now as a paradise lost.

FIFTY FIVE

# Crossing the Rubicon

Once back on the mainland I rode through Santos, an industrial city-port that connects Sao Paolo with the coast, and then into the mountains of Curitiba. I descended from the mountain tops through the dense sub-tropical cloud forest along one of the world's greatest mountain roads to the town of Paranagua. Famed for a scenic railway that makes the journey up the same mountain, those phantom clouds made my descent feel like a journey through a secret world. Emerging from the clouds I arrived at the town through an overcast drizzle. In a land with vibrancy in every plaza this was a town of eerie silence, as though its soul had been washed away by the rain. There was nothing for me here.

As I headed ever further away from the equator the frequency of stunning beaches seemed to decline, but I had one last beach to visit on the island of Santa Catarina. Florianopolis is known in Brazil and Argentina as a vacation spot for the island's numerous bays and golden beaches, and they mostly lived up to expectations. The hostel I stayed in was a gem, perched precariously on a cliff above a river at one end of a 10 mile long beach. It sported fantastic views of the ocean as well as offering free surfboard rental and free breakfast (pancakes!) until 2.00pm. This meant I could get up early, get made-to-order pancakes, go surfing and then return for a second breakfast before the cut-off time. With a second breakfast it was like being a hobbit. The arrival of two wonderful and beautiful Dutch girls, Leonie and Lidwien, then helped make this place one of my favorites. Of all the people I met on my trip they were two of the most special and certainly two of the most fun. Full of life, energy, enthusiasm and beauty, but yet humble, giving and carefree, I liked them both immensely. It sounds strange, but they showed me that at some level there was more enthusiasm and vitality inside me that remained untapped. Perhaps it was their carefree attitudes, almost like innocence, which gave me creative license, or perhaps it was the boost of confidence I felt from their acceptance. Either way, for those few days I felt energized. I was ready to tackle anything.

It was lucky I felt ready to tackle anything because when I left the island I was nearly arrested for illegally riding my bicycle across the long causeway bridge. It took a lot of talking to get out of, but for the second time on my trip I had a police escort across a bridge, again with sirens and everything. I had to promise I'd never do it again, which I thought was a pretty light punishment! Obviously I have zero reason to do it again.

From there, the next city on my route was Porto Alegre, famed for its beautiful women. They must all have been on vacation when I arrived because I didn't see a single one. Leaving in sadness I made the three day dash to the border. And then suddenly, there it was.

A short bridge crossed a shallow river, one side Brazil, the other Uruguay. I looked at my cycle computer. It had been 5,170 miles since the Venezuelan border and now, in only a few more yards, my Brazilian adventure would be over. I looked around for the border control and to my dismay I couldn't find it. But I wanted, *needed*, my passport stamped!

As with Panama, getting this stamp wasn't so easy. After much trial and error I found the border control office hidden two miles from the bridge in the middle of some non-descript residential area. The officials were somewhat surprised to see me and it took a bit of convincing before they gave me a stamp. However, as they conveniently ignored my three day visa overstay I decided I did fine out of the entire episode, although there is nothing like walking into a border office wearing bicycle shorts to help convince someone to forgive a visa overstay. Very soon I was back on the bridge and this time really was it. In a few seconds my travels in Brazil would be over.

I felt sadness and yet also relief. It had been a wonderful, fun, terrifying, awful, magical, dangerous, hedonistic, formative and irreplaceable six months. I felt as though I had seen and experienced the entire spectrum of world in those months. It was a country which had more than surpassed my expectations. Indeed, it had been a full Technicolor display and I knew I would soon be missing the vibrancy and extremism of all that was on offer. I also knew, though, that this vibrancy had taken its toll. Frankly, I was worn out. I needed a change and was ready for a little more sanity. Somewhere a bit easier, perhaps. My time in Brazil had come to an end at the right moment and I looked forward to the next chapter of my adventure. It was with that upbeat thought in mind that I clipped into the pedals for the last time in Brazil and rolled gently into Uruguay.

# Thirty Three

The differences between Brazil and Uruguay were stark and immediately apparent. The language change threw me completely. The grating harsh accent I heard was confusing until I remembered that I was hearing Spanish rather than the mellifluous flowing Brazilian Portuguese to which I had become accustomed. My Spanish had evaporated, replaced by Portuguese, so once again I could hardly speak to anyone. That was an unexpected shock.

It is perhaps strange to say, but in the damp drizzle of those few days in northern Uruguay I felt like I was cycling through rural Holland. Fields lay uniformly spaced out across a flat landscape; neat areas delineated with hedges and small groves of deciduous trees. The occasional wooden farmhouse punctuated the vista to complete this strange illusion. Towns were few, sparsely scatted along the minimal roads which crossed the north of the country, and it took two days of riding before I arrived at the first real town, a place curiously called Treinta y Tres. The name literally translates into English as "Thirty Three". I remember nothing about it apart from the name and the hunger I suffered there after arriving to find that every single restaurant appeared to be closed. A difficult end to a full day's ride. From Treinta y Tres the rural landscape began to urbanize as tendrils of industrialization reached up from the south, and after only three days I'd ridden across the entire country.

Arriving in the capital city Montevideo was like arriving in a northern European city. Maybe it was the style of the architecture or the layout of the tree-lined streets. Or maybe it was the lack of a tropical feel as with the cities in Brazil, conspicuous in its absence after my time in warmer climes. The faint smell of Montevideo's pollution didn't have that overheated equatorial tang, but rather the acidic damp smell of a wet autumn day in London. The city had neither the frenetic atmosphere of Rio nor the relaxation of the continent's far north, but rather it exuded a tangible decay of past glories, like an old woman clinging to the trinkets and traditions of her youth while the world moves on without her. Diminished and decaying and yet still proud and unbending. The architecture is slowly crumbling, the paint peeling and the buildings grey. The tree-lined pavements are cracked and the parks a little overgrown. It all felt a bit bland. For want of a better word, it felt harmless.

With all that said, however, Montevideo does have one very redeeming feature. At a wharf on the banks of the Rio de la Plate stands a large building that was once the city's main market. Built in 1885 the Mercado del Puerto, the Port Market, is nothing like anything I have seen before or since. Hundreds of small eateries stand packed closely together and many of them specialize in serving huge steaks and affiliated chunks of animal. Enormous open fires burn at the back of each stand, the large grills tended by grisly sweating men who slowly roast slabs of beef, mutton, or perhaps a whole goat. The air is thick and hazy with the smoke and smell of a hundred barbecues. A thousand voices resonate as people from all walks of life mingle and enjoy the bounty on offer, whether dock workers, businessmen, musicians or sometimes even the President of Uruguay himself. I walked around for a while, absorbing both the atmosphere and a good amount of smoke, before settling on a stool between some other customers at a random stall. It was time for a steak. My server, sweating gently in his dirty apron, skewered a great hunk of beef from the grill and carved an enormous slice onto my plate. Nothing else, no side dish, no bread. Nothing to disturb from the pure carnivorous pleasure of the meal. I ate like a glutton in Dante's Inferno. It was succulent, tender and glorious.

After a couple of days relaxing, exploring and eating it was time to leave Uruguay for its big brother, Argentina. To avoid a 500 mile detour around the river I hopped onto a high-speed ferry and zoomed up the vast Rio del la Plate to Buenos Aires. Once again I had checked by GPS to confirm I wasn't cheating. Straight off the boat I could feel the difference between Buenos Aires and Montevideo. Buenos Aires felt like the rich twin. Whereas Montevideo looked like a great European city from a past era, Buenos Aires felt more modern, more vibrant. Indeed, until the early 1900s Argentina had been one of the richest countries in the world, its wealth and sophistication giving rise to its nickname as the "Paris of the south". As I walked the streets of the city I saw that in many ways the name was well founded.

Argentina at that time, however, was far from rosy. Two years prior to my arrival the country suffered an economic crisis and defaulted on its debts, causing a collapse in its currency. While the tragic economic consequences for ordinary Argentinians have been well documented, a byproduct of the crash was a quite unique backpacking experience. It was first world quality on a shoestring budget. The shackles were off and did I make the most of it. On nights out - which was almost every night - I would begin each evening by drinking a bottle of champagne with my friends in the hostel because it was a mere $4.00 a bottle. And when I say drinking a bottle, I mean a bottle each. After six months of drinking beer each night in Brazilian town plazas to accompany my people watching I had driven my alcohol tolerance sky high and it now took me at least three bottles of wine to get nicely tipsy. After the champagne the usual plan was to get a steak dinner and some good Argentinian wine, of which there was no shortage of either, and then head to a bar. The good times were rolling.

There were many similarities between Argentina and southern Brazil, but also many small differences. One of them was the fashion sense in Argentina, or perhaps a lack of one. Now, I would never usually pass judgment on this issue, but frankly some of their trends were so weird that I'm going to anyway. My favorite fashion faux pas was the inexplicable 'rat tail' haircut. Seen primarily in Buenos Aires and the surrounding towns, the fashion was for young guys to buzz-cut their heads apart from a single small patch, and then grow a long strand out of that one area. The strand was then braided, sometimes with a little colored thread, to create a tail which was often past shoulder length. It looked terrible. It also seemed in no way necessary to have this tail emerge from the back of your head or an otherwise logical place. I saw them sprout from the top, from the fringe, or my own special favorite, from just one side. It felt as though I'd been transported back to a 1980s East German fashion show, which is saying a lot.

Even worse, this hair style - and I use the word "style" in the loosest possible sense - seemed the height of cool in these parts and no self-respecting macho hard man was without one. Machismo, that destructive man-culture of South America, had in this case taken a drunken step off the path of the reasonable and fallen into the ravine of the ridiculous. I remember stopping in a nice colonial town named Mercedes, about 70 miles outside Buenos Aires, and settled down for a drink at a cafe on the edge of the large and ornately landscaped town square. It was the kind of square with a park area in the middle and cafes lining the road which encircles it. The evening was young and the sky still glowed, the air was warm and the atmosphere was bustling. The local gang of young lads was out cruising, creating a scene reminiscent of 1950s America as they rode their scooters endlessly around the perimeter of the plaza while trying far too hard to look cool. When I say scooters, however, I mean tiny high pitched 50cc scooters with crap modified exhausts and bad paint jobs. Ridden by guys with equally crap rat tails it was about as non-macho as I could conceive. My favorite moment was seeing one particular guy who had, for reasons known only to himself, left the wire shopping basket attached to the front of his beige scooter. It looked like an old woman's shopping bike. I laughed so hard I knocked my beer off the table.

I left the rat tails and embarrassing scooters behind – thankfully - and cycled beyond the pastoral lands into the vast deserts of central Argentina. Ahead stretched the desolation of Highway 35, the so called "Highway of the Conquistadors", where inhospitable desert scrubland extended unbroken by hill or mountain to the endless horizon. There are few such bleak and featureless roads on Earth, especially for such a distance. It was so monotonous and unending that I remember passing a sign warning of an upcoming bend in the road.

"Warning! Bend Ahead!" it cried, yet beyond me the road continued straight, disappearing into the distant shimmer. Two miles later, another sign.

"Warning! Bend 500m!"

What bend requires two miles of preparation, I thought. It must be treacherous indeed! 500m later I passed the next sign.

"Warning! Bend! Turn Left!" and I did. A turn of perhaps 25 degrees swept gradually and almost imperceptibly to the left, a turn so shallow it was difficult to even notice at my slow speeds. When I later asked an Argentinian truck driver at a roadside cafe about it, he knew exactly of the one I spoke of, as there are so few on this road. Apparently a lot of accidents happen there as people trance out to the endless straight road and miss the curve. I didn't doubt him one bit.

I spent Christmas day riding 102 miles on that endless road before sleeping inside a half-constructed gas station. Luckily there was a small restaurant annex and the owners were very kind and welcoming, taking me in and preparing for me a Christmas dinner. Drinking a well-earned Christmas beer with these good people as we watched some terrible Argentinian Christmas game show on TV was deeply satisfying, and I settled down in my sleeping bag between those half constructed walls happy and contented. It had also been nice to talk to people; in the conversation I had spoken my first words in six days. But I still missed my family.

The next day was a good one, with a shining sun and only a moderately difficult cross wind. That day I rode further than I had ever done before, 128.5 miles on a 16 hour ride, which wasn't too bad considering the 80lb bike and the wind. The next day, however, began terribly as I watched images from the Asian 2004 tsunami on the news in a cafe. It was strange to get such a horrific reminder that the rest of the world was still out there.

The foothills of the Andes were getting closer and the main road turned towards the south to avoid them. As I was heading to the mountains my route became more difficult and complex to navigate, but nevertheless after two more days I crested a hill on a deserted road and there they were. For the first time on this journey I looked at the mountains of the Andes, crystal clear as they pierced the bright blue sky in all their snow-capped glory. I stopped at that crest and stared at them, so happy to be there that my eyes welled with tears. They were the final link of my journey, the beginning of the end. I could look at them rise above the bare and brown foothills and finally visualize the path to the finish; take a left at the snow and keep going until you run out of land. It was like the home stretch of a marathon as you round a bend to finally see the finishing line in sight. It is only at that point, right then and there, that you know you are going to make it for sure. Feelings of relief, pride and happiness well up inside at that moment; also a renewed determination to finish strong. Your mission changes from a multi-staged, broken-down group of theoretical milestones into a single goal, a single point of focus to which you can divert all your will. On that crest in the warm sun I felt as though I had only one more task left to complete, and for the first time in 18 months I *believed* I could actually make it.

What joy that first Andean ride! A brand new and sparsely traveled dirt road cut through the mountains as it wound around the sheer snow-capped peaks and through deep valleys. It was invigorating. I was on a secret quest along an untrodden path to destiny, and yet the prior sense of desolation was gone. Hidden in the folds of those mountains at the edge of a deep blue glacial lake I thus came to San Martin de Los Andes, a picturesque town that was an oasis after my exile in the desert. I spent a couple of days there, soaking up the slightly touristy but peaceful tranquility which I deserved.

While in San Martin I had dinner with a wonderful elderly Argentinian couple I'd met earlier on the mountain road. The meal was a very pleasurable and informative experience as we discussed the state of the Argentinian economy amongst other things. I guess sometimes, rarely, it is beneficial to have been a banker. After we talked I learned not only why everything was (relatively) so cheap for me, but also why this advantage was inversely proportional to the suffering of the Argentinian population. Many of them had seen a great collapse in their wealth and savings, making even the necessities expensive. I felt as though I was taking advantage of the situation and I have never been so willing and happy to pay for dinner as I did that evening.

From San Martin it was 100 miles to San Carlos de Bariloche, the main town in the region. The ride took me along the edge of the vast Nahuel Huapi lake, its blue waters framed by snowy mountains on all sides. I passed a small peninsular which extended into the lake, a very special place which is covered in Arrayen trees. Twisted and gnarled, with their light brown bark and citrus fragrance they create the appearance of a forest made of giant cinnamon sticks. Like the giant redwood groves in California they have a fairytale look but are even more unique, for these trees grow almost nowhere else on the entire planet. Just that little peninsular and one or two other isolated small groves in the nearby mountains. It was on the lake shore by this Disney-esque forest that I met Elke.

Elke is a wonderful person. A lawyer based in Buenos Aires, she was as sweet and beautiful as she was smart, her Germanic heritage evident in her blonde hair and blue eyes. Just like me! She was there visiting family and her young nephew, so we chatted on the shores of the lake as the little lad ran around and generally amused himself. After a few hours it was time for me to continue on and for Elke to return back to her hotel, but as luck would have it her next destination was also Bariloche. We agreed to meet at the hostel, and I said my fond farewells with a smile on my face and my fingers crossed.

# FIFTY SEVEN

# Steak and Rat

Amazingly and fortuitously, the biggest (and the best) hostel in Bariloche occupied most of the top floor of the tallest building in town. As such, the spacious communal room and balcony had an incredible view looking west across the lake to the mountains. It was quite a sight to go with your morning coffee. Watching the sun setting in the evening behind the snowy peaks from that uninterrupted vantage point with a cold beer in hand will always remain a favorite. As promised, Elke arrived the next day and it was great to share these vivid memories with her. With those two things I had more than I could ask for, but as it turned out, Bariloche had a final surprise.

"You have to visit El Boliche de Alberto," advised the man who ran the hostel when I asked him where was good to eat. "The food is great so make sure you get there early! They open at 7.00pm and there'll be a line down the street."

I was highly skeptical of that last claim. Argentinians eat notoriously late, and when I say late I mean really late. Few restaurants even open their doors before 9.00pm and barely start to fill before 10.00pm. Going out to dinner at 11.00pm isn't unusual and some bars don't even *open* before midnight. I was deeply skeptical that this restaurant even opened at 7.00pm, let alone that there would be a line. I thought it was still worth trying though, as without doubt one of the best things in Argentina is the food.

Food in Argentina generally means meat. Thousands of square miles of perfect grazing land, a small population and a restricted export market has created such quality and choice that only the best-of-the-best beef, lamb and mutton is served, even at average places. The good restaurants serve the very best of *that* selection. A group of us at the hostel decided to go to this recommended place, so some time after 6.00pm we arrived. Would you believe it, there was a line of people at the door, just as promised! A hostess was taking reservations before the restaurant officially opened so we put down a group name and went buy some beer to drink in the street while we waited. Before too long our group was called and we were escorted to our seats. The decor was surprisingly chic, with a simple yet rustic theme of warm pine tables and parquet wooden floor contrasting with darker browns elsewhere. In the center of the restaurant was the grill, called a parrija. This great plateau of stone and brick must have been 20 feet long with a great iron grill hanging along its entire length. A log fire burned furiously at one end below a tall brick chimney and the chefs carefully extracted hot embers from its base and spread them expertly along the plateau under the great slabs of meat and offal cooking slowly above. Flame grilled is for amateurs, slow cooking for hours over smoldering coals is for pros. Chefs braved the heat to busily turn the huge beef chunks or rotate the entire goats that were roasting on near-vertical spits at the far end. It was like viewing a blacksmiths foundry with a scale and industriousness that was quite something to see.

We were taken to a large table just past the parrija and the menus were swiftly distributed before the waiter returned to take our drink order. We simplified drinks by ordering some bottles of wine to share. Malbec, naturally.

"Of course, sir," replied the well-dressed server and disappeared in a flash to the wine cellar while we perused the menu. Not for vegetarians, that much was certain. We ordered our food upon his return, which I started by ordering a plate of the seasoned French fries for everyone.

"Um, is sir *completely* sure about one plate each?" responded our server, pointing our attention to an adjacent table where a plate was arriving. It was a great pyramid of fries stacked about a foot high. I saw his point.

"We'll take one between two, please."

This meal without doubt called for a steak. Luckily I'd learned the two vital secrets of steak ordering while traversing the country, and they came in useful once again. Always ask the server's recommendation, and never, *ever*, order a steak well done. Ever. If I can impart one piece of Argentinean travel knowledge to you, that is it. Indeed, some restaurants will actually refuse to serve it to you that way. Asking for well done is like asking for hot gazpacho soup or a raw chicken sandwich. It doesn't matter if you always order it that way, or can't stand it any other way. No exceptions.

I asked our server for his recommendation.

"The Bife de Chorizo is particularly good today, sir. I would suggest rare or medium rare."

Steak in Argentina is ordered not as "steak" or "filet", but with a much wider cut selection. In fact, I learned that many beef eating cultures – Britain, France, the US, for example – have different cuts and indeed different dissections of the cow, so even a fillet steak in the US is a slightly different part of the cow than a fillet in England. Argentina is no exception to such specificity. The cut called a Bife de Chorizo happened to be my favorite, having nothing to do with "chorizo", or "sausage" as it translates in Spanish. Somewhere between filet and sirloin, it includes an adjacent sliver of slightly fattier meat which in my opinion creates a fabulous combination of both tenderness and favor intensity. Recommendation accepted!

We drank the excellent wine and laughed, talked and told stories about life, love and travel. Suddenly, in a flurry of motion several mountains of French fries appeared on our table followed shortly our steaks. Did my eyes deceive me? In front of me was placed the largest steak I have ever seen. It was larger than a house brick. Now, size isn't everything, but as we all know it sure can help. This was promising, but at the same time I was a little apprehensive, and steeled myself to the disappointing possibility that this was a brick of inedible shoe leather. Picking up my fork I pushed it into the slab before picking up my knife to set about carving off a mouthful of this veritable half a cow. I never made it that far; the fork stripped off a chunk of beef so tender it rendered the knife unnecessary. I know this for certain because at one point in the meal I ate part of this steak using only my spoon, just because I could.

As the first mouth-sized portion came away with the fork, the final trepidation. The taste. Could it complete the ultimate trifecta? At that first mouthful I knew the answer. Oh it could, it absolutely could. The first bite was a taste explosion, my taste buds winning an all-inclusive vacation in the Caribbean and $500 of spending money. It was one of those moments when you close your eyes and escape into the taste. I started to wonder why people weren't lining up outside even earlier.

The meal was incredible. After a 30+oz, spoon-tender, taste sensation of a steak, most of a bottle of good wine and 3,000 calories of deliciously seasoned thin French fries it was time to pay the bill. How much would this world class indulgence cost? As we had all ordered similar things we split the bill and I got my portion. I need not have worried. It was $14, including the tip. Thank you, economic collapse. I emerged into the cool evening air a very, very happy customer.

Fabulous food is, of course, not the unique preserve of Argentinian steak restaurants. Indeed, what is most fascinating is where you find these culinary gems, for I believe they are rarely obvious and often inexpensive. I remember my travels in Laos for the Thai green curry and sticky rice, always homemade with fresh ingredients and almost always excellent, despite being sold in very basic establishments or sometime even on the street. I found it so consistently good that I ate it for lunch and dinner for 23 days straight, with the exception of one small town where the only thing available was noodle soup. In another instance, this time in Amman, the capital of Jordan, I ate at a basic, hole-in-the-wall kind of place which I'd heard was the place to go. It was nothing to look at, with linoleum flooring, white tiled walls and plastic fold-up tables and chairs. But it was packed. The restaurant sold just three things - falafel, hummus and homemade pita bread, and all three were monumental. I doubt that there is better hummus on the planet. My sister went there years later and she agrees, so it must be true!

For all such wonderful culinary experiences, I have also learned that finding good food is a fickle friend. For every lucky find I have also suffered a culinary evil, a heinous abomination from Hell's own cafeteria. These moments were born through bad luck, stupidity, poor planning, or usually all three. For one meal in Brazil I should have been alerted when my server asked me three times if I was sure of my choice after I'd pointed at some random dish on the menu.

"Sure I'm sure," was my response, to which she asked me once more. Warning signs unheeded I remained unwavering, only understanding her pity when a bowl arrived. Inside that bowl bobbed a pig's knee in some kind of vile broth, its mushy cartilage and hard bone covered in an odious soup that was the very bile of Beelzebub. It was the most unfeasibly disgusting, gag inducing, eye wateringly bad substance that has ever passed my lips, and I was very lucky that the small amount I ate only passed them in one direction.

Self-induced stupidity of unwarranted food experimentation is another risk to be navigated. A good friend of mine once took a dare on a school trip that he'd eat some ice cream from a street vendor. Unfortunately, this dare was in India on the streets of Delhi. Big mistake, as he contracted something awful that is almost never seen in the West and was ill for *two entire years* before he was finally rid of it. Fortunately he made a full recovery. Another travel rule is therefore to avoid street vendor ice cream in India. As for me, my greatest food error was probably barbecued rat on a skewer. It was being roasted on the floor in some grimy corner of a village market in Laos by a lady who did not seem quite disease free. Why did I do it, I hear you ask? I have no idea. Maybe just to say I had done it. What was the experience like? It was exactly like you would expect. Horrible, just horrible. Beyond horrible. It still had fur on it, although most had thankfully been singed off by the flames. Luckily for my health she had charred the rest of it to a cinder, leaving a layer of carbonized skin above sinew punctuated by annoying small bones. Two tiny bites and I was done. The lesson here was not to let curiosity get the best of you when it comes to spit roasted market rat.

Remember folks, you heard it here first.

# FIFTY EIGHT

# The Southern Highway

Bariloche was a good time, between eating, drinking, hanging out with Elke and adventuring into the mountains with Matt, a friendly New Zealander, and Christine, a Swiss TV weather presenter I'd also met during my time there. As was always the case, leaving such pleasant comforts and good people behind was hard to do but the last great section of my journey awaited and I now faced an important choice. Two infamous roads ran the remaining length of the Andes, Route 40 in Argentina and the Carretera Austral in Chile. Route 40 is known as a vicious destroyer of both vehicles and people, with its mostly unpaved, ungraded and unforgiving dirt ruts pushing a thousand miles through the arid gale-swept plateau located in the rain shadow east of the Andes. The Carretera Austral, on the other hand, snakes through the spine of the Andes, a thousand miles of mountain terrain and dirt road past majestic peaks, forests, lakes and rivers. It is commonly considered to be the third most spectacular road in the world after the Freedom Highway on the Nepal/Tibet border and the Karakorum Highway in Pakistan. These iconic roads can be spectacular but extremely difficult to navigate. I'd traveled the Karakorum Highway several years before and from experience knew that such roads are not to be taken lightly.

The Karakorum Highway cuts through the Himalayas between central Pakistan and China, a road so improbable that sections of it are quite literally carved into sheer cliffs a thousand feet above the raging Indus River. A thousand men died to construct this 810 mile wonder and their spectacular legacy remains deadly to this day. I was heading to the mountains on an expedition and our group was forced to undertake the journey in a rickety, overloaded minibus with so much equipment in it that we were able to lie down across the tops of the seats, supported by all the bags on the seats below. Comfortable it was not, but I managed to fall asleep as we entered the foothills towards the mountains beyond. At one point, deep in the middle of the night I awoke in the darkness and rolled over to peer out of the open window by my head. Above was a clear night sky and the Milky Way streaked from horizon to horizon, a sight that only high altitude can reveal. What caught my attention, though, was the rock face which plummeted vertically down to the rapids I could hear churning below. I could see the rock face because our bus driver periodically drove so close to the edge to avoid oncoming traffic that the road disappeared underneath the bus; we were quite literally driving with only half a tire width on the road, the other half suspended above the void. To help our somewhat precarious situation I retuned inside the bus and scooted my weight away from the cliff to add some additional counter-weight, even though I knew my fate was out of my hands no matter what I did. I finally drifted back asleep once more, this time with my fingers crossed.

Despite the potential difficulties, the Carretera Austral was the right choice for the final stretch. In any case, I had to ride several hundred miles of Route 40 before I could cut through the mountains to reach the start. As I ventured along this brutal stretch I discovered that its fearsome reputation was well deserved. That road is a bitch. In fact, it's a high maintenance, credit card spending, divorce planning, gold digging evil bitch. Barren and relatively unspectacular because of its distance from the mountains, it is also unfathomably windy. Air circling Antarctica cuts across South America at this latitude and blows relentlessly at gale force strength. I'd got a good feeling of wind speed from skydiving and the gusts I experienced here were well over 60mph, enough to push me off my feet. Standing up was challenging, a feeling you have to experience to believe. Cycling was worse. Heading down a steep decline on a rare paved section I had to pedal hard just to make any progress, even in a crosswind. At one point a frontal gust physically blew me across the road and backwards up the steep hill

I had been descending moments before. I was lucky there was no traffic at the time. You cannot compete with those forces and so I pushed my bicycle for much of the next 80 demoralizing miles. Even having this as a tailwind wouldn't have been much better; I met a cyclist coming in the other direction who said he'd worn out his brakes preventing his bike for accelerating out of control! Evil indeed. It was one mile at a time, but eventually I reached the turnoff and the shelter of the mountains once more.

The Carretera Austral is 770 miles of road carved through the extreme wilderness of the southern Andes. Flanked by glaciers, lush temperate rainforest, lakes and rivers it is mostly unpopulated and absolutely spectacular. High above the road beyond the tree line, blue glaciers cascade from the tops of jagged peaks, while far below the silence of the forest is broken only by crystal clear rivers, streams and waterfalls as they bubble and thunder through this fantastical scenery. Prehistoric ferns, monkey puzzle trees and cloud forest surround the road, appearing and disappearing in the mist. Separated from humanity, pure nature seems to extend forever.

The rivers and lakes here are unlike anything I have ever seen. The colors defy belief. Some are electric blue, so vibrant they look as though someone has poured paint into the water, truly bluer than a summer sky. Some are a milky green while still others are as clear as crystal, so transparent as to be almost invisible. Looking into one river from the road I struggled to see how deep it was, so vividly I could see the stones that bounced along its bed as though there was no water in it at all; the surface reflections were the only indication that there was more than air. It could have been 5ft deep or 50, I could hardly tell.

In the midst of this special place I then encountered something that was without doubt unique. Riding over a crest between two long mountain valleys I passed over a small non-descript bridge surrounded by dense forest. From the mountains to my left a stream flowed under the bridge, perpendicular to those long valleys, and as it passed beneath the road it was split in half by a small ridge in the middle of the river, on which rested the central pillar of the bridge. What was unique was that in this particular case the stream never recombined. The left half of the stream turned left down the valley in front while the other half turned right and flowed away down the hill behind me in the opposite direction. A small rusting sign attached to the railing explained this puzzling oddity. Right there I stood on the knife edge of the continental divide, the transition between the watersheds of the Pacific and Atlantic oceans. Rivers to the east flow to the Atlantic and those to the west to the Pacific. The divide passed exactly through that central bridge support, so the right half of the stream journeyed to the Atlantic and the left to the Pacific. An inch magnified into 2,000 miles. I have to admit it, I spit into the stream just to see some flecks go left and some right. Not very hygienic, but hey, it's not every day your spit bomb simultaneously ends up in two different oceans.

I passed through the only real town along the road, Coyhaique, and at the summit of the big climb out of the valley I made the mistake of stopping to take a photograph. Feet planted, I turned to my left, camera raised, and then 'click'. Except that the click wasn't the camera, it was my back. Just an innocuous tweak, innocuous that is until I tried to twist straight again, whereupon my back felt as though someone had rammed a metal spike through it and then glued it in place. It was excruciating and I was also stuck, as though a joint had seized. I couldn't believe what I had done. For the first four days I could barely sleep as lying down offered no relief, while getting out of my sleeping bag took 10 agonizing minutes. For three weeks I couldn't lift my arms out to my sides higher than my chest, and every position hurt with the exception of leaning forwards, arms outstretched. Very fortunately that was my riding position. Only when I randomly met a physiotherapist six weeks later who kindly gave me a massage did the pain somewhat abate and more movement return. Apparently I had most likely dislocated a disc in my back, with the debilitation further enhanced by the spasms of the surrounding muscles. While that kept me from snapping in half, given the pain I was in I don't think snapping would have felt much worse.

I suffered along the isolated road, now a singular highway where turn-offs became even fewer and farther between. In the southern stretches, the first turnoff I had seen for a hundred miles displayed a sign.

"Caleta Tortel 20km," it said. I had no idea what was in Caleta Tortel and 20km was not a minor undertaking on those dirt roads, but for some unknown reason I decided to take the fork. Two hours later the road ended at a small car park atop a steep and beautiful fjord but there was no village to be seen, indeed no buildings of any kind. Just a handful of parked cars and a break in the fence where some wide wooden steps began. I was confused but I'd come too far to stop now, so I locked up the bike and with my bag of valuables I started down the steps towards the forest and fjord beyond. The wooden planks and railings were sturdy and well maintained, a surprise given this apparent solitude, and they continued for a huge distance. After at least half a mile I reached the pine forest and the mystery began to resolve as I passed several staircases and boardwalks connecting to the main stairs like tributaries. Several small wooden houses appeared amongst the trees, and as I continued closer to the shoreline they became more densely packed. Children appeared, playing on adjacent boardwalks. This place was amazing. The whole town had been built into the steep forest and was connected only by those boardwalks. No cars, no vehicles, no roads at all. It was like entering the world of the Swiss Family Robinson, a veritable fantasy land of tree houses in the wild. I wandered around and after asking some locals I found Entre Hielos, the only hotel in town. It was a lovely place, reminiscent of an alpine ski chalet both inside and out, and the family who ran it was very kind. I stayed there for two nights and spent a wonderful day investigating. I walked the moss covered staircases winding unseen between the trees and wandered down to the small fishing boats anchored at the fjord's shores. I even found a tiny part time cafe on the main board walk. Tolly the Bear came to join me, much to the joy and amusement of all the kids in the village who passed by and saw him. There is nothing like a toy bear to break the ice. All in all, Caleta Tortel is a unique to visit, and highly recommended if you ever have the two days each way it takes to get there.

Beyond Caleta Tortel the road opened up to a wide river valley of sub-arctic ruggedness, its browns and wet greens exemplifying this harsh land, until finally, *finally*, I saw the tops of some buildings and looked upon the shores of a vast lake. The village was Villa O'Higgins and the end of the road. To continue you must take a boat many miles along the lake beyond the town, hike several miles across a narrow isthmus on a single track trail, and then take another boat across another lake to rejoin the road once more. Or fly. It is complicated, not only because of the dearth of civilization and the lack of a real destination, but also because that first boat runs just once every two weeks on a schedule determined by the captain's whim. I'd learned about this unfortunate transport bottleneck many months before, but the lack of information coming out of the village and the whims of the captain made timing the boat nearly impossible. It can be a big problem. If you mess up - or are unlucky - you face a 14 day wait in this serene yet dull village at the edge of the world. Upon arriving I immediately ascertained from my guesthouse family that the boat would leave in "about four days". Not a bad outcome in the end, especially as I could do with the rest. James was again a happy bunny.

Three days later the wife of the host family came rushing up to my room early in the evening.

"James, James, tomorrow morning is the boat!" she excitedly told me, "You must be at the dock at 8.00am, no later!"

Sold. Next morning I was up extra-early, riding the five miles of cliff-cut road along the fjord's edge to the tiny dock. I was joined by a group of three young Chilean cyclists who had arrived at the guesthouse two days before. I'd actually met them briefly a couple of weeks earlier, further back along the road, and had leapfrogged them as they rested somewhere for a few days. They were good guys and I was glad to have some company. We rounded the last corner and descended towards the jetty, and despite our early start we arrived at the dock not a moment too late! The rickety old fishing boat was nearly ready and as soon as we had loaded our gear the boat backed up from its moorings and began the glorious slow chug across the lake's mirrored surface.

As the town slowly receded I looked back from the stern and my heart sank. A distant figure could be seen riding a bicycle towards the dock, touring luggage shining red in the sunshine. He or she had made the worst mistake imaginable and missed the boat! That 15 minutes cost them another 14 days for the next boat, or at best a five day wait for the weekly flight out of town. I felt awed and a terrible pity at such bad luck, but there was nothing that could be done. I only hope that poor cyclist isn't still there.

Several hours later we reached the end of the lake's thin spur and crossed the main body to reach a small jetty on the opposing shore. Up from the jetty stood a small wooden police station that kept a precarious hold on the rocks, and on its steps waited a young policeman in a Chilean uniform. He beckoned for us to follow him inside. In the small white office, with its large desk and creaking floors, we talked a little with him about why he was there. His job was mostly to prevent smuggling, which apparently there was a surprising amount of, despite the remote location. The border in that area is also officially undefined, so a continual presence was necessary. I was skeptical but later found it was true; on a neutral map you can find a rectangle, 30 miles by 20, sitting squarely over the area to mark this disputed territory. Once again I found myself officially in Nowhere.

As well as not existing, Nowhere has its own problems. First, how to get a passport stamp. These are the business cards of the global backpacker, so the more impressive the stamp the greater the kudos, plus they are also very useful for avoiding visa overstay fines. I asked our policeman if anything could be done, and after a puzzled look he disappeared into the back office to re-emerge a few seconds later with a stamping kit.

"It's not a border stamp, but it's all we have," he said, and opened my passport to thump in the beautiful green emblem of the Chilean Gendarmerie. It was a unique border stamp and a nice addition to my bicycle customs sticker from Nicaragua and the bear picture stamp from the world's most northerly border crossing. It made me smile, that did.

It was no small feat to navigate the single track trail which wound through the hilly isthmus, our luggage and bicycles not simplifying the process, but after several hours we emerged at the grassy shore of the second lake. We were approaching civilization once more, and to the few tourists resting on the manicured grass lawn by the water it must have been inexplicable to see these guys with bicycles emerging from the forest. Several white wooden slat buildings stood in the area, one of which even had tourist information! As we walked down to the water I finally had a clear view of the horizon, and what greeted my eyes was magnificent. Towering into the sky beyond the lake stood the vast granite spires of Mt Fitzroy and Cerro Torre; bare majestic monoliths that rise 10,000ft above their surroundings to dominate this part of the southern mountains. The mass of Mt Fitzroy contrasts with the improbably thin spire of Cerro Torre, considered by many to be the most difficult mountain in the world to climb. I could see why. It is a tower devoid of features that pierces through the cold and ferocious winds which are the norm at the summit, even in summer. I had wanted to see it for many years and it did not disappoint. We sat on the grass and marveled at the view until it was time for the next boat's departure.

SIXTY

# For There Were No More Worlds to Conquer

After crossing the lake we remounted and soon arrived at the town of El Chalten, gateway to those magnificent peaks. I watched the burning bright stars and glowing moon rise above the darkened snow-peppered spires from the hostel veranda with a well-deserved cold beer in hand and wallowed in the gratefulness I felt to be there. I was back in civilization after a long, long time, and that view was my reward for making it this far. Gazing at those peaks I felt excitement at the possibility to take a closer look the next morning, so when the chill of the cooling mountain air finally seeped through my clothes and drove me indoors I found a map in the hostel common area and perused the choice of trails which reached towards it. Although certainly beautiful, none piqued my interest. I wanted altitude, to get up close and personal with the mountain, so rather than accept defeat I decided to make my own trail, figuring it out as I went along. What could possibly go wrong?

The early morning mist quickly gave way to bright rays of sunshine, the weather warm and windless. My iPod (lent to me by a wonderful chap named Erik whom I had met a few weeks before) was charged, my water bottle full and a snack was in my pocket. Conditions were perfect. Leaving town I followed a trail for the first several miles as it wound through grassy meadows and then up into the sparse alpine forests above until turning sharply away from the mountains ahead.

"Let the bushwhacking begin!" I thought, and stepped off the trail to walk across the soft forest detritus beneath the trees, with "up" as my only guide. Luckily the trees were widely spaced and the forest floor open, making it pretty easy going for the next few hours as I gained altitude to reach the stubby bushes and scrubland which clung tenaciously to life on the stony ground. The air felt thinner now and my breathing was heavier. Eventually even the scrubland succumbed and the ground became steep bare rock and scree. The summit was still far ahead but I hardened my determination; I could feel I was going somewhere exciting and the increasing exposure of the climb along the narrow ridge added some adrenaline to the trek. The ridge was segmented in places with heart stopping traverses; tiny ledges which hung tenuously over steep slopes that cascaded downwards towards the valley floor far below. I inched across them as though each one was a coin toss with my life, my resolve bound together by both a confidence in my abilities and an over confidence in my luck. Even running out of water wasn't a problem once I reached the snow line, although walking on snow in running shoes was. The taste of ice cold fresh water in my parched throat was the very ambrosia of the gods.

At last the slope flattened a little and ahead rose a small pyramid of rock at the intersection of the three ridge lines; the summit of my mountain. I clambered up the last part and sat upon the very top looking out. Below me the slope dropped several thousand feet down to a lake, from which glaciers rose up the opposing side to their birthplace on Mt Fitzroy's steep flanks ahead. From within this maelstrom of splintered ice rose the megalith of Mt Fitzroy itself, towering thousands of feet further above than where I sat as an incredible barrier of rock. Above its summit I could see wispy clouds appearing from thin air, condensing like your breath on a cold day, as strong winds rushed up the far side of the spires from the ice field beyond and cooled as they ascended. It was a stark contrast to the calm warm air which surrounded me, a contrast for which I was grateful.

As I scratched my sister's initials into the summit rock so she could be there with me, I noticed two birds circling below. It was a pleasant distraction to see evidence of life appearing in this inhospitable vista. The birds rode the thermals, rising in spirals through the clear sky until their circles brought them right past me.

It was then I saw that they were Condors! I couldn't believe it. It was a magical moment in a magical place.

The descent back was long, and in places bard to find the trail, but eventually I arrived back in El Chalten as the purple curtain of sunset fell. On the town's quiet main street I turned and looked back at the mountains once more. It was a moment I will remember forever, although I'm not sure why. Maybe it was the glow of the day's achievement, or the sadness that my time in this place would soon be over. I felt a little like Alexander the Great, at least according to Hollywood's account.

"For when Alexander saw the breadth of his domain he wept, for there were no more worlds to conquer." My eyes watered and I wiped away a joyous tear of sadness before turning to walk up the wooden steps of the hostel for the last time.

# SIXTY ONE

# The Land of Fire

I was in Patagonia. Woo! I'd actually officially been here for a while, but after a long day's ride from El Chalten to El Calafate, tourist epicenter of the region and jumping off point for the Perito Moreno glacier, it *felt* official. Famous for its visual purity, dramatic up-close views and relative accessibility, the Perito Moreno glacier descends from the Patagonian Ice Field to bisect a large lake and finish mere yards from the opposing bank (and a boardwalk of gathered tourists). It is an unrivaled vantage point to see 60ft high blocks of blue ice calve into the adjacent lake, and I was looking forward to seeing it. I had heard it was awe inspiring.

The town of El Calafate is located outside the national park that contains the glacier, about 20 miles from the ice itself, and is nothing to write home about apart from the ice cream shop. The town's only other superlative is the weather, which is terrible. Protecting your three scoop ice cream cone from icy 50 mph blasts as you leave the shop is another uniquely weird Patagonian rite of passage. After visiting the glacier (where I was suitably impressed!) those winds held me in town for a couple of days as I waited for them to abate to below 30 mph, the painful-yet-manageable threshold, and then dashed off south before they fully returned. The ride was tough and punctuated only by sparse evidence of humanity. On the first night I camped in the back yard of the only gas station for 100 miles and had to tie down my tent in about 10 separate places to stop it blowing away with me inside. Awful. After two more days of this suffering I was relieved to reach the town of Rio Gallegos and have a decent night's sleep before hopping on the bike once more for the start of the end. After quite a lot more swearing at the wind that morning I finally ran out of road, quite literally. I had reached the Straits of Magellan and the final termination of the South American mainland.

The mainland. Using that word feels strange when referring to a continent, yet here I stood on the worn concrete ramp at the water's edge as I waited for the ferry. Beyond the water I could see the shore of Tierra del Fuego, the Land of Fire, named for the tribal beach fires which were seen by those first few explorers who passed through this distant place. The narrow strait that separates the island from the mainland has been used since its discovery in 1520 by Ferdinand Magellan, the Portuguese explorer who first circumnavigated the world, and the sense of history in this place is palpable as my mind conjured images of majestic wooden sailing ships from centuries past. Magellan, Darwin and Sir Francis Drake all journeyed through the channel before me. As I thought of all those great men a knot lodged in my chest. I had come so far and now there, across the water and beyond the opposing bank, was the finishing line. The emotions ran deep, oddly reminding me of the last exam of the final year of my university degree. It is undeniably exciting, for you now can *feel* the end rather than just *know* it, as well as feel the accomplishments that this step will cement. And yet I also felt sad and afraid. I was crossing the Rubicon. I knew my life could not remain the same but must soon enter a new phase. Only at that time can you finally feel the reality of the change. With these conflicting emotions I watched some seals playing by the dock, and for a moment I wanted to swap my life for theirs, to be free of an unknown future and have certainty of tomorrow; to know what I was "supposed" to do. Knowing this is a luxury than happily and sadly very few of us can have.

The ferry was a weather-battered old car transporter, its white and blue paint streaked with rust. It was a fitting vessel for such remote surroundings. That afternoon I made the short crossing and soon landed on the windswept desolation of northern Tierra del Fuego. There were no buildings at the offloading ramp; in fact there was nothing at all, just the ramp, a small queuing area for returning traffic and a dirt road heading into the flat heather covered scrubland beyond. Remounting my bike in a cold harsh wind I could feel the desolation. With a deep breath I steeled myself and pedaled onwards, grim faced and determined to have my date with destiny at the end of the world. It was 10 hard days to cross the island and I was ready.

Tierra del Fuego is sparsely populated to say the least, and I passed through exactly three settlements in those first three days. I didn't mind though. I caught a lucky break in the weather that week and suffered no worse than sunshine and moderate winds. Over time the heather scrubland gave way to trees covered in a beautiful pale green moss, and after six or seven days the snowy mountains of the Darwin range finally appeared on the horizon. The last three days were stunning, the scenery becoming suitably impressive as inland bays and lakes also returned to the vista. It was beautiful.

As I approached the end the psychological pressure began to build. The seconds became minutes, the minutes became hours. Each day became a lifetime. It felt as though an age of man had passed in that time, but at dawn on the tenth day I crawled out of my tent, alone on a beach at one end of Tierra del Fuego's largest lake, and stood tall on the sand in just my underwear as I breathed in the invigorating cool air. My skin rippled with goose bumps from the first warm rays of sun. This was it, my final day on the road to Ushuaia. The end was so near I almost couldn't believe it was actually happening. I ate, packed up and it was time. I swung my leg over my bike and clicked into the pedals with deliberate motions, movements with an unusual weight and significance, just like the first pedal click in Alaska all those months ago. A well-rehearsed heave and I was rolling, ready to greet my fate.

The ride was pleasant and early that afternoon I found myself freewheeling downhill alongside a river between two peaks on a smooth tarmac road, a new phenomenon in those last few days. As I rounded a bend I looked up, and a huge smile swept across my face. There it was, a strip of deep azure blue shining across the horizon. It was Beagle Channel, beyond which lay the Antarctic Ocean and the end of the world. I was finally here!

# SIXTY TWO

# The End of the World

The descent took me to the channel's edge, whereupon I turned right and after a short distance along the coast entered Ushuaia, the world's most southerly 'real' town. Surprisingly large, industrial and poor, at least on its outskirts, the center was nevertheless reminiscent of Alaska with its quaint weatherworn appearance. I rode a few blocks north of Main Street and found the small hotel where my dad and sister had stayed almost two years prior to my visit. They'd told me to also stay there when I arrived, so in I went still wearing my bicycling gear and walked up to the elderly woman sitting by the reception desk.

"Hola," I said, "I was wondering if you had a room available?" The woman lowered her reading glasses and looked up at me.

"Ah!" she exclaimed. "James! You are finally here! We were expecting you last year!"

I looked at her flabbergasted, and then smiled. My memory is such that I forget what I've had for breakfast, and yet this woman had remembered my name, a guy she's never met and who may - or may not – come to visit several years in the future. She rose from her chair, took my hand gleefully in her wrinkled age-etched palm and led me to her tiny office where she fished around in a small filing cabinet.

"Here, here, I've been keeping this for you," she said, and handed me a postcard. I flipped it over to see that it was, unbelievably, addressed to me.

"HOLA!" I was greeted by my Dad's unmistakable upper case handwriting.

"IF YOU ARE READING THIS, CONGRATULATIONS! WE ARE ALL VERY PROUD OF YOU! WELL DONE!"

It was the first congratulation for my impending achievement. More than that, though, it showed the faith my family had in me to succeed, and that was a special thing. So much love. I stood there in front of the lovely old lady and began to tear up through my wide smile. My chest tightens even as I write this, such was the intensity of that moment. I felt proud, knowing that very shortly I would achieve what I had set out to do, and knowing I had done my family proud. It was a profoundly deep emotion.

With the happiest of images in my mind I finished checking in to the hotel and went to explore the town. I visited the chocolate shop on my sister's recommendation, very much necessary after the prior 10 days, as there is nothing like burning 50,000 calories to remove any guilt of eating as much good chocolate as you can handle. I also wandered into the post office, again on my sister's recommendation, to get a passport stamp from the most southerly official post office in South America. Although I think it is technically illegal to get a picture stamp in a UK passport I still considered it a must have. I also ran into another cyclist I'd met a couple of weeks prior and we grabbed a pint of Guinness at the most southerly Irish pub in the world. Hilariously, there were two Irish pubs facing each other on the street; apparently the one on the north side of the street was built first, only to be superseded by the newer pub built 20ft further south on the southern side of that same street. Ouch.

It was the morning of the last day, day 636 of my journey. I woke at dawn and looked out of the window from my bed. The weathered harbor buildings and the water beyond glowed underneath a blood red sunrise, as though the land of fire was on fire, a fitting and memorable start to my last day on the bike. After some dulce de leche croissants for breakfast (amazing!) I began the ride to the final termination of the road in South America at Bahia Lapataia, 20 miles away and six miles geographically further south than Ushuaia. The ride was longer and harder than expected, and while concentrating on the road I strangely didn't think too much of its significance until I entered a meadow area only a mile or so away from the finishing line. Suddenly it hit me, and yet through the flood of emotion I remembered a request from a friend more than two years before.

"You know what," said Andy as we sat at the kitchen table in our house in London, "You have to finish this ride properly. You should finish it with one of those skids we used to do on our BMX bikes when we were in school, right!"

"Genius!" I replied. "I guess if I'm going to do the whole ride I might as well finish in style!"

And now there it was, the last 50 yards of the road opening up to a small gravel car park at the end of the road. Accelerating to maximum speed I crossed the car park and slammed on the rear brake. The wheel locked and the back end slid out, a monstrous 25ft textbook slide ending right in front of the official 'end of the road' sign. It couldn't have gone better! I unclipped and carried the bike onto the well maintained wooden boardwalk that extended from the sign to a small platform by the water. It was the final southern viewpoint across the bay and the islands of Cape Horn, and now this really was it, my final destination and the end of the end. Propping my bike against the wooden railings I took a deep breath and climbed up to sit on the railing's wide top plank, feet dangling over the rocks below. Tolly the Bear sat with me as well, weather worn from his long adventure but nonetheless he had made it, the first of his kind to do so. I opened the bottle of champagne I had brought from Ushuaia and then glanced at my watch. It was 1.14pm on March 22, 2005. I put in my headphones and listened to some well-chosen music through a flood of pure and unadulterated joy. I had struggled so hard for so long, through all the suffering, uncertainty and weight of what I was attempting to do. Through 96 weeks of adventure, wildest happiness and deepest fear, companionship and crushing loneliness, beauty and desolation, wonder and pain I had conquered my most improbable goal and reached the end of the world.

I'd done it.

# SIXTY THREE

# The Beginning

I sat on that fence sharing my champagne with a couple of other cyclists who were there to begin a bicycle journey to Peru. Watching them at the start of their adventure I wondered what I would do next. There were so many questions and so few answers, and yet I was unperturbed. I knew that these answers didn't really matter; it was the journey to find them which was important. To progress, to learn, to live in the present and to strive for the future. As John Lennon once said, "Life is what happens while you are making plans." As I got off that fence and took one last look at the Beagle Channel before beginning the long journey back to London and the life I'd left behind so long ago, I felt I finally understood what the great man had meant.

The End.

Manufactured by Amazon.ca
Bolton, ON

10543350R00166